Social Work with Older People

Mark Lymbery

Social Work with Older People

CONTEXT, POLICY AND PRACTICE

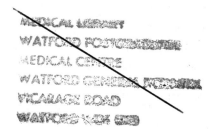

SAGE Publications
London ● Thousand Oaks ● New Delhi

First published 2005

Apart from any fair dealing for the purposes of research or private
study, or criticism or review, as permitted under the Copyright,
Designs and Patents Act, 1988, this publication may be
reproduced, stored or transmitted in any form, or by any means,
only with the prior permission in writing of the publishers, or in
the case of reprographic reproduction, in accordance with the
terms of licences issued by the Copyright Licensing Agency.
Enquiries concerning reproduction outside those terms should
be sent to the publishers.

 SAGE Publications Ltd
1 Oliver's Yard
55 City Road
London EC1Y 1SP

SAGE Publications Inc.
2455 Teller Road
Thousand Oaks, California 91320

SAGE Publications India Pvt Ltd
B-42, Panchsheel Enclave
Post Box 4109
New Delhi 110 017

British Library Cataloguing in Publication data

A catalogue record for this book is available from
the British Library

ISBN 1-4129-0204-5
ISBN 1-4129-0205-3 (pbk)

Library of Congress Control Number: 2005926013

Typeset by C&M Digitals (P) Ltd., Chennai, India
Printed on paper from sustainable resources
Printed and bound in Great Britain by Athenaeum Press, Gateshead

Contents

Preface

As the title indicates, this book is preoccupied with the context of social work with older people, policy that affects the delivery of services, and the consequent implications of both for social work practice. While it has been primarily written as an aid to understanding the position of contemporary social work with older people in both conceptual and theoretical terms, and not as a 'how-to-do-it' guide to practice, its practical focus does ensure that it will assist students to engage with the requirements for social work training specified by the Department of Health and outlined in the Quality Assurance Agency's (QAA) subject benchmark statement for social work. In addition, it can be used to enable students to practise competently in accordance with the key roles of social workers as defined in the National Occupational Standards. Although it has not been written with the specific intention to enable students to address these issues, its content is such that material relevant to all of them will be addressed.

For example, the Department of Health document *Requirements for Social Work Training* (DoH, 2002d) specifies that students must undertake specific learning and assessment in the following areas:

- human growth and development;
- assessment, planning, intervention and review;
- communication skills;
- law;
- partnership working across professional disciplines and agencies.

This book provides students with background information that will assist their fulfilment of these requirements, with particular reference to social work practice with older people.

Similarly, the QAA subject benchmark statement for social work stresses the need for students to be able to 'acquire, critically evaluate, apply and integrate knowledge and understanding' (QAA, 2000: 12) in five core areas of study:

- social work services and service users;
- the service delivery context;
- values and ethics;
- social work theory;
- the nature of social work practice.

Once again, this book contains considerable material that bears on all of these issues as related to social work with older people.

The National Occupational Standards for Social Work (TOPSS, 2002) are intended to provide a baseline for identifying the standards of practice that should be reached by newly qualified social workers. This document defines six 'key roles' for social workers, which are identified as follows:

1 Prepare for and work with individuals, families, carers, groups and communities to assess their needs and circumstances.
2 Plan, carry out, review and evaluate social work practice with individuals, families, carers, groups and communities and other professionals.
3 Support individuals to represent their needs, views and circumstances.
4 Manage risk to individuals, families, carers, groups, self and colleagues.
5 Manage and be accountable for your own practice within your organisation.
6 Demonstrate professional competence in social work practice.

Although this book is not a practice guide, it contains material that will directly assist students in meeting the majority of the twenty-one units into which the six roles are broken down. For example, the practice scenarios that are a feature of the book in Chapters 7–9 highlight issues that will encourage students to consider issues relevant to all six key roles, while providing material that bears particularly closely on key roles 1–4.

Acknowledgements

Although there is only one author listed as having written this book, its content has been directly influenced by many more. I would therefore like to take this opportunity to thank all those people whose knowledge and experience have helped to shape the book, and whose support has enabled me to bring it to fruition. In alphabetical order, these are: Marian Charles, Kevin Chettle, Hilary Cole, John Gladman, Julie Gosling, Gwen Gray, Liz Hart, John Herod, Ros Kirk, Jo Lawson, Anne Ledbetter, Pauline McCoy, Andy Millward, Maureen Murfin, Joe Pidgeon, Karen Postle, Barbara Richell, Leigh Russell, Claire Torkington. The ideas that the book advances have also been tested out on numerous student groups, which have helped to shape and refine their presentation: while anonymous, all these people have been vital in the book's formulation. I would also like to acknowledge the important role that a period of study leave played in the writing of the book, so my thanks go to Julia Evetts and Kate Wilson in the School of Sociology and Social Policy, University of Nottingham. Zoë Elliott, Anna Luker and Genevieve Murphy from Sage have all been highly supportive and patient, and I thank them for this.

On the home front, I would like to acknowledge the inestimable support that has been provided by Bruce, Max and Merlin, who have all in their different ways found ways to make me relax and focus on less cerebral pursuits. Finally, and most importantly, I would like to thank Tina for providing me with the solid domestic base which is essential for all such projects.

Introduction

It is now more than a decade since the enactment of community care policies had such a huge impact on the practice of social work with older people in Britain. Although some full length books were produced on the subject of social work with older people in the years immediately following the implementation of these policies (Hughes, 1995; Marshall and Dixon, 1996; Thompson, 1995), since the mid-1990s there has been relatively little produced in book form to examine how practice has developed. This represents a critical gap in the literature, given that the speed of organisational change with which social workers have been confronted has fundamentally altered the context and nature of practice. While the above texts do have their strengths – notably in the practice focus of each – none of them are remotely up to date as regards their policy relevance.

For example, the ambiguities that have characterised the development of care management – the model within which most practice is now framed – are little evident here, although they have been passionately argued in more contemporary literature (Carey, 2003; Postle, 2002). Similarly, all the standard books were written during the latter days of the Conservative administration, and therefore obviously could not be expected to address the issues that have become characteristic of 'new' Labour, even though one of the authors (Beverley Hughes) actually became a minister in that government. There is relatively little about partnership and collaboration, key watchwords within the 'modernisation agenda' of 'new' Labour. Similarly, there could be no recognition of the dramatic changes that have been wrought to the health and social care landscape by such developments as Primary Care Trusts, the single assessment process, intermediate care, legislation to avoid delayed hospital discharge, etc. As a result, while the existing literature on social work with older people remains useful, it is no longer sufficiently up to date to warrant detailed examination.

The paucity of literature on social work with older people in the British context is marked, particularly in comparison with the veritable flood of books that focus on various aspects of social work with children. In addition, there is a limited critical edge to the literature; most of it has featured a strong practice focus rather than a more analytical approach. While this is undoubtedly useful, it often does not help to understand the complexities that underpin the way social work with older people is organised, or the policy decisions that have had such a profound impact on practice. While this is not the case internationally, the way in which social work with older people has been depicted in the British literature has tended to take a one-dimensional view of what social work is, ignoring the more radical and collectivist approaches that have been developed in other areas of practice. In addition, this literature tends to over-simplify the complexities that will inevitably emerge in practice, while also failing to provide a coherent account of the policy and organisational context within which practice is carried out.

An element of authorial arrogance is perhaps necessary at this point, as I claim that (of course!) this book avoids these pitfalls. Certainly, some of the ground that this book covers will be familiar to those readers who are acquainted with the field. In other respects this book can claim to address issues that are not featured in the existing literature. For example, in exploring the history and development of social work in Britain it problematises the essential nature of the occupation, which is often taken for granted. Drawing particularly on the work of Payne (1996), the book identifies three distinctly different strands of social work theory and action, which have been termed the 'individualistic-therapeutic', 'administrative' and 'collectivist' orientations to practice. It argues that while these strands have been powerful within social work at different times in its development, there is little evidence that 'collectivist' ways of thinking have ever had a particular hold in work with older people. In addition, while models of social work practice drawing on an 'individualist-therapeutic' tradition were powerfully drawn in the immediate post-war era, these had relatively little purchase on actual work with older people, which has been strongly directed by administrative requirements, an orientation that is particularly evident in the post-community care world (Lymbery, 1998a; Sturges, 1996). This has created a climate of practice which can often be experienced as arid and unfulfilling by practitioners, bearing relatively little relation to the genuine needs or desires of older people.

In this context it can be hard to retain enthusiasm for the potential of social work to become more relevant to older people's needs. However, as the economic and social position of older people appears to deteriorate – a situation made more complicated by the recognition of an impending crisis regarding the income of older people in the near future (as reported in The *Guardian*, 13.10.2004) – the role of social work in upholding their value as individuals, in responding to their needs, wishes and desires, and in mediating between them and the large societal institutions to which they will increasingly require access, should become more important rather than less. The book is therefore written in a spirit of optimism, seeking to challenge the reductive assumptions that have limited the scope of social work to respond more positively to older people's needs. At the same time, it seeks to temper the idealism of this premise by identifying the realities within which practice is presently framed (Lymbery and Butler, 2004). Change cannot come into being if these realities are simply ignored, or alternatively accorded little significance, as they have served to limit the scope of what can be achieved in practice.

With the balance between idealism and reality firmly in mind, the book is sub-divided into three parts. Part I examines the context within which social work practice for older people should be examined. This section focuses on two criti-cal issues, the place of older people in society and the development of the occu-pation of social work. A book that attempts to link the two themes – as this book obviously does – needs to be clear about the nature of what is discussed. Chapter 1 therefore explores the position of older people in society, examining key issues such as demographic and population change, different ways of understanding the ageing process, and the range of needs that older people might have that call for social work involvement. This is framed within a discourse of ageism, the argu-ment being that the pervasive nature of ageism within British society serves both as a major cause of the disadvantaged position occupied by many older people, and an obstacle to resolving the discrimination that is consequently experienced. The chapter accepts that many older people never require the support of social workers, but observes that they are often in a position of emotional and physical frailty when they do.

Chapter 2 examines the history and development of social work in general terms, on the basis that this has had a major impact on the way in which all social problems are conceptualised and hence the practice response to those problems. It identifies three broad streams of thought within social work since its inception. Drawing on the ideals of the Charity Organisation Society (COS), one major theme has been the development of individual casework – initially seen as a means of putting the social theory of the COS into action, and later seen as an approach that potentially unified social work in all of its many guises. Also deriving partly from the work of the COS as well as from nineteenth century Poor Law officers, the second stream is one of social work as an element of social administration: this could be seen in much of the work of hospital almoners, and remains a feature of much contemporary social work with older people. The third stream is of social work as a form of social action, largely stemming from the work of the Settlement Movement in the nineteenth century, but which could also be readily seen in the radical social work movement of the 1970s as well as in community development, which also reached its peak at the same time. The chapter argues that these three elements can still be perceived in contemporary social work, and identifies them as the 'individualist-therapeutic', 'administrative' and 'collectivist' approaches to practice. While these elements have all been particularly powerful at different times, the chapter concludes that social work with older people has been dominated by an administratively-oriented approach (a theme expanded in more detail in Chapter 6).

Part II examines the key dimensions of policy that frame the development of social work with older people, with three chapters exploring this in more detail. Chapter 3 examines the development of community care policy in the years since the end of the Second World War. Three main themes are drawn out in this process. First, the chapter explores health and social care policy, with a particular focus on the boundaries between the two as these have been an ongoing problem in the development of policy. Secondly, it looks at the implications of the dominance of residential care in the policy response to the needs of older people. Finally, it moves on to reflect on the origins and development of community care policy, before considering how this has changed since the 'new' Labour government came to power in 1997. This overall review of policy leads to the themes discussed in the following two chapters.

Chapter 4 examines the policy emphasis given by 'new' Labour to the concepts of partnership and collaboration, which has ensured that the development of effective systems of multi-disciplinary and inter-professional working are at the core of policies for the health and social care of older people. Starting from a consideration of the nature of collaboration, the chapter moves on to discuss the place of professional groups in the delivery of health and social care, before examining how differences in power and status can create obstacles to effective collaborative working. These are then examined at three different levels – the 'structural/organisational', the 'professional/cultural' and the 'interpersonal'. From this analysis the chapter concludes by identifying ways in which these obstacles can be transcended to establish effective collaborative working, which is described as being the 'holy grail' of current policy.

On the basis that effective collaborative working between social work and health care is the most important axis in these developments, Chapter 5 explores the historical connections between the two, drawing on material throughout social work's lengthy history. In examining texts that focus on the place of social work within health settings – particularly hospitals – the chapter identifies that social workers have always had to struggle to gain acceptance for the value and independence of their work, being routinely subjected to attempts from outside to gain control over the nature and content of their practice. In addition, the chapter argues that social workers have often had to act in accordance with priorities established by others, often forcing practice into a primarily 'administrative' frame of reference. Although a somewhat more positive role has been identified for social workers within primary health care, the chapter points out that this method of organisation is far from the norm; in addition, it notes that the possibility of a more widespread adoption of this model of organisation is therefore uncertain. The chapter moves on to explore ways in which social work has had an impact on health care policies and practice, concluding with a summary of the main ways in which a social worker could have a positive impact within a multi-disciplinary environment.

The final part of the book examines the developing nature of social work practice with older people. Chapter 6 forms a bridge between the first two parts and the final chapters, by exploring the history and development of social work practice with older people, on the basis that a proper understanding of this is a pre-condition of a fuller understanding of contemporary developments. The chapter addresses the reality that social work with older people has always been a less well developed area of practice, a situation that the community care reforms did not alter, even though the needs of older people have been accorded a much higher priority than before. It argues that the administrative dominance of models of care management has in fact served to maintain the relatively low status of this aspect of work. By contrast, the chapter identifies the range of values, skills and knowledge that would be needed to work successfully with older people, drawing on a full range of social work theories and methods, and argues that a change in the way in which social work with older people is conceived could yield benefits both for service users and for social work practitioners.

The final three chapters each focus on a core issue in the organisation of a service response to the needs of older people. The chapters seek to provide practical support and guidance to social workers working within the areas of assessment, care management and intermediate care. Chapter 7 examines the central place of assessment in social work with older people. As with all aspects of social work, the act of assessment is acknowledged as being the foundation of good practice; however, the chapter argues that the exigencies of policy development in community care have created an assessment role where priority is given to carrying out the task as quickly as possible, without exploring individuals' circumstances in depth. This has led to practice that is unfulfilling for social workers, and unsatisfactory for service users. The chapter also explores the implications of two major policy developments that are being enacted in parallel – the policy to reduce delayed discharges from hospital care, and the development of a single assessment process. The themes that have been raised in the chapter are then addressed through the medium of an extended practice scenario, which gives an indication of the complexity of assessment work in practice.

Practice scenarios are also used to illustrate the practice themes in both Chapter 8 and Chapter 9. Chapter 8 explores the development of care management, one of the most significant features of social work practice in community care. Its origins in the United States are charted, along with the establishment of care management pilot projects in Britain in the 1980s. The chapter identifies the critical fact that the model of care management that has been developed under community care differs in many key respects from the projects from which it emerged, particularly in the targeted nature of the populations originally served by care management and the requirement for well developed social work skills in the performance of care management duties. By contrast, the model of care management that has come to dominate for older people has become a bulk service for large numbers of people, where highly developed social work skills are almost an irrelevance to the success of policy. The chapter argues that a more imaginative response to the needs of older people is possible, and outlines organisational arrangements that might help to bring such change about. The themes of the chapter are then brought together in a practice scenario, which focuses on the extent to which timely, sensitive, skilled social work interventions can make a genuine difference to the lives of service users and carers.

Chapter 9 concentrates on the role of social work in relation to the development of intermediate care, one of the major policy priorities in health and social care for older people. The chapter outlines the genesis of intermediate care, focusing particularly on the wealth of small projects that sought to rehabilitate older people. It illustrates how these individual projects coalesced into the overarching framework of 'intermediate care', despite the fact that the evidence base that should theoretically have demonstrated the effectiveness of particular forms of service provision was relatively sketchy. The chapter goes on to discuss the role of social work within the provision of intermediate care. It suggests that a clear analysis of the role of social work in helping older people recover their capacity to live independently has not yet been undertaken, despite the plethora of research which focuses on the occupational roles of therapists in the process. The chapter seeks to rectify this omission by identifying how a social worker can play a major creative role in the provision of intermediate care through a combination of the three main dimensions of social work activities. As in the previous two chapters, the dimensions of this work are illustrated through a detailed practice scenario, which outlines the way in which a social worker can contribute to the intermediate care process in both residential and community settings.

Three explanatory notes are important at this point. The first is that while the book focuses on social work practice in the British context – and seeks to have a broader relevance to practice on an international level – the particular policy and legal context to which it refers is essentially that of England. The reality of the last few years has been a gradual divergence of both law and policy within Britain. The implementation of the *Royal Commission on Long Term Care* (Sutherland Report, 1999) is a case in point; although it was decided not to implement the recommendation of free personal care in England, the opposite decision was taken in Scotland (see Chapter 3), thereby creating a clear policy divergence with major long-term implications. As a result, therefore, an author has to balance the competing demands of establishing an argument that is grounded in a clearly defined policy and legal context with the requirement to make the text as broadly applicable as possible. It is hoped that the specificity of the former does not detract from the wider applicability of the argument to other policy and legal contexts.

The second point relates to the practice scenarios, and the role they play within the text. As the above chapter summaries indicate, these scenarios have been devised to highlight the general issues produced in the preceding discussion. Inevitably, this has meant that some issues have been highlighted and others have been less developed. It is not the intention of the practice scenarios to engage with all the issues that will confront social workers in day-to-day practice. For example, none of them throw up issues of abuse, a major concern for social workers with older people in the context of *No Secrets* (DoH, 2000a). In addition, none of the three practice scenarios generate issues relating to Black or Asian service users: certainly, the dynamics of the issues generated would have been different had this been the case. Their purpose is rather to illustrate important themes in practice, rather than encapsulate all of the possible issues with which a social worker will engage. The patterns of critical reflection that they encourage should be transferable to other situations encountered throughout practice.

The third point refers to other ways in which the text has been worked upon with the intention of making it more comprehensible for its readership. Each chapter contains a summary of the main issues to have emerged from its content; in addition, most separate sections within chapters also feature a boxed summary of the main learning points. Within Chapter 4, the various precepts for successful collaborative working are also illustrated through a practice example drawn closely from the author's own research (Lymbery and Millward, 2000, 2001). The aim of this example, as with the practice scenarios mentioned above, is to ground the analytical debate in genuine practical applications.

PART 1
Context

Older People and Society

From the available evidence, old age would appear to be a stigmatized social identity. Even those who are chronologically old may disassociate themselves from 'old age'. (Pilcher, 1995: 102)

This chapter focuses on the place of older people in British society. Any capable social worker must understand the nature of ageing in order to work successfully with this group of people. This implies an understanding of the physical, biological and psychological manifestations of the ageing process; however, it also requires a grasp of two elements that are perhaps less well understood, as the experience of living as an older person cannot be fully comprehended by reference to the above three factors alone. The first of these is the political, social and cultural status of older people in contemporary society. As we will see later in this chapter, there are a number of ways in which older people are perceived as problematic, and a range of reasons that have been advanced to explain this. The chapter will argue that the theory of 'ageism' (Bytheway, 1995) can help to explain how many views that are prejudicial to the well-being of older people are perpetuated within society. The second are the subjective experiences of older people – what Thompson (1998) has termed the 'ontology' of ageing. As Biggs (1993) has explained, we cannot reach an understanding of subjective experiences of ageing if we are incapable of penetrating the inner lives of people who have become old. In addition, we need to understand how the impact of structural and cultural factors can create individual problems and difficulties for older people. The chapter will argue that an effective social work practice with older people cannot be developed unless we first understand the way in which all of the above factors can combine to affect an individual older person and her/his life.

The need to examine social work with older people will be made more pressing by demographic changes in the twenty-first century. For example, there will be an increase in the numbers of older people, both in absolute terms and as a proportion of the overall population (Shaw, 2004). There will also be a higher proportion of people categorised as dependent – both children and older people – within the population. However, the 'dependency ratio' – the proportion of people defined as economically unproductive and hence 'dependent' expressed as a proportion of those of working age in society – is likely still to remain within the boundaries that had been considered normal through the twentieth century (Tinker, 1997). It is interesting that the increase in longevity which characterises modern British society is not treated as 'one of the great successes of modern times' (Wilson, 2001: 1). Instead, there has been a focus on the problems that this could create in terms of the increased burden on the rest of society, particularly health and social care services. A crude determinism dominates the debate, where the subtleties of demographic change are underestimated or simply ignored (Pilcher, 1995). While it is clear that there will be a gradual increase in the numbers of older people requiring some level of support and assistance from health and social care services into the middle of the twenty-first century, the increased amount of need may well not reach the levels that some have forecast. In addition, no account is taken of the positive contributions that older people make to society in a range of different ways (Wilson, 2001). However, on the basis of current knowledge, it is reasonable to assume that social work services for older people will be even more required in the future than they are at present.

The chapter commences with an analysis of the nature of ageism, as it is a concept that informs the rest of the content of both the chapter and the overall book. It then considers the various ways in which ageing can be understood, moving from individual to structural considerations. Having surveyed the subject in broad terms, the chapter then summarises the range of needs that all older people experience, before considering the specific circumstances that are liable to require the assistance of a social worker. The chapter emphasises that only a minority of older people will require this level of support. This is an important corrective to the tendency of professionals to fix their understanding of ageing on the examples of the most disadvantaged and distressed people as if they represent the totality of the ageing experience (Biggs, 1993). In conclusion, the chapter notes the deficits of current services in responding to need, setting up links between this chapter and the remainder of the book.

A word on terminology is important here. Over time, the language that refers to older people has undergone a gradual transformation. For example, the phrase 'the elderly' was used in health and social care for many years in an unreflective way, without consideration of the fact that it depersonalised the people to whom it referred. As a result, an alternative conception was long overdue – but agreeing what such a term might be was problematic, given the contested nature of language. In many ways, the changes in terminology reflect a similar shift that has occurred in relation to other groups, notably people with physical or learning disabilities. While it is in the nature of language to have a certain measure of elasticity, these changes came about largely because the terminology deployed by professionals was challenged by the people to whom it referred. This has encouraged a greater degree of caution about language, and a wider understanding about the impact of previously unchallenged constructions. As a result, in line with most authors in the social work/social policy field, I have fixed on the term 'older people' as being the most accepted current usage. For example, two standard texts in this area (Marshall and Dixon, 1996; Tinker, 1997) have changed their titles as successive editions have been produced, both (currently) deploying the phrase 'older people' that is suggested here. The use of 'older people' may well prove unacceptable in future, reflecting the continuing growth of language; however, it seems sensible to deploy similar terminology to that which is most current both in academic and practice circles.

AGEISM

Ageism has been simply defined as the unwarranted application of stereotypes to older people (Bytheway, 1995). In the way it is used in this book it is different from a more generalised form of age-related discrimination, which could affect people at all ages. The distinctive quality of ageism, in British and other western societies at least, is that it is a process whereby older people are systematically disadvantaged by the place that they occupy within society. Thompson (1995) has argued that the discrimination faced by older people can be manifested at three levels, the 'structural', 'cultural' and 'personal' (Thompson, 1995; see also Thompson, 2001, for a more general application of this analysis).

While this position does have considerable analytical clarity, it fails to engage satisfactorily with the fact that these levels are interconnected in terms of an individual's actual lived experience. For example, the way in which an older person could be treated when raising a question about her/his pension may easily contain aspects of all three of Thompson's levels. The way in which the pensions system operates is part of the overall 'structural' oppression of older people; the fact that their demands for a decent standard of living are seen as representing a burden on the state is indicative of the way in which the presence of older people is seen as problematic. The idea that we are living with a 'demographic time bomb', further explored below, is an example of an ageist construction of older people, as it completely ignores the positive contribution that older people can make within society in favour of seeing them as creating a forthcoming crisis (Pilcher, 1995; Wilson, 2001) through their continued existence. At the 'cultural' level the people charged with responding to the individual's question may carry stereotypes about older people that inform the way in which they act. If the stereotype is that older people become unable to deal with relatively simple matters, the behaviour at the 'personal' level is likely to be patronising; if a contrasting stereotype is held that older people are awkward and cranky, the behaviour might shift to be more defensive and obstructive. In such a case, the three levels at which ageism might be manifest continually reinforce each other and can become indistinguishable in practice.

The following bullet points give an indication of the more common and insidious ways in which ageism can be made manifest, with particular reference to the provision of health and social care services.

- *In the policies of government, both at national and local levels.* As an example of this, it has been argued (Grimley Evans and Tallis, 2001) that the *National Service Framework for Older People* is inherently ageist because it works on the assumption that older people do not merit expensive hospital care. (This is particularly ironic given that the reduction of age-related discrimination is a key aim of the framework!) Similarly, given that the primary motivation for community care was to curb the social security budget (Lewis and Glennerster, 1996; see also Chapter 3), this can be seen as a policy constructed on the ageist basis that cost considerations have precedence over the quality of lives of older people, the majority of people affected by the policy. At the local level, it is worth noting that while the bulk of a social services department's budget is spent on the care of older people, this amounts to the smallest amount *per capita* of all the main service user groups.
- *In the way in which services for older people are organised and staffed.* As Chapter 3 will argue, the development of health and social care policy for older people has often been poorly organised and developed, with ageist assumptions at its heart (Means and Smith, 1998). The scandalous treatment of older people in institutional care in the immediate post-war years, highlighted by Townsend (1962), was a particularly striking example of this. The development of social work for older people, addressed more fully in Chapter 6, is another example of how policy and practice have had an ageist underpinning, as it has long been the least professionally developed of the various forms of social work practice (Lymbery, 1998a). Much day-to-day practice with older people is in fact carried out by staff without professional qualifications, often paid on an hourly basis, many of whom work in the independent sector where the pressure to carry out tasks within a defined time period is intense. These sorts of arrangement are scarcely in the best interests of older people, and attest to the fact that they are treated in a way that reinforces their relatively low social value.
- *In the differential development of understandings about the abuse of older people as opposed to the abuse of other groups, particularly children.* While the abuse of children has become a preoccupation within social services, the abuse of adults and older people has never been given the same level of priority. Although the publication of *No Secrets* (DoH, 2000a) has ensured that policies have been put in place the better to manage issues related to adult protection, their impact has been variable (Mathew et al., 2002). The 'discovery' of the abuse of older people occurred many years after the equivalent

discovery of the abuse of children, and yet was trivialised by the ageist terms ('granny-bashing'!) by which it was originally described. Even now, it does not have the shock value of child abuse; there are fewer headlines if an older person dies as a result of abuse or neglect than if the same fate befalls a child.

• *In the attitudes and values of those staff employed to work with older people.* As noted above, a wide range of staff are employed to work with older people, both in residential and nursing homes and in the community. The fact that many of these staff do not have professional qualifications renders them more susceptible to stereotyped and demeaning impressions of older people.

• *In the language deployed to describe older people.* This issue ranges from the casual stereotyping in everyday parlance (variations on the themes of 'silly old fool' and 'old dear') to the more insidious and dehumanising references to older people by professionals. There is also a tendency, particularly in health care settings, to refer to people by their condition rather than their names, another depersonalising and essentially dehumanising act.

It is particularly important that practitioners are enabled to understand the ways in which older people's lives are affected by factors at the structural and organisational levels, hence avoiding a reductive biologically-based view of ageing. Social workers have an occupational tendency to focus first on the needs of the individual, and can easily allow themselves to ignore wider structural issues. Practitioners must also identify other forms of power and oppression to which older people could be subject. Ageism does not operate in a vacuum and hence in isolation from other forms of oppression. Instead, these forms of oppression can combine to create even more difficulties for the older person. As a result, it is important for social work practitioners to be able to recognise and challenge multiple forms of oppression, of which ageism will be a major element.

SECTION SUMMARY

This section has explored the issue of ageism and its impact on older people. It has discussed the following issues:

• The nature of ageism and its centrality as a concept in respect of the needs of older people.
• Drawing on Thompson (1995) the various 'structural', 'cultural' and 'personal' aspects of ageism.
• The connections between ageism and other forms of oppression that older people might experience.
• The various ways in which ageism can be made manifest.

WAYS OF UNDERSTANDING
THE AGEING PROCESS

This section will summarise different approaches to understanding the ageing process. It will start at the individual level, working outwards from this to focus on older people in the context of society. The content of this section is a necessarily condensed version of material that can be found in standard texts on gerontology and social gerontology (see, for example, Bond et al., 1993a). Its purpose is to examine the experiences of ageing through a variety of theoretical prisms. The overall intention is to present the issues of which social workers need to be aware if they are to pursue their roles successfully.

A note of caution is appropriate at this point: while the chapter does start its survey with the impact of biological ageing it is imperative not to perceive older people only in terms of what happens to them physically as they age. Such an attitude can lead to what has been termed 'biological reductionism' (Biggs, 1993), where the complexity of an individual's life and experiences is reduced to the apparent verities of what will inevitably occur to the physical body. Of course, there are observable physical changes when one ages; it is important to know what these are and to understand the impact that these might have on the individual and others. Although ageing is a physical fact, it is not inherently problematic. The vast majority of people are quite able to manage the process of ageing without requiring the support of social workers. It is therefore important to see older people in a more rounded light, not simply as the collection of problems that a purely physical/biological approach might seem to encourage.

PHYSICAL/BIOLOGICAL CHANGES

The process of human ageing is affected to a large measure by certain universal truths, which have their basis in biological fact (Briggs, 1993). For example, there are four facets of ageing that have been generally accepted:

- That it is *universal*, in that it will inevitably affect all people.
- That it is *progressive*, a continuous process throughout life.
- That ageing is *intrinsic* to the human organism.
- That it is *degenerative* in a biological sense (Strehler, 1962; in Bond et al., 1993b).

However, while particular diseases may be associated with the process of ageing, ageing is not in itself a disease, although Briggs (1993) points out that the distinction between 'ageing' and 'disease' is often quite narrow and arbitrary. For the sake of clarity, this sub-section will focus on those processes that can clearly be accounted as part of the 'normal' process of ageing, not all of which will necessarily involve the intervention of health and social care services. Indeed: 'Decline in physiological function may be of little consequence to an older person until they cross some threshold so that they are no longer able to carry out necessary activities' (Briggs, 1993: 56). However, some aspects of biological ageing – for example, recovery from a stroke, the onset of dementia – will almost certainly require this form of assistance.

The first sub-group of issues is concerned with decline in sensory functioning. For example, many older people – approximately one in three people over the age of 65 (Briggs, 1993) – experience some measure of hearing loss. While there are numerous ways in which this loss can be compensated, it can also create some practical and psychological problems, particularly when the loss of hearing has an impact on day-to-day living. An even higher proportion of older people experience some impairment of vision: indeed, practically all older people need spectacles to assist them in some aspect of their lives (Briggs, 1993). For the majority, the difficulties that the impairment creates can be managed relatively easily; however, approximately one in four older people have continuing difficulties that the use of spectacles alone cannot resolve. In particular, older people are much more likely to develop *cataracts* (a compression of the lens in the eye, leading to reduced vision) or to experience problems due to the onset of *glaucoma*, raised pressure of the fluid in the eyeball, usually leading to a gradual loss of peripheral and later central vision.

Similarly, there are a number of ways in which changes to our biological makeup affect the bodily appearance as we age. Two of these represent the most obvious physical signs of ageing. The first of these is wrinkling of the skin, due to a gradual degeneration in its elastic tissues. This is more severe where an individual has been extensively exposed to strong sunlight, and also varies according to ethnicity. The second of these is that the skin and (most noticeably) the hair tend to lose their pigment with age. Neither of these observably common experiences of ageing are usually, in themselves, problematic. Similarly, an inevitable decline in muscle power is associated with ageing, although this can be compensated to some extent by maintaining physical activity. Weight-bearing exercise can also help to preserve bone density, the reduction of which is a significant feature of ageing, especially for women. Many women experience *osteoporosis* – an extreme thinning of bone density – following the menopause, due to changes in the hormonal balance. This renders the individual more prone to fractures and is also the cause of skeletal and postural problems, which can – in more severe cases – affect the functioning of internal organs such as the heart and lungs. Many people also experience a form of arthritis as they age. The more commonly experienced is *osteoarthritis*, which is usually caused by wear and tear on the major weight-bearing joints such as hips and knees. In the worst cases affected joints can be replaced, although the replacements only have a limited lifespan. The less common form is *rheumatoid arthritis*, which usually affects the smaller joints such as hands and wrists, but is often experienced as more painful.

The internal functioning of the body also alters with age in a variety of ways. For example, changes in kidney and bladder function are commonly experienced. The operation of the kidneys generally starts to deteriorate from the age of about 30 years, without necessarily creating a problem in later life. There is often a weakening of bladder function associated with ageing, with older men experiencing problems with the prostate gland and women being particularly susceptible to stress incontinence. In both of these cases effective medical intervention can help to maintain bladder function; however, more serious and irreversible bladder problems can also be created by a range of diseases: for example, incontinence is strongly associated with recovery from a stroke and also with dementia.

Changes are also generally experienced in respect of the heart and lungs during the ageing process. For example, heart muscles degenerate with age, thereby becoming less effective and often requiring additional support to regulate the rhythm of the heart. In serious cases, this can lead to heart failure, where the heart is no longer sufficiently effective to pump blood around the body. Similarly, the lungs become less efficient with age, creating problems with breathing. A combination of the above two occurrences can render it difficult for an older person to maintain the healthy level of exercise that can help to control the rate of physical decline in respect of muscle tone and bone density, noted above. Problems with circulation can be exacerbated by *atherosclerosis*, the 'furring up' of arteries. This is particularly prevalent in developed societies, aggravated by a number of factors including high fat and salt diets, high blood pressure, smoking, etc. which are characteristic of countries such as Britain and the United States. The range of problems that can be created by this process include one of the largest causes of death in industrialised societies, coronary heart disease.

Older people are more likely than younger people to be affected by various forms of hormonal imbalance, such as diabetes and disorders of the thyroid gland. In addition, as noted above, older women are particularly susceptible to *osteoporosis*. As well as the difficulties that this can create deriving from reductions in bone density, noted above, it can also create physical changes – for example, thinning of vaginal walls and vaginal dryness – that can adversely affect sexual functioning. Similar physiologically-based sexual problems can also afflict men in later life, due to reductions in the production of testosterone.

Finally, a number of physiological effects can result from disorders to the brain and nervous system. The process of *atherosclerosis*, noted above, can affect the blood supply to part of the brain causing a stroke. As we shall see, this is a major cause of death and illness amongst older people. This process can also lead to one of the two main forms of dementia. Perhaps the most commonly feared disease affecting older people is *Alzheimer's disease*, a degenerative condition of the brain's nerve cells. This affects around 2–3% of those aged over 65, rising to around 20% of those aged over 80. The prognosis for people with *Alzheimer's disease* is poor, with a gradual loss of memory leading to increasing levels of behavioural difficulties over a number of years. There are also other sorts of disease that can affect the brain's ability to function. For example, *Parkinson's disease* causes selective degeneration in the nerve cells that release the chemical transmitter 'dopamine'. While this disease can affect people in their middle years, it is particularly associated with old age.

This sub-section has indicated the main physical and biological changes that are likely to occur for older people. Although some of these may precipitate the involvement of health and social care services, most such involvement will be brought about by 'abnormal' as opposed to 'normal' ageing – the presence of illness and/or disease. There are also other aspects of ageing that affect this; the following sub-section considers one of these, the psychological impact of ageing.

PSYCHOLOGICAL CHANGES

Unlike the picture created by the examination of biological changes that occur during the ageing process, a study of the psychological impact of ageing presents a more varied set of outcomes. As Coleman (1993a) has observed, psychological ageing is not necessarily negative; however, the dominance of biologically derived understandings of the ageing process has ensured that the negative effects are emphasised over the positive. This is not aided by the 'folk' conceptions we often hold of older people being forgetful and not quite 'with it'. In reality, there are psychological gains as well as losses in the ageing process; often the two balance each other out.

There are two main areas in which the popular belief is that older people experience a considerable decline in their ability to function. The first of these is in respect of intellectual ability. However, the evidence suggests that there is minimal decline in intellectual functioning up to 70 years, with some people showing no decline at all, although there is an increased likelihood of some decline in intellectual functioning in very old age (Coleman, 1993a). As with physical activity, it has been suggested that the maintenance of mental 'exercise' can help the brain to function as well as it can. Further research has shown that there may be changes in the nature of one's intelligence with age. For example, while there may be a decline in what has been termed 'fluid' intelligence (that is, the ability to solve new and unfamiliar problems quickly) this may be balanced by the stability (and possibly even increase) in 'crystallised' intelligence (that is, the way an individual can bring her/his experience to bear on a problem). This also links to the 'common-sense' attribution of wisdom to older people, a perspective that is particularly common in societies that value, even venerate, age and experience (Slater, 1995). Of course, as with many issues that affect the experience of ageing, intellectual functioning may be affected by biological events, such as Alzheimer's disease.

Memory loss is popularly believed to be the other key aspect of decline in psychological functioning in old age. While there are changes in memory function, they cannot all simply be labelled as indicative of deterioration and decline. However, there are some areas of decline that do appear to affect most older people. For example, as Coleman (1993a: 75) points out: 'difficulties occur for older people when they have to process novel information . . . especially if they have to deal with other problems and distractions'. This could relate to older people's reduced capacity for 'fluid' intelligence, noted above. Despite this, it can be concluded that the reduction in the efficiency of an older person's memory is less sharp than might popularly be understood. Of course, if an older person is affected by conditions such as dementia, memory functioning will deteriorate markedly; even here, as Jones (2004) has argued, the nature of memory loss is more complex than has hitherto been acknowledged. However, the general points about memory loss do relate to 'normal' as opposed to 'abnormal processes of ageing. In addition, there will be a wide variety of experiences within the broad category of 'older people', just as there are within the wider population.

As Coleman (1993a) has indicated, older people retain a considerable ability to learn new tasks and skills – with the possible *caveat* that not all older people have the *desire* to learn a repertoire of new skills and abilities. In addition, many older people tend to underestimate their abilities, perhaps believing that speed of recall (the exercise of 'fluid' intelligence where they may experience difficulties) is a better proxy for the ability to assimilate new knowledge, rather than the more sophisticated act of making sense of complex information (the exercise of 'crystallised' intelligence) (Slater, 1995). Indeed, as reported by Coleman (1993a) older people can often make good sense of a mass of apparently contradictory information. On balance, therefore, during the course of 'normal' ageing older people retain much of the capacity for learning and memory that they possessed as adults. While there are age-related changes, these do not constitute a major obstacle to the ability to function effectively in later life.

Another key element of psychological change amongst older people concerns the extent to which their personality alters as they age. While a range of research has been carried out on the response of older people to their changed circumstances, the findings do not all point in one direction (Coleman, 1993b). For example, there is a body of research that suggests that people have enduring personality characteristics that endure into old age (Slater, 1995), although this is often accompanied by suggestions that older people do change some facets of their behaviour and interests (Coleman, 1993b). By contrast, the influential research by Cumming and Henry (1961) hypothesised that older people undergo a process of disengagement with the external world, preferring to withdraw into themselves. While the general theory of disengagement has been criticised for its apparent justification of policies that actively exclude older people (Estes et al., 2001a; Pilcher, 1995), at the psychological level it does accord with other research that suggests that people tend to become more introverted and inward-looking as they age (Coleman, 1993a).

A possible corollary of this is that older people are more likely to experience depression than younger people (Slater, 1995). However, some caution about this conclusion is warranted on two counts. First, it does not appear that older people are any more likely to become seriously clinically depressed (Coleman, 1993b). Secondly, it is difficult to be entirely accurate about the incidence of depression since the basis for diagnosis varies from clinician to clinician (Coleman, 1993b) and the suspicion exists that older people are more likely to confuse the symptoms of depression with the symptoms of an illness with a physical cause (Slater, 1995). Given that the older one gets, the more one is likely to experience a range of losses and other negative life events, it is perhaps not surprising that older people can become depressed. Indeed, in the light of this Slater (1995) suggests that it is remarkable that depression is not more common amongst older people.

This partial survey of the psychological impact of ageing reveals a similar picture to that of the previous sub-section: that although older people experience some psychological changes regarding issues such as intellectual functioning, cognitive ability, memory and learning, the impact of these changes is less dramatic than might be popularly believed. There is nothing about the process of ageing that leaves older people inherently less able to cope with the psychological demands of everyday life. Indeed, older people seem to be remarkably resilient in the face of these pressures. In the face of this evidence, combined with the fact that biologically driven theories of ageing also fail to explain the place of older people in society, we need to consider wider structural issues that affect ageing – particularly the way in which the experience of ageing is socially constructed, and the place of older people in the political and economic context of society.

SOCIAL CONSTRUCTIONIST PERSPECTIVES

As Thompson (1995) suggests, the process of ageing can be understood in more ways than simply focusing on the biological and psychological. He argues that various elements that make up our understandings of old age are socially constructed. Indeed, whereas the physical signs of ageing are slow to accumulate, the various social constructions of ageing are applied suddenly, and are experienced as particularly problematic as a result (Biggs, 1993). The first of these is the construction of 'retirement', which has become central to the experience of older people and which defines most clearly the point at which one officially becomes an 'older person'. As Phillipson (1982) has argued, the concept of 'retirement' was primarily created to meet the needs of the capitalist economy, ensuring that work would be redistributed from older to younger people. This has been particularly important in times of high unemployment – the 1930s being a classic example – when defining people as surplus to economic requirements was helpful in appearing to reduce the numbers of people defined as 'unemployed'. The construction of the concept of 'retirement' was also assisted by passage of pensions legislation in the first part of the twentieth century; although this was heralded as a socially beneficial event for older people, it also created a safety net for older workers, meaning that employers no longer needed to accept any sort of responsibility for their longer-term welfare (Phillipson, 1982). While retirement can have beneficial consequences for individuals and their families, it is a fact that the older one becomes the more likely one is to join the ranks of the poorest people; for example, 37% of pensioner couples over the age of 85 are in the bottom quintile of net income, as opposed to 24% of those aged between 60 and 74 (ONS, 2001).

By the early years of the twenty-first century, retirement has become something that practically all older people will experience. Indeed, in the 1980s, the growth of unemployment heralded a rapid growth in the experience of early retirement, prompted by the politically unacceptable reality of mass unemployment (Phillipson, 1993). Concerns about the impact of demographic change, particularly the projected shortage of people of working age in the middle of the twenty-first century (Shaw, 2004), have led to an ongoing debate about the need to harmonise retirement ages and to 'allow' older people to work longer. Both of these moves will potentially increase the numbers of people available for work, thereby helping to reduce some of the projected difficulties in respect of the dependency ratio.

The experience of retirement from paid employment is therefore a major part of the way in which society constructs old age. However, the experiences of older people are also mediated by various other socially constructed artefacts – for example, 'class', 'gender' and 'race' (Thompson, 1995). Older people from the 'working class' experience ageing in a qualitatively different manner than people from the middle and upper classes, as the effects of earlier disadvantage and inequality are magnified by getting older. Therefore, while not all older people are at an increased likelihood of experiencing poverty, those people so afflicted are disproportionately from the working classes, who were more likely to be in poorly paid employment without the benefits of an occupational pension, and hence reliant on the state pension as their primary source of income. At the same time, these same people are more likely to experience poor health (Townsend et al., 1992), while their housing quality is also significantly worse than for the population at large. For example, 13.9% of people over the age of 85 live without central heating as opposed to 7.0% of those people between the ages of 50 and 64 (ONS, 2001). Similarly, 39.2% of those over 85 live in rented accommodation, which often provides the worst form of housing available, as opposed to 19.8% of those people aged between 50 and 64 (ONS, 2001). At the same time, increasing numbers of the very oldest people (i.e. those over the age of 85) live alone (ONS, 2001). The financial hardship of many working class older people also has an impact on their leisure activities, as they are more likely to be reliant on public transport, which is often inadequate – particularly in rural areas. At the same time, they are likely not to have sufficient disposable income to engage in a number of leisure pursuits. A combination of all of these factors means that older people of working class background are far more likely to come to the attention of social services than others. In particular, economic strength in old age means that an individual does not have to approach social services for assistance, given that this can be purchased direct.

As far as 'gender' is concerned, it is vital to recognise the impact that this has on the lives of older women, who greatly outnumber men amongst older people, particularly at 75 years and beyond. In 2002, there were almost 4.2 m people over the age of 75 in Britain, 61.35% of whom were women and 38.65% of whom were men (adapted from ONS, 2001). With the increased numbers of women in the workplace they are likely to experience all the issues that relate to retirement in the same way as men. In addition to this, women are significantly more likely than men to have caring responsibilities that will continue into old age (Evandrou, 1997), as women have long been assigned the role as 'carers' within British society. As Hughes and Mtezuka (1992) have observed, when older women require care themselves this 'natural' order is in fact overturned. The gendered assignation of caring roles to older women is mirrored by other assumptions about the nature of older women. Within a society fixated on the physical attractiveness of women, the loss of this commodity renders older women 'invisible'. Indeed, the cultural references to older women tend to portray them as crones, harpies and witches (Hughes and Mtezuka, 1992), hardly the most positive of points of reference. It should also be added that gendered expectations of behaviour can also affect older men, who may be given little opportunity to express their emotional responses to the losses of old age.

'Race' is another important variable in considering ageing in British society (Blakemore and Boneham, 1994). While the majority of post-war immigrants were predominantly adults and younger people, the first generations of immigrants are progressively ageing, ensuring that they are now a larger proportion of the older population as a whole (Blakemore and Boneham, 1994). In addition, there are many 'invisible' minorities – from Irish and eastern European backgrounds – who also have needs that are particular to their group, which may not be adequately met. As a way of conceptualising the experience of older people from ethnic minorities, Norman (1985) has suggested they are subjected to a form of 'triple jeopardy', often experiencing forms of discrimination based on class and race, in addition to oppression based on age. It is the interlocking nature of these forms of oppression that create particular problems for such older people.

There are also numerous culturally bound images of ageing that are common within society. It is rare, for example, that any action by an older person – other than the Queen or Rupert Murdoch! – is deemed to be worthy of news coverage. When older people do appear in the news the coverage is likely to be patronising and hence demeaning (Aldridge, 1994). Similarly, there are relatively few positive images of older people to be found in the visual media – in films, television and advertising. Indeed, despite the numbers of older people in society, advertising directed specifically at them is 'ghettoised' into specialist publications and daytime television. Although older people do inhabit the pages of quality literature (see Johnson, 2004) their presence in the more popular forms of media are few and far between. Although most television 'soaps' contain older characters, often portrayed by highly skilled actors, the story-lines that they tend to be given are more limited in their scope than the younger characters'. In general, forms of popular culture seek to play commonly accepted attitudes and forms of behaviour back to its audience, rather than seeking to challenge and change perceptions: in this way the inherent 'conservatism' of much of its coverage can be readily explained.

THE POLITICAL ECONOMY OF AGEING

The development of the above concept is particularly associated with the writings of Estes (1979) in the United States and Phillipson (1982) in Britain. An essential element of their argument is that mainstream thinking has constructed age as exclusively an individual problem, ignoring the impact of broader social structures on the way in which each individual experiences her/his ageing (Estes et al., 2001a). By contrast, Estes (1979) and Phillipson (1982) have argued that it is also important to understand the ageing process in western societies. They have suggested that older people are seen as inherently problematic primarily because they represent a drain on resources, to which they no longer contribute actively either as tax-payers or as parents raising the next generation of tax-payers. Because of this, older people are accorded a lower status in a capitalist society than other 'productive' citizens.

Estes (2001) has suggested that there are three ways in which this dominant view is perpetuated:

- Through the creation of cultural images and representations of ageing (which was addressed in the previous sub-section).
- Through an appeal to the requirements of the economic system.
- Through focusing on ageing as a 'rational' problem amenable to 'technical' problem-solving, without consideration of the conflicts and disagreements that might underpin the debate.

The latter two points have been well exemplified in the debate concerning the supposed 'demographic time bomb', where the essential 'problem' is defined as the fact that the economy cannot sustain increasing numbers of older people. If one were to accept this economic argument, it follows that some form of technical 'solution' might be proposed. Two of these have already been trailed in Britain. The first is a 'harmonisation' of retirement ages for men and women, to take place between 2010 and 2020 (Shaw, 2004), which is in fact an increase in the pensionable age for women from 60 to 65. The second is the outline proposal that all people should be allowed to work beyond the retirement age should they and their employers so desire. Both of these changes would have the result of reducing the numbers of people claiming their pensions and hence allaying the fears about the unproductive numbers of older people in society. While there are rational arguments in favour of both proposals, the fact remains that they are both driven by economic calculations. To be more credible, they need to be placed within the context of a fundamental debate about the most appropriate way to structure society in order to ensure the best quality of life for older people.

The essential tenets of the political economy approach to the study of ageing are usefully summarised in the following quotation:

> In the political economy perspective, social policies pertaining to retirement income, health and social benefits and entitlements are seen as products of economic, political and sociocultural processes and forces that interact in any given socio-cultural period. (Estes et al., 2001a: 40)

Estes and colleagues (2001b) are particularly critical of those theories of ageing that do not take these factors into account. In their view, this has resulted in policies that treat old age as a 'disease' and older people as primarily therefore a medical problem; these policies are reinforced by the various forms of practice – in health and social care services in particular – which only treat older people in relation to their presumed medical problem, failing to respond to them as individual citizens. They suggest that the dominance of the medical paradigm for understanding ageing has acted to suppress the development of alternative forms of understanding, and effectively ignores the influence of four critical factors on ageing:

- Income and education;
- Safe and supportive housing environments;
- Opportunities for meaningful human interactions;
- Public financing for rehabilitation (Estes et al., 2001b).

The effects of inequality on health outcomes have become more widely recognised (Townsend et al., 1992), but public policy has not been widely constructed on this knowledge. In fact, although there has been increased public finance available for rehabilitation and intermediate care – an extra £900m was promised in the *NHS Plan* (DoH, 2000b) – this is less about the inherent benefits to older people of enhanced rehabilitation than it is an economically driven attempt to free up beds in hospitals. Therefore, in a number of ways, the political economy approach reminds us of the marginal status of most older people in society. However, this too can only provide a partial understanding for social workers, as it fails to engage with the areas of difference between the experiences and outlook of people from similar economic and social circumstances. An examination of the nature of identity in old age is therefore a necessary element in our overall understanding.

IDENTITY AND AGEING

With the changes that will inevitably affect the ageing body, combined with the acknowledgement that the organisation of society profoundly affects the experience of ageing, it is important to establish a sense of how each older person experiences her/his personal encounter with old age. For example, Nolan et al. (2001a: 9) have suggested that the increased frailty of extreme old age creates an 'existential challenge' for older people. Thompson (1998) has discussed the need to establish a different way of looking at the individual older person, suggesting that more work is needed to establish an understanding of what he has termed the 'ontology' of ageing. Indeed, models of ageing that derive from the biological, social constructionist and political economy perspectives have relatively little to say about the way in which the process of ageing may be experienced by the individual.

In examining what effect ageing might have on the identity of the older person, Biggs (1999) has suggested that three critical factors – drawn from a combination of sociological and psychodynamic theory – should be considered:

- Ageing takes place in a potentially hostile environment which over-emphasises productivity and consumption.
- Societal changes occur very rapidly, necessarily impacting on the identity of the individual older person.
- Despite all the changes to which an ageing person is subject, an 'inner self' will tend to continue.

Although the self-confidence and self-image of older people may well be more fragile than for younger people, which can lead to the internalisation of negative societal attitudes, he suggests that the essential characteristics of an individual's identity will remain, despite being subjected to numerous challenges and assaults. Taking this insight into account, it would seem that a vital role for a social worker is to contribute to the maintenance of an older person's sense of identity under circumstances where events will conspire to threaten it. In addition, while the individual identity will be affected by social and economic factors, it will not be predetermined by such factors. Each individual will respond differently to identical sets of occurrence; in working to assist somebody at a time of change or transition in her/his life the uniqueness of this response needs to be recognised and form the basis of future work. It will be difficult to help a person through fundamental changes in her/his life without grasping how those changes are perceived by the individual.

The theory of the 'life course' (Hockey and James, 2003) has been advanced to link the individual experience of ageing with the structural factors that have a major influence on this. Here, it is argued that a fuller understanding of the process of ageing can be gained through connecting a number of factors that combine to construct each individual's experience. For example, each person belongs to a 'cohort' (Pilcher, 1995) of people, who share similar experiences due to their membership of a group of people comprised of people of similar age. In addition to this, people can claim memberships of other groups that are not dependent on their age – their gender, class, race, etc. These factors will create other sets of experiences which will differ from the first. An understanding of the individual experience of ageing is generated from an understanding of these influences, together with the specific psychological makeup of the individual, her/his family background and experiences, etc. Identity, therefore, is a complex entity moulded from these various elements.

THE NEEDS OF OLDER PEOPLE AND THE SOCIAL WORK ROLE

As the preceding section makes clear, there are numerous issues that could lead to a reduction in the quality of life experienced by older people. While this section will not attempt to itemise all the eventualities that could precipitate changes in an older person's circumstances that might call for the involvement of health and social care services, it will identify some key general themes. In so doing, it will draw directly on the insights generated through the previous section.

ILLNESS, DISABILITY AND PHYSICAL FRAILTY

Undoubtedly the single event that is most likely to promote the involvement of health and social care services is the onset of physical illness, a growth in the level of disability experienced by an individual, or an increased level of physical frailty. As the previous section indicated, older people are more likely to be subject to various manifestations of any one of the three above. For example, 67% of men, and 74% of women, over the age of 85 have a long-term illness or disability that limits their activities (ONS, 2001). Given the expressed policy intention is for care services to be designed to maintain people in their own homes for as long as possible – an aspiration expressed in both *Caring for People* (DoH, 1989) and the *NHS Plan* (DoH, 2000b) – there is an urgent role for services to function in such a way as to allow that policy aspiration to be met. The fact that there has been a reduction in the proportion of people in long-stay institutional care (ONS, 2001) is some evidence that there have been genuine moves in that direction. Problems that would previously have caused the automatic admission of an older person into long-stay care – hip fractures, strokes, heart disease, etc. – are now increasingly managed within the person's own home. Social workers are an integral part in the process by which assessments are made concerning an older person's ability to manage at home, the nature and extent of care support that is required, as well as the contributions from family and other care-givers (see Chapter 7). They also have a key role in the continuing management of care packages (see Chapter 8). In addition, the proliferation of 'intermediate care' services that enable older people to maintain their independence and autonomy also creates a potential role for the social worker (see Chapter 9), although this has been relatively little developed as yet.

Where problems stem from deterioration in the physical health of an older person, the social worker needs to have a general understanding of the causes and effects of the conditions that have caused the problems. For example, it is important for a social worker to understand that the nature of life-threatening conditions for older people changes with age. While cancer is the main cause of death for those people between the ages of 50 and 64 years, other factors predominate for older people. There is an increased likelihood of heart disease or related problems of the circulatory system, as well as an increased likelihood of respiratory problems (ONS, 2001). However, they also need to recognise where specialist knowledge about specific aspects of a person's condition is required. For medical matters that require the knowledge of a doctor this may appear self-evident; however, there are also other aspects of health and life-style where other forms of expertise will be needed. For example, the area of diet and nutrition is a vital factor in the maintenance of good health (Copeman and Hyland, 2000) while physiotherapy can play an active role in the recovery of an older person's independence (Randall and Glasgow, 2000). In neither case would a social worker be expected to have the specialist knowledge to carry out these tasks, but they do need to understand how important they may be for an older person's overall welfare. Similarly, the contributions of nursing, occupational therapy and podiatry will also be an essential component of a co-ordinated response to the changing physical needs of older people. This argues for a multi-disciplinary approach to the organisation of the response to the needs of older people. However, as explored in Chapters 4 and 5, there does need to be some caution about the potential for collaborative working to resolve some of these historical problems.

DEMENTIA, DEPRESSION AND OTHER COGNITIVE IMPAIRMENTS

Social workers will almost certainly become involved where there are significant levels of cognitive impairment in an older person. For example, where there is progressive dementia it will become increasingly difficult for an individual to maintain her/his level of independence – creating problems both for the person concerned and also for any carers that are involved. The disruption caused to normal, everyday patterns of living will become so intense that additional levels of support will almost certainly be required.

One of the key practical problems lies in understanding the various forms of dementia and their effects. In addition, social workers often confront difficulties in securing accurate information on which to base care plans, as many people are broadly characterised as having 'dementia' or being 'senile', without any detail about the nature of the condition being communicated. This creates a particular problem because, as noted with respect to physical illness and disease, there are many aspects of the various cognitive impairments where the social worker will be reliant upon others for detailed information. The aetiology of dementia is a complex subject, on which specialist medical guidance is required. This chapter can only give general guidance about the most commonly encountered forms of dementia, their likely prognosis and possible options for the provision of care services.

As Goldsmith (1996) has pointed out, dementia is not in itself an illness, but a syndrome that is caused by a number of other illnesses. Of these, the numerically most significant is *Alzheimer's disease*. Indeed, in many people's minds, there is an automatic connection between the two. However, there are numerous other causes of dementia that can afflict older people. The second most common is *multi-infarct dementia*, caused by a succession of small 'strokes', in which parts of the brain are starved of a blood supply. In addition, much less commonly, a number of other conditions can cause dementia, illustrating the complexity of diagnosis and treatment. It is therefore vital to establish the nature of dementia in each circumstance, as this will necessarily affect the nature of the treatment provided. The importance of social workers possessing this general level of understanding of dementia cannot be underestimated. Certainly, it would be impossible to construct a viable care plan without clarity about the likely progress and effects of Alzheimer's disease, for example.

Similarly, a social worker is well advised to encourage a service user who appears to be depressed – or that person's carer – to seek specialist advice and support, as this is likely to reap benefits that are beyond the individual social worker's capabilities. In all such circumstances, the social worker has to recognise the limits of her/his knowledge and professional role. However, within these limits the social worker still has an important role to play and her/his skills will be of the utmost importance. The experience of any cognitive impairment – particularly dementia – is acutely distressing for all concerned, requiring a high level of skill on the part of all practitioners involved.

WORKING WITH CARERS

While many of those defined as 'carers' provide care for a range of people, it is in respect of older people that their numbers are particularly significant. It was estimated that approximately 3.4 m people were providing significant levels (in excess of 20 hours per week) of care for people in the 1990s, roughly half of which were living in the same house as the person cared-for (usually a spouse) with the other half living elsewhere (Evandrou, 1997). While the gender composition of the former group was broadly even, the latter group comprised significantly more women than men, reflecting the gendered nature of caring (Arber and Ginn, 1991). While people have many motivations for carrying out a caring role – reciprocity, obligation, expectation, lack of alternatives, etc. – there is little doubt that some of the conditions that can affect older people have a profoundly distressing impact on carers as well. In addition, the sheer volume of work undertaken by informal carers is a vital component of the entire system of care, without which it could barely function.

In recognition of this the 'new' Labour government instigated a *National Strategy for Carers* (DoH, 1999) to co-ordinate policy in relation to carers. While the concept of a 'carer's assessment' has long been a feature of community care, its impact was constrained by the fact that no resources were allocated to meet the needs that could be identified. Although the Carers (Recognition and Services) Act 1996 obliged local authorities to provide an assessment for each carer who requested one, an obligation that was reinforced by the passage of the Carers and Disabled Children Act 2000 (DoH, 2001b), practice was still heavily circumscribed by a lack of resources. Even the additional resources promised in the *National Strategy for Carers* (DoH, 1999) only scratched the surface of the problem. In fact, the guarantee that carers could receive an extra £50 a week by 2050 (!) was faintly risible (DoH, 1999), an archetypal promise of 'jam tomorrow'.

In practice, social workers involved with older people are particularly well aware of the needs of carers, especially the fact that support for the carer is often a prerequisite for enabling an individual to remain at home. At the same time, social workers are also aware that there may be problems and tensions in the caring relationship – the needs of the service user and carer should not be presumed to be identical, and conflict may be anticipated in many cases. Negotiating, and potentially mediating, between the potential conflicts is a key role for social workers, as Chapter 6 will explore in more detail.

TRANSITION AND CHANGE

This sub-section is closely connected to the one that follows. Older people experience numerous transitions in later life, many of which are concerned with various aspects of loss. Social workers are likely to become involved with older people at precisely such a point – when they are no longer capable of managing their lives independently and require the support of paid carers, or when they can no longer live in their own home, needing to transfer to sheltered accommodation or some form of institutional care. By the nature of social work's role with older people, practitioners will normally become involved with older people at precisely the points at which some form of transition is needed.

Two examples of this are the process of discharge from hospital (see Chapter 7) and admission into long-term care. Both of these events occur when people are at their most vulnerable, feeling powerless to affect their lives in a positive way, and often subjected to well-meaning but destructive guidance from family members. The balance between autonomy and protection – at the root of much contemporary social work with adults in general, and older people in particular – looms particularly large here. Many family members understandably emphasise the need for safety in decision-making, often believing that residential or nursing homes will be 'safer' places than the home. By contrast, many older people are loath to give up their independence and are desperate to remain in their own homes. As one older person who had experienced some weeks away from home put it: 'more than anything in the world I want to go home, back to *my* home' (in Hart et al., 2005). Here the identity of the older person is clearly bound up in being able to return to live independently in what she was clear was *her* space. A key role for the social worker is being able to manage and negotiate the conflicts that may arise in such a situation.

BEREAVEMENT AND LOSS

While bereavement and loss are an inevitable part of life, they are experienced most by older people. The older one becomes, the more likely it is that many of the people to whom you have been close in life – spouse, friends, relatives – will die. While many people will be profoundly affected by any one of these events, other older people are able to take even multiple bereavements in their stride. Therefore, a social worker must not assume that the experiences and emotions of every older person will be identical – s/he must start from the specific experiences of each person and work alongside her/him in accordance with this.

In addition, it is likely that each transition experienced by an older person will be accompanied by some form of loss. For example, if an older person requires assistance with many activities of daily living – bathing, cleaning, shopping, etc. – s/he may also experience a sense of loss of those abilities that had previously been taken for granted. If the person becomes unable easily to leave the house, there may also be a sense of loss regarding social activities. In addition, any admission to sheltered housing or institutional care implies a loss of home and/or independence. As we shall observe in Chapter 6, the nature of social work with older people has historically provided limited opportunities for practitioners to engage with these issues, leaving a number of emotional and psychological needs unaddressed.

ABUSE AND PROTECTION

As noted earlier in this chapter, the publication of *No Secrets* (DoH, 2000a) has ensured that the issue of the protection of adults from abuse and harm has assumed a higher priority in the provision of services for older people. The establishment of Adult Protection Coordinators in many locations has meant that more allegations of abuse are being addressed within Social Services Departments (SSDs) (Cambridge and Parkes, 2004). However, the establishment of procedures does not define the appropriate course of social work action; rather they provide a framework within which effective practice can take place. This must be directed by what the social worker uncovers in the process of working through the issues. For example, in some cases, abuse may have taken place within the context of a long-standing abusive relationship. In others, it may have only developed later in life, and be exacerbated by the disinhibiting effects of dementia. Yet again, the abuse could involve other family members, or be aggravated by alcohol dependence. It may be of markedly different types, ranging from direct physical or sexual abuse, to more indirect forms such as financial abuse (see Bennett et al., 1997).

Given the range of possible circumstances within which the abuse has taken place, and the complexity of relationship dynamics that may underpin it, the social worker's task is replete with complexity. Clearly, the first priority will be to seek to maintain the abused person's personal safety, but the number of possible ways in which this could be achieved are legion. As in much of social work practice, the core dynamic underpinning abuse is the balance between protecting the individual from harm while simultaneously seeking to maximise her/his autonomy. Social workers have a pivotal role in ensuring that older people are able to live safely, in managing the investigation processes in cases where their safety is threatened, and in ensuring that their autonomy is maintained.

CONFRONTING AND CHALLENGING OPPRESSION

Social work has a clear commitment to challenging and confronting injustice (see Chapter 2 for more on this theme). However, as delineated in this chapter, older people experience some forms of oppression which derive from deep-seated attitudes and social policies which social workers cannot directly affect. This is not to suggest that practitioners can therefore have no role in seeking to combat wider forms of injustice, but rather to point out the (perhaps obvious) fact that change at such a level is not liable to come about quickly. It is politic for social workers to be patient and take a 'long view', where the detail of their own practice might help to improve the general status of older people. If older people and their families are able to experience their involvement with social workers as an empowering process this can potentially have beneficial wider consequences.

Although this chapter has foregrounded specific aspects of disadvantage that older people will experience – with particular emphasis on ageism – it should be remembered that there are many other forms of oppression that could be encountered. The chapter has already focused upon issues around race, class and gender, but these do not represent the only forms of oppression that older people might encounter. As Pugh (2002) has highlighted, for example, there are a number of relatively unexamined issues relating to social work undertaken within rural settings. For older people, the likely increase in social isolation that often accompanies old age can be exacerbated by the physical isolation of many isolated rural communities. Similarly, there is an increasing need to consider the needs of older people with intellectual disabilities, as an increasing number of such people are living into old age, with particular difficulties generated by a combination of their age and their intellectual disabilities.

As I shall argue later in the book, there are forms of practice that can be developed which can have a more direct impact on the oppression of older people. Many of these derive from the 'collectivist' traditions within social work outlined in Chapter 2, moving beyond the administrative responsibilities of most statutory social workers. In reality, simply carrying out statutory duties, as transformed into agency policies and procedures, is unlikely to challenge the forces of injustice and oppression that confront older people, even where these duties are carried out with exemplary consideration for the principles of empowerment. Therefore, this book will argue that a broader conception of the social work role is needed – which clearly has implications for the organisation of social work, as well as for social work practice itself. However, if one accepts that the range of older people's needs encompasses the wider structural and societal issues elaborated above, it becomes incumbent on social work to organise itself so as to ensure that they also can be addressed. Simply defining social work in a restricted way as the commission of statutorily defined duties will not go far enough to meet older people's needs.

CONCLUSION

This chapter has outlined the place of older people within the context of British society, and the nature of the problems that might be encountered when people age. The perception of ageing on which this chapter has drawn is strongly influenced by Riley (1986), who argued that in the study of age it is vital to retain a 'dynamic emphasis', where several different levels of analysis – for example, structural, organisational, familial, group and individual – are seen as intersecting and interconnecting. In her view, the appropriate study of ageing requires the integration of several academic disciplines, as it is from these disciplines that specific knowledge can be generated. For example, an understanding of biology and psychology forms an essential base for the study of ageing, but these understandings are insufficient unless supplemented with knowledge from a range of other disciplines, of which sociology and social policy are particularly important, and to which anthropology, economics and history also contribute.

What has been outlined represents an 'ideal' response to the needs of older people; as Chapter 6 will outline, the current practice of social work within the statutory sector does not necessarily address all of the areas of difficulty emphasised here. A more complete reaction to the needs of older people requires social workers to exercise a wider repertoire of responses, drawing on a level of creativity that has not always characterised social work practice with older people. However, before being able to accomplish this task, it is important to understand the different elements of what social work actually is, which is the task of Chapter 2. Chapter 6 will then apply this understanding specifically to social work with older people.

CHAPTER SUMMARY

This chapter has addressed the following issues:

- Demographic changes to the population at large, commenting that concern about the effects of the 'demographic time bomb' may be over-stated, given current population projections.
- The importance of the concept of ageism in seeking to understand the treatment received by older people, individually and collectively.
- A number of ways in which the ageing process can be understood, touching upon physical and biological changes, psychological changes, social constructionist and political economy perspectives, with consideration given to the combined impact of these on the identity of an older person.
- The areas of need that older people have that might call for the involvement of social work, relating these areas of need back to the various ways in which the problems of older people can be understood.

The History and Development
of Social Work

Is becoming a social worker primarily to be understood in terms of the 'helping', 'caring' or therapeutic content of the job, or according to the official, bureaucratic, legal and even potentially coercive powers and responsibilities it entails? (Jordan, 1984: 13)

The purpose of this chapter is to analyse the establishment, growth and development of social work in Britain, from its origins in the nineteenth century to its position at the start of the twenty-first century. It is written on the assumption that understanding the history of social work is helpful when seeking to explore options for its future direction. This is particularly important when the social work role is under question, as it undoubtedly is in relation to work with older people. Ensuring that forms of practice are developed that pay full attention to its history and potential might form a useful corrective to the overwhelmingly 'administrative' nature of much contemporary social work.

As the above quotation from Jordan (1984) indicates, there are different ways of interpreting the growth and development of social work as an organised activity. Following Seed (1973), three strands in its development are charted. The first of these is the focus on *individual casework*, which originated in the work of the Charity Organisation Society (COS) (Woodroofe, 1962; Lewis, 1995). The second is the role of social work in *social administration*, particularly (although not exclusively) involving various forms of relief from poverty. Although much of this originated from the Poor Law (Jordan, 1984), it was also promoted in some of the work of the COS. The third is the focus on *social action*, which has been particularly identified with the growth of the Settlement Movement, both in Britain and the United States (Rose, 2001).

Although these three strands will be addressed separately for analytical purposes, they have often been interconnected. If one examines the origins of social work, for example, many key figures spanned these themes. For example, Octavia Hill was closely associated with both the COS and the Settlement Movement

(Bell, 1942), while Canon Barnett was originally a supporter of the COS before establishing the first settlement at Toynbee Hall in East London as an example of what he then considered to be the most effective way of bringing about social change (Mowat, 1961). Both Hill and Barnett actively engaged in more general processes of social reform, meaning that they were at different times 'case-workers, group workers and reformers' (Cormack and McDougall, 1955: 21). The close complementary working of the Poor Law and charity was a vital prerequisite for the effective operation of the COS (Bosanquet, 1914), while some practitioners – notably hospital almoners (Bell, 1961) – brought together casework and financial administration. These links and connections have reappeared throughout the history of social work, albeit in a range of different guises.

INDIVIDUAL CASEWORK

Most historical accounts identify the COS as the initiator of the social theory that led to the formation of the occupation of social work (see, for example, Seed, 1973). A particular element of the work of the COS was its focus on individual casework. As this section will demonstrate, this has been perhaps the most consistent theme running through the entire history of social work. This section will therefore examine the ways in which individual casework developed, starting with its origins in the COS before moving to consider how it flourished in the years immediately following the Second World War into the present day.

One of the key contributions of the COS to social work was its clear – if perhaps partial and misguided – view of the cause of many social problems in Victorian Britain. London, as graphically portrayed by Bosanquet (1914: 5), was seen as beset by a 'mass of chronic pauperism, beggary and crime', behind which lay 'an appalling amount of genuine misfortune'. In the view of the COS, existing services for the relief of poverty actually made matters worse (Bosanquet, 1914), due to the inadequacy of the Poor Law combined with the counterproductive impact of the vast growth of charitable organisations. In the view of the COS, this combination stripped people of the will to fight against the circumstances in which they found themselves; by not making any distinction between those who did and did not merit support, it was held that the system in effect encouraged all people to throw themselves onto the combined ministrations of the Poor Law and charity rather than maintain their independence. The COS maintained that this weakened the family and hence had a profoundly negative impact on society at large.

To put their social theory into effect, the COS established systems and structures that enabled action in accordance with its principles. First and foremost, it insisted on proper coordination of charitable endeavour to avoid overlap and competition between organisations (Webb, 1926). To support this, an understanding was reached about the respective roles and purposes of the two arms of welfare, charity and the Poor Law (Bosanquet, 1914; Lewis, 1995). Charity was to be the first port of call for people in need, with the Poor Law and its institutions functioning as a general safety net beneath the charitable institutions.

The next priority for the COS was to establish an organisational structure and a system to assist people who appeared to have some level of need. While the COS did not originally intend to provide charity directly, but rather to coordinate the charitable provision of other organisations (Mowat, 1961), District Committees of the COS soon became established to provide relief on their own account (Bosanquet, 1914). The critical task was to oversee a process whereby a judgement could be made concerning the eligibility of applicants for support. This was accomplished by judging whether an applicant was considered to be 'deserving' or 'undeserving' (Seed, 1973) of assistance. Even though the terminology used by the COS changed in later years (to 'helpable' and 'unhelpable'; see Lewis, 1995), a moral dimension is clearly evident; this has had a continued impact on social work.

It is in this process of investigation where the roots of social work practice can be clearly divined. If charity was to be properly directed, there needed to be a full, 'scientifically' organised (Woodroofe, 1962) examination of the circumstances of individuals and families who presented for a service. The basic techniques of 'casework' that the COS instigated have continued applicability. For example, judgements had to be based on a detailed assessment of the applicant's circumstances, requiring home visits. The COS termed this 'taking down the case', a process that is clearly analogous to the preparation of assessments in contemporary practice. The COS issued guidance about how the process of 'taking down the case' should be organised; again, this role is broadly analogous to the guidance routinely issued by governments and employers to assist organisations and managers come to grips with changes in policy and practice. Following the assessment, a judgement was then to be made concerning an individual's eligibility to receive a service, which has its exact parallel in the existence of defined 'eligibility criteria' in current practice.

If services were to be provided, they could be of many different types, as is evident in the case histories that the COS cited in support of their work (see Bosanquet, 1914). The COS did not simply dispense financial charity, but also sought to find creative ways of maintaining and enhancing people's independence as such approaches were more in line with their governing philosophy. Although there was considerable variability between District Committees in terms of the number of people served and the quality of the investigations undertaken, the number of cases which the COS investigated was surprising to many, indicating that the organisation was uncovering a large amount of unmet need within society (Mowat, 1961). However, its general approach was not popular, as is evident from the defensive tone throughout Bosanquet's (1914) history. While the COS took pride in the efficiency of its system, for many others it appeared harsh in the extreme. In addition, the COS was markedly hostile to other organisations involved in the provision of charity, as well as to other perceptions of the causes of poverty (Webb, 1926). It was apparently difficult to criticise the work of the COS – even in relatively mild terms – without provoking an antagonistic response; for example, the differences of view between the COS and Canon Barnett were addressed in a peculiarly arrogant and defensive manner (see Bosanquet, 1914: 297).

In addition, the success of the COS in fulfilling its mission was also called into question, despite the robust way in which it sought to protect its position (see Bosanquet, 1914: *passim*). Throughout its period of peak influence – up to the outbreak of the First World War in 1914 (Lewis, 1995) – it was never able to escape from a paradox that it had itself created: 'The fact remained that the "unassisted" might be those who most needed help but least deserved it . . . while those helped, the respectable and provident, ought least to have needed help' (Mowat, 1961: 37). In addition, it was claimed that the perceived harshness of the COS approach actually promoted rather than curbed 'unscientific' charitable activity (Lewis, 1995). It was also argued that the COS had not actually managed to classify the deserving and undeserving poor accurately, and that the charity that was dispensed was quite inadequate to combat need. As Webb concluded: 'the administration of the Poor Law . . . supplemented by charitable assistance according to the tenets of the C.O.S. . . . had next to no effect either on the poverty or on the misery of the poor' (1926: 251). These were powerful criticisms, which the COS struggled to combat successfully. In addition, the tide of opinion was shifting against the belief that the relief of poverty and distress was primarily an individual responsibility. In British society, following the cataclysm of the First World War, there was a much stronger level of acceptance that the provision of welfare was a matter for the state as much as the individual and the family. However, the influence of the COS on the development of social work was vast; in fact, it effectively created the occupation of social work, as well as defining many of its core tasks. The COS also recognised that effective work required a level of training of those people undertaking it. Indeed, one of its most significant legacies to social work was the development of systematic programmes of education and training for the role of the social worker. (As we shall see, it has this in common with the Settlement Movement.)

With a diminution of the influence of the COS, a separation therefore appeared between the practice of individual casework and the social theory from which it originated. This was certainly a difficult time for social work in Britain (Seed, 1973), as it sought to establish a role and function that was separate from the specific ideas of the COS. One of the effects of the separation of social work methods from a broader social theory was a fragmentation in the occupational processes that sustained it (Seed, 1973). For example, different branches of social work – psychiatric social workers, hospital almoners, etc. – operated separate systems of education and training, and in effect created parallel routes into the occupation. The search for an alternative rationale for social work was a preoccupation for much of the next part of its existence (Lewis, 1995).

The importation of a collection of ideas from the USA was to have a particular importance in this respect. The first of these was the detailed codification of the process of 'social diagnosis' undertaken by Mary Richmond (1917), which was an early attempt to establish a common base for all social work practice. Richmond asserted that: 'in essentials, the methods and aims of social case work were or should be the same in every type of service' (1917: 5). Central to this was the act of assessing needs, which should be based on a systematic process of gathering 'social evidence' from a range of sources – the individual, family members (individually and collectively), and outside sources such as schools, doctors, employers, etc. The key contribution of Richmond to the development of social work was in the detailed, 'scientific' organisation of data that she propounded, which represented a major step forward along the path first outlined by the COS.

The second major import stemmed from the popularity of psychologically-based theories in American social work from the 1920s onwards. Cormack and McDougall (1955) suggested that the introduction of treatment methods deriving from related disciplines did little to suggest that a social worker possessed unique expertise and was hence worthy of professional status; it appeared that a social worker was doing nothing that could not equally well be accomplished by many other occupations – and even mature people of good sense lacking any qualification at all. Nevertheless, the adoption of psychologically-oriented insights increased the focus of social work on the workings of the mind, as is apparent from the content of one of the most significant post-war textbooks on social casework in Britain (Morris, 1955).

The attraction of 'universal applicability' for social work approaches was obvious, particularly given the occupation's fragmentation in the first half of the twentieth century. A focus on social casework informed by psychological theories offered the prospect of unifying these disparate elements. Indeed, the first 'generic' training course for social workers was established for precisely this purpose (Younghusband, 1955). The increased confidence that this gave to the social work world should not be underestimated – it suffuses all the contributions to Morris' seminal text (1955). For example, Younghusband is somewhat patronising to the pioneers of social work practice who (somehow!) managed to operate without the knowledge of 'unconscious motivations, behaviour patterns, the transference situation, client–worker relationships, social maladjustment, obsessional behaviour, the need to express feelings of guilt and aggression, reactions to deprivations in childhood' (Younghusband, 1955: 198) that were the stock in trade of the 'modern' practitioner. She is clear that social work practice had developed for the better as a result of the increased knowledge that social workers had of the innermost workings of people. In addition, she is in little doubt of the greater levels of skill and knowledge that could be required of the social worker. The scope of the social work task, as Younghusband (1955) defined it, was greatly increased – indeed, it was ambitiously framed. However, there was an element of unreality in her description: only a small minority of people could receive the sort of service she identified (Lewis, 1995). It was difficult for social workers in statutory agencies to accommodate these requirements into their daily work, as Rodgers and Stevenson (1973) made clear. Even in voluntary organisations, the ideals of individual casework were difficult to put into practice. However, the way in which the social work task was theorised represented an elaborate updating of its key elements.

However, it was this very ambition that caused one of the most notable attacks on the developing occupation of social work. In her book *Social Science and Social Pathology* (1959) Barbara Wootton excoriated what she saw as social work's obsession with methods drawn from psychiatry and psychology. The essence of her critique was that the fascination with psychology and psychiatry created a 'fantastically pretentious façade' for the occupation, resulting from 'a tendency to emphasise certain aspects of social work, while playing down others that are potentially at least as valuable' (Wootton, 1959: 271). She identified the rhetoric that accompanied descriptions of social work practice as particularly worrying, and mocked the idea that social work could actually achieve the sorts of change its advocates appeared to propose. Her preferred remedy was that social work should rediscover a more modest focus on helping people by acting as what she termed a 'middleman': mobilising, organising and coordinating the services of a huge range of other professional colleagues, and by guiding people through the mass of legislation and policy that could affect them. In this way, Wootton suggested that the social worker could once again be essential to the effective functioning of the welfare state.

While this was a witty and stimulating critique, Wootton's analysis did not engage fully with the reality that confronted social workers. Her conception of the limited role of social work offered little that could assist, for example, an abused child, a person with a mental health problem, or people who had experienced bereavement (Lewis, 1995), all of whom would require an approach that was more in line with that suggested by the advocates of individual casework. In addition, Wootton's perception of the role of social work did not accord with the reality of what practitioners actually did – vividly conveyed by Rodgers and Stevenson (1973) – but related more closely to the rhetoric of those whose role it was to promote the development of social work. In reality, practice already contained much that drew on social work's administrative origins, as I shall explore in the following section. Younghusband (1955) certainly recognised that social workers required knowledge of resources and the ability to coordinate them effectively, even if she downplayed this aspect of the social work role. In that sense, Wootton's critique was built on somewhat insecure foundations. However, it strongly influenced subsequent attacks on social work from the political

Left (Bailey and Brake, 1975) and Right (Brewer and Lait, 1980). These will be addressed in forthcoming sections.

With the benefit of hindsight, the 1950s represented the period where individual casework was most highly prized within social work. However, as we have seen, one key problem with this formulation was that it did not equate to much of the actual practice of people employed as social workers, particularly those working within statutory settings. For such people, there remained an emphasis on the efficient administration of relief; this will be the focus of the next section. In addition, it moved the occupation a long way from its origins as a social movement (Seed, 1973); the idea that social work can be seen as a movement interested in securing social change is the focus of the section after that. In terms of work with older people it had relatively little impact; the role of social worker has always had more of an element of administrative requirements.

SECTION SUMMARY

The section has engaged with the following themes:

- The establishment of the COS and its enormous influence both on general social policy and also the development of the occupation of social work.
- The differences between the COS and its critics about the causes of social problems, and hence the most appropriate ways of responding to them.
- The fragmentation of social work in the early part of the twentieth century, following the reduction in influence of the COS.
- The attempt to establish a common base for social work practice.
- The increased influence of theories deriving from psychology and psychiatry within social work practice, and the argument that these could be universally applied within all social work settings.
- The various ways in which such an approach could be subjected to criticism, focusing particularly on the devastating critique of Barbara Wootton (1959).

SOCIAL WORK AS SOCIAL ADMINISTRATION

As various commentators have noted (Seed, 1973) social work has its earliest roots – even pre-dating the formation of the COS – in the work of the Poor Law relieving officers, whose duty was to administer the system that had first been created through the Poor Law Act of 1601. The importance of their role was given additional stimulus by the Poor Law Amendment Act of 1834, which emphasised the element of deterrence through the formal introduction of the concept of 'less eligibility'. This meant that the conditions of relief would consciously be made no better than was available to the lowest paid worker, in order not to make such relief more attractive to those who might be eligible for it and hence discourage their desire to engage in productive labour. The Poor Law was administered on a local level by Boards of Guardians, which gave rise to considerable variation in the way in which it was managed across the country. All Boards of Guardians required some basis of making judgements about the eligibility of applicants to forms of relief, which were generally financial. Relieving officers were widely employed to accomplish this end in the early years of the nineteenth century. By contrast with the COS or the Settlement Movement it was not generally argued that these officers required a formal period of education and training to accomplish their tasks: as a result their quality was variable. Although a National Poor Law Officers' Association was formed in 1884, seeking to improve the status and quality of the occupation through better professional training, this had little effect on the low public esteem in which it was held (Crowther, 1981). However, the 1929 Local Government Act did manage to achieve some degree of change for this group of staff, as the responsibility for managing the Poor Law transferred to the direct control of local government, with the relieving officers redesignated as public assistance officers (Crowther, 1981). In their location, as well as in some of their work, the influence of these staff on the development of social work was considerable. Elements of social administration were also contained in the role of workers within the COS. For example, although much assistance was other than financial, direct financial support was provided in some instances. In addition, the role of hospital almoners – addressed more fully in Chapter 5 – contained elements that were explicitly concerned with financial administration (Bell, 1961), which was a staple of their work until the establishment of the NHS in 1948.

As noted in the previous section, even where the rhetoric of casework most affected social work in the 1950s it was accepted that the social worker needed to have a good understanding of the range and scope of resources that could be made available to an individual or family (Younghusband, 1955). Indeed, the conception that the social work role was, at least in part, concerned with humanising the administration of social services (Rodgers and Stevenson, 1973) was well accepted. This general perception lasted through reorganisation in the early 1970s, which coincided with a rapid increase in the numbers of qualified social workers. In reality, irrespective of the rhetoric of individual casework (or, indeed, the rhetoric of the later radical social work) much of the practice of social workers was concerned with responding to the minutiae of people's lives in a practical and pragmatic fashion.

Throughout this period, there is little doubt that the administrative elements of the social work role far outweighed the elements that derived from casework, particularly in respect of older people (Younghusband, 1978). It was in recognition of this that very little practice with older people was actually carried out by qualified staff until the passage of the National Health Service and Community Care Act 1990 (Lymbery, 1998a). Even though this legislation increased the numbers of qualified staff employed to work with older people, care management – the dominant form of social work practice with older people – particularly emphasised the administrative role of the practitioner (Sturges, 1996). The social work role was increasingly restricted to the act of assessment, leading to the establishment of care packages and the rapid closure of the 'case' (Lymbery, 1998a). Arguably, these trends have made social work with older people into a particularly dispiriting enterprise for many practitioners (Carey, 2003; Postle, 2002).

Although the 'administrative' elements of social work have a long history, it is the development of 'casework' that has been more frequently cited as the main contributor to the development of the occupation of social work. However, the origins of social work in social administration are apparent, and this focus for practice remains evident. This is in direct contrast with the conception of social work as a form of 'social action', the subject of the following section, which is relatively little in evidence.

SECTION SUMMARY

This section has discussed the following issues:

- The development of an administrative approach to social work.
- The persistence of this orientation to practice throughout the twentieth century.
- Its particular dominance in the delivery of social work to older people following the introduction of community care.

SOCIAL ACTION:
THE SETTLEMENT MOVEMENT
AND BEYOND

The earliest example of social work as a form of collective social action in Britain can be found in the work of the Settlement Movement, established by Canon Barnett in the 1880s. The Settlement Movement was underpinned by a number of beliefs that it shared with the COS. Both were based on similar moral principles, even though different forms of practice stemmed from these principles; a belief in the value of education and example underpinned the values of both. In addition, both accepted that financial assistance was insufficient to combat problems within communities and individuals. Similarly, both had their origins in the sense of obligation of the more privileged to those less fortunate than themselves, and shared a strong belief in the purpose and value of education, establishing training courses in conjunction with universities (Jordan, 1984; Seed, 1973).

Gilchrist and Jeffs (2001) have indicated that the movement was based on three linked ideas:

- The need to develop scientific research on the causes and effects of poverty.
- That the 'settlers' could help to broaden the lives and horizons of people and communities through education.
- That they could also enhance leadership within local communities.

As this outline indicates, its practice differed from the work of the COS. For example, it was not predicated on resolving immediate individual needs, but rather sought to work through the community and the group to improve general social conditions. Critically, the vision of Canon Barnett was different from that of the COS on one key point, relating to the social theory that underpinned the Settlement Movement. Barnett came to believe that the root causes of poverty and distress could be located in social structures more than in the defects of individual character; he termed the action that followed this diagnosis 'practical socialism' (Barnett, in Lewis, 1995). His vision was that people of education – the movement attracted women as well as men (Matthews and Kimmis, 2001) – could establish a relationship with people of a different class to their mutual benefit. The residence requirement for 'settlers' was critical for this; while most worked outside the community for their paid employment, they spent other time undertaking forms of community service and development (Rose, 2001).

To the modern reader, there seems at least as much unifying as dividing the COS and the Settlement Movement – and some early pioneers like Octavia Hill supported both (Bell, 1942) – but the division was deeply felt by the COS at least (Bosanquet, 1914). The explanation for this can be located in the clarity of the COS vision: if the analysis on which it was based was accurate, then only one possible set of responses could logically follow. Any divergence from this path was treated almost as apostasy.

Although the Settlement Movement initially expanded quite quickly in Britain – and with even more speed in the USA – its growth did not outlive the main establishing pioneers. By 1914 there were 46 settlements; these were a mixture of women-only, men-only and mixed establishments. However, as the education and training of 'settlers' developed, the pioneers tended to be replaced by 'professionals', who saw their role as consolidating the innovations that they inherited, rather than devising new ones (Rose, 2001). As a result, as Seed (1973) pointed out, the nature of the movement gradually changed, losing much of its radical edge.

With the decline in significance of the Settlement Movement paralleled by the advance of individual casework, there was little connection in social work practice in the middle years of the twentieth century to the strand of social action and community development that had motivated Canon Barnett and his followers. Indeed, the 1950s and early part of the 1960s represented the almost total eclipse of collective action as part of social work. However, a coherent critique of the contemporary state of social work was mounted from the late 1960s onwards, focusing on the failures of a practice that 'pathologised' the individual while ignoring the material and social causes of poverty and disadvantage. The establishment of the radical journal *Case Con* in 1970 was a key moment in this process, providing a focal point for an alternative conception of the potential of social work.

This was more fully articulated in a variety of texts in the late 1970s and early 1980s, of which Bailey and Brake (1975), Jones (1983) and Simpkin (1983) are a representative sample from the UK. They are part of a movement that became known as 'radical social work' after the title of Bailey and Brake's important text. Although there were differences amongst the proponents of radical social work, particularly in the way in which they addressed issues of inequality that were other than class-based, they shared an understanding of the causes of human problems that sought to shift the focus of social work intervention in a profound way, moving away from an individual to a collective response to problems.

While influential within the academy and within certain areas of practice, ultimately radical social work as a 'movement' foundered on some barely recognised contradictions. For example, while its analysis of social problems was a necessary corrective to the highly individualised understandings within 'casework', it was much less effective in guiding social workers towards alternative models of practice. As Cohen (1975) observed, the emphasis on structural causes of disadvantage did not necessarily enable individuals to address the specific problems that they encountered. In addition, the radical social work agenda appeared to assume that social workers had more capacity to challenge and change policy than was realistic, given their occupational location (Langan, 2003). Certainly, employers did not expect their staff to foment revolution, despite the apparent inducement so to do within some radical social work material! This was particularly true from the 1980s onwards, a difficult period for the development of more progressive forms of social work. Finally, the early analyses of the radical social work movement were heavily class-based (see Jones, 1983), with relatively little attention devoted to issues of race, gender, disability, sexuality, etc. This meant that it did not connect sufficiently well with groups of people – practitioners and service users alike – who could have been allies.

It is perhaps significant that the radical social work movement was relatively short-lived, failing to surmount either the challenges provided by the changed social and political climate of the 1980s or the different sorts of critique mounted by Black people, women and disabled people. It had less impact on social work than it had intended, but the sorts of analysis that it engendered have proved to have a continuing influence. Its impact on social work with older people was particularly limited (Phillipson, 1989). As an attempt to re-focus social work onto its potential to operate as a social movement it was only partly successful, but it certainly helped to draw attention to various issues – the impact of poverty, the potential of community – that had been long neglected.

SECTION SUMMARY

This section has focused on the following issues:

- The origins of a more community-oriented approach to social work through the development of the Settlement Movement.
- The lengthy period in the middle of the twentieth century when there appeared to be little emphasis on social action as a part of social work.
- The rebirth of social action in the 1970s and beyond in the form of community development, influenced by the thinking of the radical social work movement.
- The failure of radical social work to have a lasting impact on social work practice.

THEMES AND ISSUES IN CONTEMPORARY SOCIAL WORK

The purpose of this section is to analyse key elements of contemporary social work, drawing on themes that were identified in the previous sections. It represents a condensed version of a complex debate, focusing on specific controversies in social work in the recent past. It starts with a consideration of the politically inspired critiques of social work that were generated in the 1960s and 1970s. It continues with an analysis of the Barclay Report (1982), concentrating particularly on the debate engendered by the dissenting reports by Pinker and Hadley et al. It then moves on to consider the ways in which social work has been challenged by groups of the people it exists to serve, fuelled by the growth of the 'new social movements' from the 1980s onwards. Finally, the section suggests a way in which the various types of social work practice can be understood that provides a conceptual framework for the remainder of the book.

The political critique of social work that had particular force from the 1960s on was from the 'radical social work' movement, the outline of which was sketched in the previous section. It rejected what it saw as the pathologising elements of individual casework, notably the common assumption that poverty was the result of personal failure rather than economic forces. (In this respect, the argument replays themes that were explored in the disputes between the Fabian Society and the COS in the late nineteenth century.) It pressed for the establishment of a form of practice that re-engaged with the economic basis of disadvantage, drawing on ideas of community development and social action that are traceable to the Settlement Movement. Radical social work largely rejected the notion of individual casework, believing that this distracted from the central mission of social work, which it saw as combating poverty and disadvantage.

The critique from the right was of a different order, focusing on the fundamental ineffectiveness of social work. Brewer and Lait (1980) contended that social work was imprecisely defined, encompassing too broad a range of roles and functions. They argued that it should be much more narrowly focused and defined, and followed Wootton (1959) in questioning the essence of social work's claims for professional status, believing that social workers were 'valued but *essentially subordinate* employees of the traditional health and welfare agencies' (Brewer and Lait, 1980: 8; emphasis added), whose role was basically to carry out the practical work of such agencies. Brewer and Lait (1980) further suggested that the diffuse, over-ambitious and ill-defined aims of social services departments ensured the futility of much practice, and that the poor quality of the education and training offered to social workers further compounded the problems. Their conception of social work had the practitioner occupying a predominantly bureaucratic position, with 'professional' training replaced by a form of apprenticeship.

These criticisms of social work found a ready audience within certain sections of the media and politics, not to mention the medical profession. However, their analysis is contaminated by the prejudiced language in which it is conveyed, with constant disparaging barbs directed to all and sundry within social work and a dismissive tone towards all knowledge that is not based in hard, scientific certainty. For example, in discussion on the selection of students, the authors suggested that 'only graduates in maths, physics or chemistry, with firsts or upper seconds, should be accepted for training, since to attract them one would need to put on courses with intellectual content' (Brewer and Lait, 1980: 41). In addition, their insistence that social work training had taken a strongly psychoanalytical direction is largely out of line with the realities of the late 1970s, however true it might have been of the 1950s. Indeed, their insistence that the influence of radical left-wing academics was such that students were 'having to regurgitate their tedious and irrelevant nostrums to obtain a certificate in applied social studies' (Brewer and Lait, 1980: 114) appears to contradict their very claim of psycho-analytical dominance within the social work academy.

The debate that this critique engendered concerned the essence of social work; it was extended through the process of the Barclay Report (1982), which sought to clarify the role and tasks of social work. As is often the case with large committees, not all the parties to the Barclay Report were able to agree. The majority report contained a strong focus on the elements of 'social care planning' within the social work role, which was contrasted with the element of 'counselling' that the report identified as its other core strand. The most far-reaching recommendation of the majority report was for the creation of what it termed 'community social work', where practice and policy would become more responsive to the needs of a community, defined in terms either of locality or of 'shared concerns' (Barclay Report, 1982, 13.38–13.41: 208–9). In the committee's view, this would require a change of attitude and orientation by social workers (Barclay Report, 1982, 13.38–13.41: 209–11).

Critical areas of contention were laid out in two contrasting minority reports, one of which was largely the work of Roger Hadley (Brown et al., 1982), the other being solely the work of Robert Pinker (1982). Hadley and colleagues advocated for the extension of the notion of community social work, the most controversial of the recommendations of the main report. They argued that the central role of social work should be to support informal caring networks; in order to do this, they suggested that a community-oriented approach had to be developed. In their view, such an orientation required four conditions to be met:

- *Localisation*: 'statutory services must be local enough to operate at street and village level' (Brown et al., 1982: 227).
- *Integration*: three kinds of integration were suggested – integration within each social services department, integration between the department and other service-providing agencies, and integration between the department and social networks.
- *Wider roles*: to accomplish this fundamental shift, staff roles had to be defined much less narrowly than before.
- *Greater autonomy*: 'local social services teams will need a larger measure of discretion to develop these approaches than they have been formally accorded' (Brown et al., 1982: 229).

There had been a number of projects that had explored this sort of practice (see, for example, Hadley and McGrath, 1981), and the alternative view adopted by Hadley and colleagues was firmly in this tradition. However, this conception of the social work role did not fit comfortably with the increasingly coercive nature of social workers' activities, particularly in respect of child protection. Pinker took a diametrically opposite position, contending that social workers had no mandate for the sorts of activity that could be grouped under the banners either of 'community social work' or 'neighbourhood social work'. He argued that both the majority report and the minority appendix of Hadley and colleagues were based on fundamentally flawed premises. The concept of 'community' on which they founded their analysis was not clearly defined, there were fatal ambiguities in the concepts of accountability that were deployed, and unresolved tensions between the principles of 'specialism' and 'genericism' within social work practice. By contrast, Pinker recommended that social work would be more securely defined in a manner that was limited by its statutory remit. In a memorable turn of phrase he characterised community social work in the following terms:

> It conjures up the vision of a captainless crew under a patchwork ensign stitched together from remnants of the Red Flag and the Jolly Roger – all with a licence and some with a disposition to mutiny – heading in the gusty winds of populist rhetoric, with presumption as their figurehead and inexperience as their compass, straight for the reefs of public incredulity. (Pinker, 1982: 262)

While the Barclay Report did not have the impact on social work that had been widely anticipated, it encapsulated an ongoing debate within social work between those who argued for a wider involvement of the occupation in social action and those who took a more limited view of its role and functions. Although framed in different terms and language, this dispute echoed earlier debates about the essential nature of social work. Given the political climate into which the Report was catapulted, it is little surprise that the more restricted vision of Pinker was to characterise social work practice in the following years.

In the 1980s there were challenges to social work from groups – women, Black people, service user groups (including people with disabilities and people with mental health difficulties), the advocacy movement, etc. – who had been subject to the services of social workers. These challenges have been usefully summarised by Taylor (1993), who argued that the groups share common purposes, despite their obvious differences, in their focus on issues such as diversity, universalism, power and rights. The tests that these movements have posed for social work served to expose fundamental elements of the occupation's self-image.

- A key underlying theme is that their criticisms highlight the fact that social work has often failed to live up to its more lofty ideals. Given that an important principle of social work has always been its ability to respond positively to the most disadvantaged sections of society, this condemnation highlights a dismal failure within the occupation.
- The groups have also highlighted social workers' inability to work effectively in practice with individual disabled people, black people, gays and lesbians, etc.

In combination, these concerns helped to create a climate of uncertainty and doubt within social work, attesting to the fact that it was an occupation in some disarray.

The final part of this section will seek to understand how the various themes that have characterised social work through its history can be placed into a conceptual framework that will help to govern the subsequent discussion. Working on the assumption that disputes about the nature of social work are really disputes about the nature and causes of, and solutions to, social problems (Jordan, 1984), the different perspectives on social work therefore represent alternative views on the role that the occupation plays within society. In this respect Mullaly (1997) has differentiated between broadly 'conventional' and 'progressive' perspectives on the role and functions of social work. In the 'conventional' view – which he suggests is, and always has been, held by the majority of the profession – the structure of society is believed to be fundamentally sound. The broad role of social work is therefore either to help people adjust to existing social structures, or to amend those structures in a limited way. In the minority 'progressive' view the purpose of social work is different, being primarily to contribute to a fundamental social transformation, on the basis that the problems of individuals are caused by inequitable social structures rather than individual inadequacy or weakness. In the foregoing debate about the origins of social work, the efficient administration of relief and most individual casework can be placed within the 'conventional' perspective. Indeed, support for the *status quo* was a central part of the role of the COS. In addition, there is relatively little in the literature on individual casework that argues for a more radical social vision. By contrast, the Settlement Movement contained the seeds of a more critical perspective; it is therefore no surprise that many future socialist politicians – including the future Prime Minister Clement Attlee – were active in this movement in their youth (Matthews and Kimmis, 2001). This critical perspective became more explicit in the radical social work movement.

An alternative way of conceptualising different perspectives on social work has been devised by Payne (1996). He has suggested that three 'general perspectives' on social work can be identified: 'individualist-reformist', 'socialist-collectivist', and 'reflexive-therapeutic' (Payne, 1996: 2). The discipline of social work is held to contain elements of these three perspectives, with one or another being influential at different times. For example, the reflexive-therapeutic perspective was particularly powerful in the USA in the early part of the twentieth century (Woodroofe, 1962), being imported for British consumption in the years following the Second World War (Morris, 1955). The socialist-collectivist perspective was especially prominent in the radical social work literature in Britain in the 1970s and early 1980s (Bailey and Brake, 1975). By contrast, most social work in contemporary Britain is more within the individualist-reformist tradition, which has been influentially articulated by Martin Davies, who claimed that, 'although social workers have many roles . . . they are all subsumed under a general theory of *maintenance*' (Davies, 1994: 57; his italics). That this has become the dominant perspective is far from being a matter of chance, as it accepts the basic structures of society and sets limits to the social work role that circumscribe its focus.

While these are helpful ways of conceptualising the place of social work, they do both over-simplify some of the inherent contradictions that characterise daily practice. To take Mullaly's (1997) split, even if a practitioner were to espouse a 'progressive' view of social work, s/he must necessarily frequently *act* in ways that support the framework of society: the legislative and statutory basis of social work requires no less. Similarly, it is at least conceptually possible for a social worker to practise in accordance with all of Payne's (1996) 'general perspectives' on social work at different times: they are not mutually exclusive. In reality, the bulk of what a social worker actually does in practice with older people in Britain will fit within the individualist-reformist perspective, simply because the key statutory and policy requirements of the agencies within which most of them operate – carrying out community care assessments, arranging for safe and speedy hospital discharges, etc. – lend themselves to this orientation to social work. However, a social worker should not forget that there are other perspectives on which to draw. For example, s/he might recognise that an older person needs additional support to come to terms with loss and bereavement, or that a carer for a person with dementia has a particular need for counselling to come to terms with the changes that dementia engenders. Both examples are of work that fits within a more therapeutic tradition. Similarly, on different occasions a social worker might perceive the need for collective action, for example by supporting a group of carers to meet, or by enabling the formation of service user groups to argue for better services.

This book makes an argument for a broad view of social work, encompassing all three perspectives identified by Payne (1996). It argues that it is unrealistic to construe social work as simply about a process of social reform, as individuals in genuine need require more immediate help to assist them with their problems. However, to perceive social work simply as a succession of individual 'cases' is likely to lead to safe but sterile practice. Indeed, not all of the problems confronting older people can be seen as relating to the individual, as identified in Chapter 1; such a conception ignores the collective experiences of older people, and the structured oppression that they experience within society (Bytheway, 1995). A skilled social work practitioner must be able to identify the approach that most suits the circumstances with which s/he is confronted, being sufficiently flexible to respond to them in different ways according to their nature and cause.

Therefore, to adjust the terminology deployed in this chapter, drawing particularly on Payne (1996) and Seed (1973), social workers need to be capable of working in three different but complementary approaches:

- Working with individuals, in both problem-solving and therapeutic ways. For the purposes of this book, I have labelled this the *individualist/therapeutic* approach.
- Working as a go-between, ensuring that resources are mobilised to meet need, with particular stress on the tasks of liaison and coordination. In this book, this has been termed the *administrative* approach.
- Working with groups and communities, to construct creative and new types of response to problems, including the development of new services and resources. This has been termed a *collectivist* approach.

This approach recognises that human problems are complex and that the ways of responding to them are manifold. An *individualist/therapeutic*, an *administrative* or a *collectivist* response may be indicated at different times; the practitioner has to retain the capacity to identify what approach is more likely to be effective, and at what time. In addition, and this is particularly true for practice with older people, the functions of agencies need to be constructed in ways that allow for this element of flexibility on the part of the social worker. As I will explore further in Chapter 6, the way in which social work with older people is currently constructed forces the practitioner into an administrative response, irrespective of need.

It is apparent that, in taking this line, I have also defined my position in relation to Mullaly's (1997) 'conventional' and 'progressive' orientations. In his terms, this would be within the 'conventional' camp, since it does accept the legitimacy of the present social order. This is less a statement of personal political beliefs than it is a recognition of the nature of social work practice within British society. Pinker (1982) was surely correct in pointing out that social workers have no mandate to work against the system that employs them; in addition, most service users would not necessarily appreciate their concerns being transformed into political tools. However, in the context of social work practice with older people, the approach advocated does move beyond the limits of what has customarily been accepted as normal for this group. There has historically been scant opportunity for the development of therapeutic approaches to practice, and little evidence of collectivist work. It can be argued that these failures are an expression of the low value accorded to older people within society at large as well as within social work (see Chapters 1 and 6).

SECTION SUMMARY

This section has examined numerous debates within contemporary social work, including:

- The politically inspired critiques of social work that led to the development of the radical social work movement.
- The publication of the Barclay Report (1982), and in particular the debate that was engendered by the two minority reports.
- The critique of the effectiveness of social work that was mounted in the 1980s, particularly through the impact of vocal groups representing the very people served by social work.
- Various ways in which the practice of social work can be understood, drawing particularly on Mullaly (1997) and Payne (1996).
- It concludes by proposing a way in which social work can be analysed that forms the conceptual framework that governs the rest of the book.

CONCLUSION

This chapter has engaged with the history and development of social work, identifying the main strands that have contributed to contemporary policy and practice. It has suggested that there are three dominant traditions of social work – *individualist/therapeutic, administrative* and *collectivist*. It has argued that social workers need to be enabled to use all of these approaches, and to make a judgement about which one would be more effective in different sets of circumstance. Although this argument would potentially apply to all aspects of social work, in this book it is applied specifically to social work with older people.

In respect of social work with older people, as Chapter 6 will demonstrate, there has been relatively little history of the use of any approach to social work other than *administrative*. Since the implementation of community care policy in particular, this has led to sterile and unimaginative forms of practice. It is the contention of this book that this should not continue: that the needs of older people will be more effectively met if social work practice draws on the *individualist/therapeutic* and the *collectivist* traditions as well. However, for this to happen there would need to be an overturning of much of what underpins contemporary practice. It is also suggested (in Chapter 8) that a fundamental shift in the way social work is organised could help to facilitate such a change.

CHAPTER SUMMARY

The chapter has addressed the following issues:

- The influence of the Charity Organisation Society in the development of social work, with particular attention to the way in which social work practice was seen as the way of putting the social theory of the organisation into practice.
- The gradual decline in the importance of the COS, the fragmentation that this engendered within social work and the post-Second World War growth in therapeutically-oriented social work practice.
- The critique of such practice mounted by Barbara Wootton (1959), alongside a recognition of the reality that not all social work practice approached the 'ideal' promoted by many within the social work academy.
- The roots of social work in forms of social administration, focusing particularly on the role of the social worker in arranging for services and resources to be provided for service users.
- The development of a conception of social work as a means to affect social change, focusing on the principles that underpinned the Settlement Movement, moving on to the development of the radical social work movement in the late twentieth century.
- A range of themes, issues and critical debates (Adams et al., 2002) within contemporary social work, touching upon the critique of social work from the political left and right, the split within the Barclay working group, and the growing influence of service user voices on the development of social work.
- The chapter has suggested that there are three main elements in the development of social work – the *individualist/therapeutic* approach, *the administrative* approach and the *collectivist* approach.
- It has further suggested that these approaches are not inherently in conflict with each other, but that the *administrative* approach has come to dominate practice with older people.

PART II
Policy

Community Care Policy

With the implementation of the community care reforms in 1993 it is easy to assume that community care was 'invented' or 'created' in 1993. In fact this is a term that has been in use among policy makers for a considerable period. (Victor, 1997: 6)

The purpose of this chapter is to chart the way in which policy affecting community care has developed in the years following the Second World War. In so doing, themes that will form part of the analytical framework of the remainder of the book will be developed. The chapter focuses particularly on the impact of community care in the 1990s and discusses in depth the policy developments advanced by the New Labour government from 1997 onwards. Since much social policy that affects older people has been comprised of piecemeal and *ad hoc* developments (Nolan et al., 2001a), it is not fruitful to examine it *as if* it had been constructed with a clear idea about its direction and desired end point. While the *National Service Framework for Older People* (DoH, 2001a) represents an attempt to create a unified policy structure within which health and social care services can be developed, it builds on a markedly incoherent policy legacy as this chapter demonstrates.

The chapter reviews the key elements of policy and law in the post-war years, leading up to the implementation of community care. The chapter will note that while these policies have encouraged closer collaborative working between health and social care, they have been advanced without a full understanding of the various factors that have obstructed such developments in the past. This gap between governmental policy intentions and the reality of their delivery is a critical issue for the book overall. The chapter begins with an analysis of policy from the perspective of the boundaries between health and social care. Using the creation of the National Health Service (NHS) and the passage of the National Assistance Act 1948 as its starting points, the first section looks specifically at the blurred boundaries between health and social care services, arguing that the so-called 'Berlin Wall' (DoH, 1998a) is a product of a long-standing lack of clarity about the roles and functions of health and social care, which has in turn affected the quality of collaborative working. It then examines the development of collaborative working in this period, before considering the development of services – particularly residential care.

HEALTH AND SOCIAL CARE POLICY IN THE IMMEDIATE POST-WAR YEARS

BOUNDARY ISSUES: CONSTRUCTING THE 'BERLIN WALL'

One of the outcomes of the National Health Service Act 1946 and National Assistance Act 1948 was a division of organisational responsibilities for health and social care that rested on an apparently straightforward, but in fact highly contentious, distinction: the newly established NHS would take responsibility for people's health needs whereas their social care needs would be addressed through the Welfare Departments established in local authorities. One of the significant policy consequences of this is financial: in British social policy, health services are free at the point of delivery whereas social services potentially attract a charge from the user of the services. For example, the National Assistance Act 1948 required local authorities to extract a contribution from service users towards the costs of local authority-provided residential care.

As Means and Smith (1998) argue, the essential problem is the difficulty of differentiating clearly between health and care needs. In turn this has generated an extended period of what Lewis (2001) has termed 'hidden policy conflict' between health and social care agencies. There are three themes that are particularly relevant to this:

- Health and social care agencies have been organisationally separate for several decades; each organisation manages its own budgets and has its own operational priorities.
- These budgets have proved increasingly inadequate to respond to the total level of need within society. This has created a mismatch between supply and demand (Salter, 1998), which has to be managed by each organisation as best it can.
- This task is rendered more complex by the contrast between the 'absolute' rights of people to health care, balanced by their 'contingent' rights to most social care (Salter, 1998). This is also complicated by the differences in charging policies for health and social care, noted above.

In practical terms, as there was considerable ambiguity in the definitions used the separation between heath and social care needs did not clarify the organisational and budgetary responsibility for older people, many of whom existed on the borderline between the first two categories, leading to conflict over which agency had the duty to respond to an individual's needs. Indeed, Lewis (2001) has argued that both health and social care agencies sought to avoid accepting this responsibility, with health services being particularly effective in this respect. She also commented that this process continued unacknowledged for several decades, for two specific reasons:

- That a public acknowledgement that the policy created an increase in local authorities' responsibilities would have provoked immediate demands from these authorities for a comparable increase in funding.
- That a public admission that there had in fact been a shift in responsibilities would have led to accusations that the original ideals of the NHS were being betrayed.

Therefore, it is the separate organisational and budgetary priorities of health and social care agencies which created these problems, which have had a continued impact on the development of health and social care policies for older people. As a result, the existence of the 'Berlin Wall' can be seen as the outcome of decades of policy relating to health and social care rather than the result of operational practices.

However, collaborative working between health and social care was relatively slow to develop during this period, although large numbers of social workers were employed in hospitals (Younghusband, 1978) and some were attached to general practice (see, for example, Collins, 1965). Joint working between health and social care was conceptualised through a model of comprehensive rational planning (Lewis and Glennerster, 1996), similar to that which existed in the wider NHS of the time (Klein, 2001). The NHS reorganisation in 1974 gave particular focus to this, as it fully separated the organisational structures of health and social care services, removing public and community health services from the local authority and hospital-based social workers from the health service. Elaborate systems of joint planning were established following this reorganisation but with limited outcomes (Webb and Wistow, 1987).

One reason for this was that there was relatively little financial incentive to develop far-reaching joint projects. The joint finance that had been introduced to 'oil the wheels' of partnership working was time limited, with substantial financial responsibilities left to be picked up when it lapsed. This was particularly problematic from the late 1970s when the parlous state of public finances created budgetary pressures. As a result, both sides were cautious in their approach to joint planning, reluctant to adopt the ambitious undertakings that were needed to transform the health and social care landscape. These problems created a substantial barrier to the development of effective partnership working, which were aggravated by a range of other issues which will be explored in more detail in Chapter 4.

RESIDENTIAL CARE AND ALTERNATIVE FORMS OF PROVISION

The artificial distinction between health and social care was not the only problem area in community care policy in this period. Another central difficulty stemmed from the fact that residential care was presented as the best – and in many cases, the only – response to people whose circumstances required social care support. There was little development of alternatives to residential care – in fact, older people were effectively excluded from the wider range of welfare services that were created for children and for narrowly defined groups of adults with disabilities (Means and Smith, 1998). It is hard to resist the conclusion that this represents an acceptance of the limited potential and value of older people, which is ageist in its nature (Bytheway, 1995; see also Chapter 1).

The priority given to residential care in the 1948 Act was, in its own terms, riddled with problems. While residential care was the preferred solution to the needs of older people requiring some measure of support, there were insufficient numbers of good quality care homes. Townsend's (1962) survey revealed that what homes there were could be sub-divided into three broad categories:

- The large group of institutions that had existed under the aegis of the Poor Law, transferring to local authority control with the passage of the 1929 Local Government Act. These were often poorly designed, inadequately staffed and actively disliked and feared by many of the older people who may have had to enter them. The lamentable quality of such institutions was not amenable to rapid change, as Townsend's study (1962) illustrates.
- Converted properties, regarded at the time as the easiest and quickest means of increasing the numbers of available places (Means and Smith, 1998). Again, as Townsend (1962) recognised, there were many problems with this sort of development. Often, the buildings which lent themselves most readily to conversion were located in isolation from community facilities. In addition, the nature of the buildings themselves limited what could be achieved through conversion, leading to a layout that often represented an uneasy compromise between the ideal and the possible.

- Purpose built homes, which could therefore have avoided the inherent problems of the first two groups. However, as Townsend (1962) reported, this group did not necessarily improve the standards that could be expected by those people who lived within them. While this stemmed in part from inadequate guidance about building standards, a greater problem lay in the fact that costs and completion rates were of more importance than considerations of quality (Means and Smith, 1998).

In general, therefore, there were three main problems with the residential provision for older people following the implementation of the National Assistance Act 1948.

- The quality of residential homes was poor, leading to unsatisfactory experiences for many older people.
- There were too few places for the level of need in the population at large. The construction and/or conversion of homes did not keep pace with the increasing numbers of older people in need of residential care.
- This was exacerbated by the transfer of responsibility for many older people from the health service – particularly hospitals – to the newly created Welfare Departments in local authorities (Townsend, 1962).

These problems characterised local authority residential care for many decades. Into the 1980s, former public assistance institutions remained in operation, although very much in the minority. There were large numbers of converted properties in use alongside purpose-built residential care homes of variable quality. At this point, the financial difficulties within local authorities effectively curtailed their capital building programmes, leaving a stock of residential care homes of largely inadequate quality. Although the 1980s saw the rapid growth of private sector homes, making up the shortfall in public provision, they too were beset by problems of quality. Initially, most belonged to the second group noted above, being conversions of large Victorian houses; they could not easily provide the standards of care – single rooms, a high number of *en suite* bathrooms – that were increasingly demanded.

Townsend (1962) was as much concerned with the lack of development of alternatives to residential care as with its overall poor quality. As charted by Mandelstam (1999) the introduction and expansion of domiciliary support for older people was gradual in nature, enabled by successive pieces of legislation that incrementally increased the range of services available to people in their own homes. However, various acts did permit the establishment of home help services and meals-on-wheels, for example, thus providing the basis for much current care provided in people's own homes. Although there was a gradual expansion of domiciliary services, this also served to emphasise the problem of coordination between the different parts of the health and welfare system (Ham, 1999). The organisational responsibility for these types of service was also separate. While residential care, home help and meals services were all provided by the local authority, two different parts of the health service – hospital and primary care – were involved. As the policy direction towards community care became more evident in the 1980s, a major shift in the organisation and funding of both health and care services became inevitable.

SECTION SUMMARY

This section has examined policy regarding the care of older people in the immediate post-war years. It has identified a number of issues and problems:

- The creation of the 'Berlin Wall' between health and social care services, which the chapter has argued has been primarily caused by legal and policy decisions which have created incentives for each organisation to act in its own interests rather than for the common good.
- The level of joint working between health and social services organisations did not develop to the extent that had been envisaged, leaving a fragmented and patchy range of services in place.
- The dominance of residential care as a service option for older people remained unchallenged, even though developments in law and policy did allow for the establishment of a wider range of domiciliary services.

THE ADVENT OF COMMUNITY CARE

As a result of the various issues explored in the previous section, it became increasingly apparent that firm action by government would be needed to improve the situation – the question that remained to be addressed was the nature of the action to be taken. This section explores the development of community care, both as a concept and as a policy.

ITS ORIGINS

As Victor (1997) has observed, it is hard to be precise about the origins of community care policy. There was specific concern about long-stay hospitals for people with learning disabilities and mental health problems from the 1950s onwards; this instigated a general shift in the provision of such services away from large institutional bases in favour of care provided in the community (Means et al., 2003). In addition, welfare services were poorly coordinated, which placed obstacles in the way of a coherent response to people's needs (Audit Commission, 1986). The spiralling cost of residential and nursing home care in the independent sector, which experienced an unprecedented boom following changes to supplementary benefit regulations in 1980, also created cause for concern. Large numbers of people were accommodated in residential and nursing home care, irrespective of need, at the public expense (Lewis and Glennerster, 1996). The extent of the cost incurred as a result of this should not be underestimated; in 1979/80 a sum of £10m was spent from the income support budget to support people in independent sector care, which increased to £744m in 1987/88 as a consequence of the change in supplementary benefit regulations (DoH, 1989). By the time of the full implementation of community care in 1993 this had mushroomed to over £2bn (Lewis and Glennerster, 1996). It was assumed that many of the people entering residential and nursing home care in the independent sector did not need to be there, and that the public money that was deployed to support them could be better used elsewhere.

Following Lewis and Glennerster (1996), one can therefore conclude that the policy of community care would not have been established were it not for these budgetary problems. Lewis and Glennerster (1996) argue that the 'deep normative core' of community care was to seek a measure of financial control over the costs of independent sector residential and nursing home care, with all other issues secondary to this. However, other elements also motivated the community care reforms, as Lewis and Glennerster (1996) recognise. The growing realisation of the nature of the problems within the care system was a key element in this.

In this respect, the conclusion of the Audit Commission (1986) that community care existed more as an aspiration than a reality was particularly significant. This report recognised that many problems stemmed from the organisational and budgetary complexity that characterised health and social welfare for adults. For example, it criticised the fact that there were numerous funding sources and hence priorities for the development of services. It also focused on the lack of funds to facilitate the transfer from a hospital-based to a community-focused service, while highlighting the fact that the social security system created a perverse incentive in favour of residential care, which worked in opposition to the desire to create more community-based alternatives. In addition, the report observed that there were major organisational problems that contributed to policy failures in community care. In summary, therefore, it suggested that care arrangements for groups and individuals were neither organised nor coordinated, and that the overall funding of policy was equally confused.

Recognising the range of problems that beset community care, the Government sought to resolve them by appointing Sir Roy Griffiths to undertake a review of the issue; he had previously reported successfully (in the eyes of ministers at least!) on the problems of management within the NHS (Griffiths, 1983). His subsequent report was clear on one specific point – that community care needed to be taken more seriously as a government policy. He was particularly scathing about the lack of coordination of community care, which occupied much of his attention. To resolve this, Griffiths (1988) recommended both that local authority social services departments should function as the lead agency for all community care, and that these organisations should develop as enablers and purchasers of care, and hence move away from seeing themselves as monopolistic providers of services, to ensure the continuation of a vibrant independent sector. As a means of controlling the budgets for community care, social services departments were to have the responsibility for assessing the care needs of any individual who may be in need of care services.

There were a number of difficulties with Griffiths' plan:

- His proposals placed local authorities at the heart of community care; this was problematic for the Prime Minister of the day, given her rooted antipathy to local government (Lewis and Glennerster, 1996).
- They rested on a distinction between health and social care which is, as we have seen, not at all clear in practice.
- Although the report acknowledged the role of informal carers, its proposals contained little in the way of practical support for them.
- The heavily ideological and contentious promotion of the 'mixed economy' of care in the report was treated as if it was 'entirely unproblematic' (Victor, 1997: 17).
- Griffiths' key proposals for the establishment of a Minister for Community Care and a ring-fenced budget for its implementation were both seen as politically awkward: neither were part of the final policy.

Having received the Audit Commission Report, and then appointed Griffiths to review policy options in response to it, the Government had taken steps to identify the nature and scope of the problem. The next stage was to advance a policy that would address the various issues that had been identified. There was a lengthy delay before its response appeared, as officials and ministers grappled with the central problem of how to frame the policy in such a way as to be politically acceptable to the Prime Minister (Lewis and Glennerster, 1996). In the event, some 18 months after the publication of the Griffiths Report, the White Paper on community care finally emerged (DoH, 1989).

CARING FOR PEOPLE

The White Paper contained six key objectives for service delivery, which are as follows:

- to promote the development of domiciliary, day and respite services to enable people to live in their own homes wherever feasible and sensible . . .
- to ensure that service providers make practical support for carers a high priority . . .
- to make proper assessment of need and good case management the cornerstone of high quality care . . .
- to promote the development of a flourishing independent sector alongside good quality public services . . .
- to clarify the responsibilities of agencies and so make it easier to hold them to account for their performance . . .
- to secure better value for taxpayers' money by introducing a new funding structure for social care . . . (DoH, 1989: 5)

The order in which these objectives are specified is interesting, and not a little misleading. Normally, when constructing any list there is a tendency to order it from the most to the least important: this is not the case here. The nub of the reforms is actually contained in the final objective, the establishment of a new funding structure for community care that removed the existing financial incentive in favour of institutional care. In this respect it is worth noting that Griffiths' primary purpose was to 'review the way in which public funds are used to support community care' (Griffiths, 1988: iii), plainly indicating that financial motivations were central to the government's thinking. The intention of policy was to scrap the system that enabled people to enter residential and nursing homes in the independent sector with funding from the social security budget. Since there was no means of containing this budget, it was imperative that a replacement system was introduced with in-built control mechanisms. The simple expedient of passing this responsibility to local authorities with a cash-limited budget achieved this goal effectively. It would henceforth be impossible for local authorities to allow the expansion in numbers of people entering residential and nursing homes, for no other reason other than that they could not pay for such an increase.

All the other objectives stem from this starting point. Indeed, they make more logical sense if they are addressed in reverse order. For example, while the desire to clarify lines of accountability reflected both the need to resolve the organisational confusion that Griffiths had identified and to make agencies accountable for the performance of their responsibilities, it also contained a key financial message. If lines of accountability were more clear-cut, then it would, in theory at least, be easier to work out the financial responsibility for the provision of services. The establishment of a 'flourishing independent sector' has been seen as indicative of the second level of priority in community care (Lewis and Glennerster, 1996). To enable this, a far-reaching organisational shift was required within social services departments, with the widespread introduction of what became known as the 'purchaser–provider' split. In other words, an organisational separation developed between the parts of a department responsible for the assessment of need and those other areas responsible for the provision of services, such as the various forms of domiciliary and residential care. One core action that compelled this shift was the requirement that 85% of the Special Transitional Grant (STG) that was introduced to support community care had to be spent in the independent sector (Lewis and Glennerster, 1996). While the government did not introduce a fully ring-fenced grant, as noted above, the STG was a partial step in this direction. In total, £399m was made available in 1993/94, the first year in which community care policies were fully operational. For the following year, an additional £651m was transferred, with an extra £518m in 1995/96. Although each instalment was only ring-fenced for the first year, there was actually little prospect of much of it being lost to community care: since the bulk was spent on placements in residential or nursing homes, most of it was committed from year to year. The cumulative total for the first three years of implementation was therefore £1,568m, plus £140m which was made available to assist local authorities with the infrastructure required to implement the policy.

As Lewis and Glennerster (1996) noted, this was not an ungenerous settlement; however, it still represents much less than would have been spent from the social security budget, particularly given the rate of increase that prevailed during the late 1980s/early 1990s. Lewis and Glennerster (1996) estimated that an expenditure of less than £625m *per annum* in the early years of the policy would correspond to significant savings for the government. The size of the grant was carefully calculated to ensure that the government could safely claim that the policy had been adequately funded; in addition, a key purpose underpinning the requirement to spend 85% in the independent sector was the government's desire not to alienate the providers of private residential care by ensuring that any drop in income was both gradual and relatively slow. However, there has been a continuing tension between the cash-limited funds administered by local authorities and the desire of independent sector providers to maximise their income.

The centrality of assessment and care management to community care appeared to be an important professional gain for social work within the legislation. If the haemorrhaging of money into residential and nursing homes were to be staunched, this would require a detailed and accurate assessment of need – to be carried out, by and large, by qualified social workers. In addition, it was widely felt that the advent of care management, which had been actively developed in various pilot projects by the Personal Social Services Research Unit (see Challis and Davies, 1986) as a professional, highly skilled activity, would provide a shot in the arm for social work – particularly since the majority of care managers would be qualified social workers. As originally envisaged, there was reason to expect that the introduction of community care would have a beneficial impact on the role and status of social work.

In the light of these four objectives, the first two have their own logic. Controlling the costs of community care could only realistically be managed by reducing the level of dependence on expensive institutional care. In turn this would require a greater level of recognition and support for carers than had been the case. The government understood that encouraging older people to remain at home for longer periods would also carry financial benefits. This also served to attract practitioners to the policy, as they were well able to support what appeared to be its primary objectives.

Responses to the White Paper were mixed. While the academic community gave the White Paper a markedly hostile response (Hudson, 1990), there was a more positive reception within social services departments. In the extended period between the Griffiths report and the White Paper many observers had predicted that the pivotal role that Griffiths had proposed for local authorities in community care would not be accepted. The fact that local authorities were given a key role in the policy was something of a relief, particularly since the policy also appeared to hold out the promise for a better deal for vulnerable adults. This more positive perception was sorely tested in the forthcoming years as the problems of implementation mounted (McDonald, 1999).

COMMUNITY CARE: SUCCESS OR FAILURE?

Given that I have followed Lewis and Glennerster (1996) in ascribing primary importance to the financial basis of community care, it is no surprise that I also follow them in my conclusions concerning the overall success or failure of the policy. On the economic front, community care policy has succeeded on a number of levels. It halted the escalation in costs on independent sector residential and nursing home care that had characterised the 1980s through the simple expedient of making local authorities responsible for a defined budget. In addition, while financial problems did surface from the mid-1990s onwards, the way in which the funding had been organised ensured that central government was able to distance itself from any local difficulties. Given the primacy of economics in the entire policy, this success is highly significant.

Whether other aspects of the policy have been successful cannot be so clearly defined, however. Indeed, success on one set of criteria may in fact lead to failure elsewhere. Nowhere is this more evident than in the case of care management and assessment. For those people who were excited about the positive contribution that care management could potentially make both to the lives of vulnerable people and to the growth and development of the social work profession, the past decade has been a period of great disappointment. The primary role for care managers has been related to the economic purpose of rationing scarce resources, leading to a negation of much of the potential of the role (Carey, 2003; Lymbery, 1998a; Postle, 2002). The effects of this are a key element of this book, considered in more depth in Chapters 7 and 8.

On the ideological level, there was pressure in the early stages for social services departments to institute a separation between 'purchasing' and 'providing' services, which was heavily promoted in the official policy guidance (DoH, 1990). There has certainly been an increase in the amount and proportion of care provided within the independent sector, which implies that there has been the establishment of a 'mixed economy' of care. As will be explored further in the following section, this aspect of policy has altered its dynamic with the accession of the 'new' Labour government in 1997. The political emphasis on 'partnership' (Glendinning et al., 2002) emphasises cooperation rather than the notion of competition that underpinned the original policy. As a result, there is a gradual move to replace the fragmented systems that characterised the early days of community care with integrated teams and joint working. However, the fact that the majority of care is now provided within the independent sector is unlikely to change.

Another factor that has worked against the creation of a market in social care is the continuing dispute about the costs of care between local authorities and the independent sector. The fact that there has been a squeeze on the numbers of people entering residential and nursing home care, combined with the fees paid by local authorities, has created major problems for some care providers that affect both residential and home care. It would seem that the intention to create a market within social care has been only partially successful, although a much higher proportion of community care services are now provided by the independent sector.

A similar duality is visible in relation to the desire both to develop a greater number of non-residential options for older people and to target these developments on 'those people whose need for them is greatest' (DoH, 1989: 5). It is undoubtedly the case that there is now a greater range and variety of home based care, although this was relatively slow to progress following implementation in 1993. The primary reason for this is because local authorities were forced to commit a large proportion of their budgets on residential and nursing home placements in advance of the development of alternative forms of care, despite the encouragement of the Audit Commission to do the reverse (cited in Lewis and Glennerster, 1996). In addition, the concentration on those in greatest need has been at the expense of people with lower levels of need. The value that such people place on relatively low levels of support (Clark et al., 1998) has counted for little, as the focus has inexorably shifted onto those with higher levels of need, particularly in relation to personal care. That this led to a relative lack of investment in prevention and rehabilitation has had serious consequences for policy (Bauld et al., 2000). It has also had unwelcome repercussions, creating a conflict with another objective of community care, the high priority given to the provision of practical support for carers. Although it was possible for SSDs to assess carers' needs, carers did not have the absolute right to support that their advocates argued should be present. Therefore, the benefit of having their needs assessed was fatally compromised by the lack of available resources to meet these needs. While support for carers has been subsequently strengthened by other forms of legislative and policy change, this aspect of policy has been much less well developed than others.

The relationship between social care, health and other agencies is another aspect of policy that has seen an uneven level of development. There has been relatively slow progress towards the 'seamless service' that had been emphasised in policy guidance on community care (DoH, 1990). There have been numerous exhortations to improve collaboration – particularly in the *Policy Guidance* (DoH, 1990) – but these were insufficient to bring about major policy changes. There remained substantial obstacles in the way of effective joint working – not least the ever-present fact that the organisational priorities of each separate body may conflict with the other. The point made by Salter (1998) is applicable here; the separate lines of accountability for each organisation can lead to policy that is to the direct benefit of one party, not necessarily both. Community care policy has magnified these problems rather than resolving them, as a higher proportion of frail older people (who would hitherto have been defined as the responsibility of health services) have become the responsibility of social care services. This shift has been exemplified by the increase in the number of social care-funded places in nursing homes by contrast with the run-down in the number of long-stay hospital beds for older people (Means et al., 2002). In addition, the problems around delayed discharge of older people from hospital have gradually assumed greater significance in policy terms. While this was recognised as an important issue in the implementation of community care – it features strongly in the *Policy Guidance* (DoH, 1990) – it was only in the early years of the twenty-first century that it became a major policy priority.

SECTION SUMMARY

This section has examined the introduction of community care, with particular reference to the following subjects:

- Its genesis in the 1980s through a succession of key reports (Audit Commission, 1986; Griffiths, 1988).
- The nature of the policy, with particular reference to the objectives of the Community Care White Paper (DoH, 1989), and its reception.
- The various and potentially competing definitions of success that could be applied to the policy.

COMMUNITY CARE POLICY AND 'NEW' LABOUR

Although community care policy was initially the product of a particular political approach to resolving problems in the delivery of welfare, the 'new' Labour administration of Tony Blair has been responsible for its development from 1997. This section explores the way in which policy has progressed since then.

POLICY THEMES – PERFORMANCE AND PARTNERSHIP

This section will first explore key themes of welfare policy in general, moving on to consider how it is responding to the needs of older people. In this respect, the chapter builds on a body of literature that has analysed the impact of 'new' Labour social policies (see, for example, Dean, 2003; Glendinning et al., 2002; Lister, 2001; Powell, 2000). The rhetoric of the Labour party leading up to its election in 1997 carefully positioned its social policies as standing between the 'old left' and the 'new right' (Powell, 2000), in an attempt to convince the electorate that they were materially different from either. This was labelled the 'third way', seeking to chart a middle course between the dominant ideological approaches to welfare that preceded it. While this is not the place for a detailed examination of the various constituent elements of the Third Way (see Giddens, 1998; also Jordan with Jordan, 2000, for a more critical view), the values that appear to underpin it are important for an understanding of the way in which social policy has developed since 1997.

Powell (2000) and Lister (2001) argue that there are two characteristics of 'new' Labour that have significantly affected the nature and impact of its policies. The first of these is the populist tendency to court the electorate rather than lead it (Lister, 2001). This has tended to create policies that appear to reflect the sensibilities of *Daily Mail* editorials rather than the values that had hitherto characterised the Labour party, as the interpretation of public opinion on which this is based is inherently self-interested and reactionary (Lister, 2001). As Dean (2003) has observed, the 'new' Labour approach to social policy draws on core 'myths' about the nature of welfare, particularly the pernicious view that state provision of welfare breeds a 'dependency culture', a perspective that has been transferred wholesale from the lexicon of the New Right.

This has been combined with a pragmatic approach to policy-making, which derives from no particular ideology or intellectual pedigree. Emphasis is therefore placed on 'what works' in an unashamedly eclectic approach to the formulation of policy (Powell, 2000). In addition, the government has been preoccupied by the need for 'modernisation' – the White Paper *Modernising Social Services* (DoH, 1998a) being a clear expression of this. Indeed, understanding the nature of this document is a critical route towards an understanding of 'new' Labour's aspirations for social services. It sets out the government's general intentions, underpinned with a clear statement about the meaning of the 'third way' in social care, which would move 'the focus away from who provides the care and places it firmly on the quality of services experienced by, and outcomes achieved for, individuals and their families' (DoH, 1998a: 8).

However, some commentators have detected direct ideological and practical continuities between the policies of past Conservative governments and 'new' Labour (see, for example, Jordan with Jordan, 2000). As noted above, 'modern' – including the many words that derive from this root (modernising, modernisation, etc.) – is a key word in the vocabulary of 'new' Labour (see, for example, DoH, 1997a; DETR, 1998; DoH, 1998a). In this sense, 'modernising' means more than simply 'bringing up to date': it also carries a rhetorical message conveying the idea that the proposed policy represents a decisive break with the past.

Two characteristic themes of 'new' Labour social policy have been the emphases on performance and partnership. The primary way that the government seeks to ensure the delivery of improved performance in social services is through the Best Value system, introduced throughout local government (DETR, 1998). The rationale for Best Value is that it should secure continuous improvement in the way in which local authorities' functions are exercised. It depends upon measuring the performance of such authorities against a set of performance indicators and by requiring authorities to establish Best Value reviews to assess their performance in all their functions. The rhetoric surrounding the introduction of Best Value was typical of the way in which 'modernisation' was introduced. While it was trailed as representing a decisive break with the past (DETR, 1998), it retained many features in common with the systems of competitive tendering which it replaced (Sanderson, 2001). Its particular contribution has been to strengthen the framework whereby performance can be measured within local government (Sanderson, 2001). The Performance Assessment Framework – the set of performance indicators against which the quality of social services' operations are measured – is a critical part of the Best Value system. This process is supplemented by Joint Reviews, which are carried out by the Audit Commission and the Social Services Inspectorate (Humphrey, 2003) and which are intended to provide objective external evidence of the progress made by a given department. This amounts to an apparent obsession with performance – evidenced in the publication of league tables and 'star' ratings for all sorts of public services – which has served to focus the attention of managers and practitioners on those elements of service provision that are measurable, which may be different from those things that are most important.

This point is particularly significant in relationship to the theme of partnership, which is critical to the 'new' Labour reform of public services. Indeed, so significant is the concept that it occupies a chapter in the *Modernising Social Services* White Paper (DoH, 1998a); there is another full chapter on this theme within the *NHS Plan* (DoH, 2000b). Clarke and Glendinning (2002) have suggested that partnership has become the organising framework for public services, replacing the New Right-inspired emphasis on markets, and the preceding dominance of bureaucratic hierarchies, as the most appropriate organisational structure for the delivery of welfare. Given this, the lack of conceptual clarity about the nature of partnership, noted by numerous commentators (see, for example, Clarke and Glendinning, 2002; Huxham, 2000), is particularly problematic.

This lack of clarity is hardly aided by the almost promiscuous dimensions of partnership; as indicated in the White Paper, this could encompass more or less any combination of agency – social services, health, education, housing, employment, myriad private and voluntary providers, etc. (DoH, 1998a). However, Wyatt (2002) is surely accurate when he identifies that the key dimension of partnership – particularly relating to services for adults – is between health and social care. It is undoubtedly true that health and social care agencies are mutually dependent, which makes improving their ability to work together a matter of some importance (Clarke and Glendinning, 2002). As far as services for older people are considered, *Modernising Social Services* is only one of a sequence of documents that have discussed the need for closer partnership working. For example, the *Partnership in Action* discussion document (DoH, 1998b) advocated the development of pooled budgets, integrated provision and lead commissioning responsibilities as mechanisms to improve the quality of joint working between health and social services organisations. These proposals were incorporated into the Health Act 1999, and have become popularly known as 'Health Act flexibilities'. They became particularly significant in the development of services following the publication of the *NHS Plan* (DoH, 2000b), which contained a chapter on the relationship between health and social care that appeared to change the direction of policy in a radical way.

Until this point, the message from government on organisational structures had been that structural reorganisation would not resolve the problems that obstructed partnership working (see, for example, DoH, 1998a). However, the *NHS Plan* (DoH, 2000b) carried a forceful message in *favour* of structural change; the extent of this can be judged by the legal power conferred on the Secretary of State (in the Health and Social Care Act 2001) to compel such change if inadequate progress had been made towards joint working, and to force the creation of joint Care Trusts. Hudson and Henwood (2002), in a somewhat puzzled response, observed that this approach broke with past policy, making the identical point that had been made in several previous governmental publications: 'structural integration evidently does not guarantee well-coordinated practice on the ground' (Hudson and Henwood, 2002: 163). At this juncture, the government appeared to be pursuing a policy of what Hudson and Henwood (2002) termed 'compulsory partnerships' and 'compulsory restructuring'.

This shift into a more coercive attitude towards partnership development did ensure a widespread use of the Health Act 'flexibilities', although very few Care Trusts have come into being. Even where they have been developed, difficulties have emerged (see, for example, Callaghan, 2003), deriving from the fact that health and social care organisations have separate criteria for success, which is also defined and measured in different ways. The consequences of apparent poor performance can be serious: many senior managers in both health and social care have lost their jobs following poor performance, while some partnership arrangements have also been halted as a result (Callaghan, 2003). These pressures graphically illustrate the paradox at the heart of partnership working, where organisations are forced into an introspective process through performance measurement, while at the same time being required to establish a much more active sense of partnership working (Charlesworth, 2001). Ultimately, therefore, most organisations in health and social care have come to the view that structural change does not represent the best way forward for them, while accepting the need to establish improved systems of collaboration.

NATIONAL SERVICE FRAMEWORK
FOR OLDER PEOPLE

The government has published a series of National Service Frameworks for a range of user groups, with the intention to establish the essential components of service responses to the needs of each. For the purposes of this chapter, the *National Service Framework for Older People* (DoH, 2001a) will be given particular attention. It should not be treated in isolation, however, as there have been other relevant developments in respect of policy for older people. In particular, it is important to locate the priorities of the *National Service Framework* within the context of the government's national objectives for adult services, spelt out in the White Paper *Modernising Social Services* (DoH, 1998a). Seven specific objectives were set out, particularly emphasising the centrality of concepts such as autonomy, independence, protection and support for carers. The emphasis on independence and autonomy is further developed in the *National Service Framework*, and is consistent with global policies on the care of older people (Nolan et al., 2001a). The focus on support for carers is consistent with the approach of all governments following the publication of *Caring for People* in 1989. The importance of partnership working is emphasised in these objectives, and the shape of future policy developments, such as *Fair Access to Care Services* (DoH, 2002e), can also be discerned in these objectives.

The *Report by the Royal Commission on Long Term Care* (Sutherland Report, 1999) is also a significant document in charting the government's progress towards integrated health and social care policies for older people. The Royal Commission was set up by the 'new' Labour government in December 1997, in recognition of the continuing problem of financing long-term care. The Commission's remit was to 'examine the short- and long-term options for a sustainable system of long-term care for elderly people, both in their own homes and in other settings . . . and to recommend how, and in what circumstances, the cost of such care should be apportioned between public funds and individuals' (Sutherland Report, 1999: ix). There were two main recommendations:

- That the costs of long-term care should be split between living costs, housing costs and personal care: 'Personal care should be available after assessment, according to need and paid for from general taxation. The rest should be subject to a co-payment according to means' (Sutherland Report, 1999: xvii).
- That the Government should establish a National Care Commission to monitor trends, including demography and spending, ensure transparency and accountability in the system, represent the interests of consumers and set national benchmarks.

The first recommendation caused the most controversy. Even within the Commission there was dissent – two members would only sign the document if their objections, and alternatives, were noted. (These objectors provided a useful pretext for the government to avoid full implementation of the recommendations.)

The core objection was that the proposal would add an extra burden to the public purse without actually providing any more care than was currently available. It was also argued that making the care element free would increase demand; on this basis, the financial projections in the report were said to be unrealistically low. It was further suggested that the proposal would be of most benefit to the better off, who could afford to pay the care fees, at the expense of the worst off, for whom it would have been effectively free anyway. The Royal Commission insisted that change was imperative, with the majority urging the government to 'implement our proposals as soon as possible' (Sutherland Report, 1999: xxii). However, the Government failed to act for an extended period following the publication of the report, fuelling suspicions about its motives and intentions.

When it finally did respond, the Government did not accept the proposal that all personal care should be provided free of charge. Instead, it argued that nursing care would be freely available in all nursing homes, but that personal care as well as other living costs would still attract a charge. This implies a neat separation of nursing care from personal care, which is – as we have seen – far from straightforward. It also required an extensive process of assessment to place people into particular bands of nursing care. However, under its devolved powers, the Scottish Assembly agreed to implement the recommendations in full; this created a situation where different, incompatible policies were put into effect across Britain.

The National Service Framework (NSF) for Older People was published in 2001; it was intended that this should provide the basis for all health and social care services for older people. There are four general themes within the NSF, with eight standards being linked to these themes. The first broad theme is 'Respecting the Individual', and the two standards attached to it are both central to social work concerns. Standard 1 is 'Rooting out age discrimination', and applies equally to health and social care services. Arguably, social work has a stronger commitment to responding positively to issues of discrimination than other related occupations (Thompson, 2001). Standard 2 is 'Person-centred care', stressing that people should be treated as individuals and proposing a pattern of integrated service delivery, including single assessments, etc. Again, given the fact that social services departments are responsible for large numbers of assessments under community care, this standard is clearly central to social workers (see Chapter 7).

The second general theme of the NSF is 'Intermediate Care', which is also the title of Standard 3. It requires the development of services to prevent unnecessary hospital admission, enable avoidance of long-term care, and aid early discharge from hospitals. There is little literature that has specifically explored the contribution of social workers to intermediate care, despite the fact that they are seen as a crucial occupational group in the NSF. This will be explored in more detail in Chapter 9.

The NSF also contains some themes and standards that are less directly relevant to social care and social work. For example, the third general theme is 'Providing evidence-based specialist care', and four separate standards are attached to this theme: Standard 4 relates to 'general hospital care', while Standard 5 relates to 'stroke' care, both of which are primarily the responsibility of the health service. Standard 6 focuses on 'falls', with particular emphasis on their reduction. However, Standard 7 focuses on 'mental health and older people' and is also defined as a joint health and social care responsibility; clearly, older people with mental health difficulties create major issues for social care. The fourth general theme is 'promoting an active, healthy life'; Standard 8 relates to this, and is 'the promotion of health and active life in older age', which is seen as the primary responsibility of health supported by social care services. As this book will argue, the first three standards are particularly significant for social care, and each builds on strengths that are arguably greater in social care than in health. For all of them the social worker could play a vital role as part of the multi-disciplinary team.

POLICY PRIORITIES IN SOCIAL WORK WITH OLDER PEOPLE

As far as the policy priorities that govern work with older people are concerned, many of them require the concerted efforts of health and social care organisations to ensure that they are met, as acknowledged in the White Paper (DoH, 1998a). There are two particular themes that will increasingly impact upon the work of social workers.

The first of these is the general theme of independence and rehabilitation. The overarching goal of 'Promoting Independence' is a particular priority for government, and has consequently been a significant feature in most policy documents that focus on the needs of older people (see, for example, DoH, 2000, 2001a). One mechanism for bringing about this change was the extension of the policy of 'direct payments' to encompass older people in 2000. In principle, the development of direct payments has been seen as a means to increase people's direct control over the way in which they want to live their lives (CSCI, 2004a). However, direct payments have not become widely used, despite the regulations that came into force in April 2003 requiring local authorities to offer direct payments to all people in receipt of community care services. Only around 12,600 people were estimated as being in receipt of such payments in September 2003, of which fewer than 2,000 people were over 65 (CSCI, 2004a). Although uptake has increased, it was much lower than desired at the political level. As a result, urgent action has been called for at policy and practice levels (CSCI, 2004a). Indeed, the government's intentions for social care include the development of direct payments as a core element of a response to the needs of all adults (DoH, 2005).

In another example of the promotion of independence – this time, specifically for older people – the NHS Plan promised an additional £900m by 2003/04 for various forms of 'intermediate care' (DoH, 2000b). The *National Service Framework for Older People* (DoH, 2001a) places such care at the centre of the response to the needs of older people, bringing together a range of initiatives that consolidate the focus on rehabilitation. As often with government policy – as witnessed by the earlier discussion on the meaning and purpose of the six key objectives of community care – its commitment is based on a number of over-lapping issues. While it is framed as being in the interests of older people as well as in accordance with their wishes, it is also concerned with the desire to save money within the NHS by reducing the overall length of hospital stays, on the basis that maintaining people in hospital beyond the time when they need that level of medical care is financially wasteful.

The 'problem' of delayed discharge has been one of the most pressing issues within health and social care policy in the first part of the twenty-first century (Glasby, 2003), as was emphasised with the establishment of the Community Care (Delayed Discharges etc.) Act 2003. This Act introduced a system where social services departments have to reimburse health service organisations to compensate for any delays in discharge arrangements for patients in acute beds (DoH, 2003a). The 'problem' of hospital discharge has been regarded as signifi-cant for several decades (Glasby, 2003), but it has not proved easy to rectify. There are many reasons for this, including significant structural and organisa-tional barriers, as well as failures of inter-professional working (Glasby, 2003). These will be discussed more fully in Chapter 7.

The second theme focuses on the development of effective systems of assess-ment and care management. In this book, a chapter will focus on each of the core elements, assessment in Chapter 7 and care management in Chapter 8. The reason for this is the fact that there has been an uneven development of the two concepts in work with older people, despite the fact that they were closely linked both in *Caring for People* (DoH, 1989) and in subsequent guidance (DoH/SSI, 1991a). While assessment of need has become the dominant element of social services policy, as once again emphasised with establishment of a single assess-ment process (DoH, 2002a), care management has been much less well devel-oped (Gorman and Postle, 2003). The contention of this book is that older people need both an improved quality of assessment and care management processes, and that the role of qualified social workers within these processes can help to improve them.

SECTION SUMMARY

This section has explored the development of community care policy by the 'new' Labour administration. It has addressed the following issues:

- The general way in which social policy has been interpreted by 'new' Labour.
- The particular emphasis given to performance and partnership within this policy.
- The specific detail of the *National Service Framework for Older People* (DoH, 2001a).
- The policy priorities for social work with older people that can be extracted from the above, in particular the focus on assessment, care management and intermediate care.

CONCLUSION

As this chapter has demonstrated, health and social care policy has undergone significant changes since the foundation of the welfare state. While the needs of older people have always received some level of recognition, they gradually shifted more towards the centre of policy towards the end of the twentieth century. In the early part of the twenty-first century, the publication of the *NHS Plan* (DoH, 2000b) and the *National Service Framework for Older People* (DoH, 2001a) have ensured that older people can no longer be relegated to the fringes of debate about health and social care policy. However, the fact that the needs of older people are now at the heart of policy does not mean that services for them will improve magically. The scandalous conditions in residential care for older people, first outlined by Townsend (1962), may have improved, yet the health and social care world remains dominated by unresponsive and unimaginative forms of institutional care. In addition, there is little evidence that practice with older people is seen as a popular and fulfilling career direction for social workers.

In examining the development of health and social policy for older people, two key themes have emerged:

- Good quality services will be reliant on the ability of a range of different professional groups to work together effectively. This depends on a clear understanding of the nature of inter-professional collaborative working. This will be explored further in Chapter 4. The three practice issues that are the subjects of Chapters 7, 8 and 9 (assessment, care management and intermediate care) all depend on this form of working.

- A clear appreciation of the relationship between social care and health care is required, including an understanding of the way in which this relationship has developed over time. Chapter 5 will explore the historical relationships between social work and health, particularly the medical profession.

CHAPTER SUMMARY

This chapter has addressed a number of salient issues in the development of community care policy since the Second World War. These include:

- A discussion of the nature of the 'Berlin Wall' between health and social care services, concluding that the creation of this barrier was more the result of legislation and policy choices than the action of the different groups themselves.
- However, it has also outlined the problems that have existed in collaborative working, which are further developed in the following chapter.
- It has identified the over-reliance on mostly poor quality residential provision for older people, combined with the slow development of community-based alternatives to residential care.
- In charting the development of community care policies, the chapter has identified the primacy of financial considerations in their formulation, and outlined the various reports that led up to the establishment of community care with the passage of the National Health Service and Community Care Act 1990.
- Given the financial priorities of community care, the chapter has argued that the policy has been successful from this perspective: however, it also notes that other aspects of community care have been less successfully developed.
- The chapter has charted the main contours of the 'new' Labour response to health and social care, noting the emphasis on partnership that has suffused numerous policy documents.
- It has outlined the key elements of the *National Service Framework for Older People* (DoH, 2001a), indicating the policy priorities – the single assessment process and intermediate care – that this document has generated.

Partnership, Collaboration and Inter-professional Working

... significant social issues necessarily sit within the 'inter-organizational' domain and cannot be tackled by any organization acting alone. (Huxham, 2000: 338)

The purpose of this chapter is to explore the mechanics of partnership, collaboration and inter-professional working, given their centrality to effective practice with older people. As outlined in Chapter 3, 'partnership' has become a concept that is characteristic of 'new' Labour policy in a range of arenas (see Glendinning et al., 2002). However, achieving meaningful partnership is particularly complex for health and social care services, as the different management, organisational and financial arrangements that govern each make their establishment highly problematic. In addition, for partnership working to be successful, it requires a good quality of collaborative activity: this is complicated by a range of factors that have affected the development of the various professions involved in the delivery of service.

This chapter will commence by examining various issues in the development of professions within health and social care, with a particular eye on the differences and potential incompatibilities between them. (These will be further developed in Chapter 5.) Employing a framework first developed by Beattie (1994), the chapter analyses collaboration from three linked perspectives. The first of these focuses on 'structural/organisational' arrangements, including issues such as autonomy, accountability, pay, management and planning. The second perspective examines 'professional/cultural' issues, stemming from the mix of social and professional ideologies of the different groups. The third perspective explores the impact of 'interpersonal' dynamics within collaborative working. Beattie (1994) has argued that while none of these perspectives – if taken individually – can necessarily explain all the problems which could arise in collaborative working, a fuller understanding is made possible by combining insights from the different levels. Without wishing to minimise the importance of the other two perspectives, particular attention is given to the 'professional/cultural' dimension, as this is the area which is perhaps least understood both by practitioners and managers. While the chapter accepts the argument that there is a close interconnection between issues such as organisational structures, professional cultures and personal values (Johnson et al., 2003), the framework is a useful way to analyse the nature of collaboration (see Lymbery, 1998b; Lymbery and Millward, 2000).

Having established the difficulties that may be encountered when seeking to extend collaborative activity, the chapter will then specify the elements of effective collaboration. These have a particular bearing on the practice-related chapters (Chapters 7, 8 and 9) as it is not possible to practise effectively in social work with older people without also being able to function successfully in a multidisciplinary, inter-professional environment. Therefore, understanding and being able to handle the context within which practice takes place – as well as managing the nature of the practice itself – is an essential skill for an effective social work practitioner.

A note on definitions is important here. There is a high degree of imprecision in the language used to describe the range of activities that are encompassed within these terms (Huxham, 2000). Indeed, the terms 'partnership' and 'collaboration' are often used interchangeably, with a consequent potential for analytical confusion (Whittington, 2003). In a search for clarity, in this book the term 'partnership' is deployed when two or more agencies have established arrangements that enable them to work together. By contrast, 'collaboration' refers to two activities – the process of working together to establish a partnership and the process of working together to achieve the desired outcomes of a partnership. Therefore, amongst other things, 'partnership' is an outcome of collaborative processes: indeed, a 'partnership' could not be developed without close collaboration. Further, 'collaboration' is the activity that gives practical expression to a partnership.

THE NATURE OF PROFESSIONS IN HEALTH AND SOCIAL CARE

The purpose of this section is to establish an analytical grasp of the nature of professions in health and social welfare. This is vital because successful collaborative activity implies a good quality of inter-professional working; however, the history of inter-professional work creates doubts and concerns about the extent to which this may be achievable in practice (Hudson, 2002). The section will commence with a brief summary of influential ways of considering the nature of professions, leading to an analysis of the status of the key professions in health and social care, with specific reference to medicine and social work. The core argument is that the differential levels of power and status of these professions can have a major impact on the quality of inter-professional working.

Ways of conceptualising professions changed greatly in the latter stages of the twentieth century. For example, in the 1950s and 1960s, the most influential strain of sociological thought on professions was based on a 'taxonomic approach', which sought to list the traits that characterise a profession (Greenwood, 1965, cited in Wilding, 1982). Following this approach, the archetypal professions were held to include law and medicine, while in an influential analysis Etzioni (1969) classified occupations such as social work, nursing and teaching as 'semi-professions', since they did not possess all the traits which characterised a 'full' profession.

However, there are limits to the utility of trait theories; they do not define the essential nature of an occupation, but the characteristics of those occupations which have been able to secure a measure of control over the nature and conditions of practice (Johnson, 1972). This allows for some differentiation between those occupations such as medicine whose professional status is generally accepted and those whose claims to professional status are more contested – which would include both social work and nursing. Three issues particularly affect social work in this respect:

- As with nursing, social work is heavily dependent on other professions – particularly medicine – for defining the nature and extent of its work. This is particularly true in relation to practice with older people.
- The fact that most social work practice has been located within the hierarchical and bureaucratic structures of local government has limited the extent to which a professional status could be claimed. It has been suggested that the nature of bureaucratic control is such that levels of professional discretion and autonomy cannot apply in this sort of environment (Johnson, 1972).
- Social work is possibly unique amongst aspiring professions in that it has long contained an element of its membership fundamentally opposed to the desirability of professionalisation. Much of this resistance has been political in origin, with the radical social work movement particularly active in this respect (Jones, 1983; Simpkin, 1983).

It is worth exploring this final point in a little more detail. Should social work aspire to 'traditional' professional status, or is that an inappropriate goal for the occupation to pursue? Ehrenreich has neatly summarised the concerns that many have had about the process of professionalisation, with the clear implication that 'traditional' professional status is not one to which social workers should aspire:

If 'professionalism' means a frantic search for status, abjuring social action, kowtowing to upper-class financial saviors, evaluating theory for its occupational benefits, defending turf against other professionals, maintaining agency or 'professional' concerns as prior to those of clients, then 'professionalism' hardly seems a desirable or respectable goal for social work. (Ehrenreich, 1985: 229–30)

However, a revised process of professionalisation could legitimately become a goal for social work (Hugman, 1998a; Lymbery, 2001). Following Larson (1977), it is suggested that a form of 'new professionalism' could emerge; the characteristics of this would be an attempt to break down the barriers between social work professionals and laypersons, alongside an active process of seeking greater involvement of those who use services in decisions that affect their own lives. This implies working to establish relations of 'trust' between social worker and service user or carer. Hugman argues that a 'professionalism in which skills and knowledge were based on responsiveness, openness and service could not accrue and exercise the same social power as that based on autonomy, exclusion and status' (Hugman, 1998a: 191). The core of the 'new professionalism', therefore, would lie in the values of empowerment, advocacy and anti-oppressive practice, all of which should be considered as central to the social work role.

Whether or not social work can be defined as a profession, Larson's theory (1977) of the 'professional project' would suggest that social work – in common with other comparable occupations – has long sought professional status. She has argued that the attempt to organise and control a market for their services is characteristic of all aspirant professions: the more that this can be managed the more 'occupational control' a profession will be able to exert. Within Britain, social work's status as a 'state-mediated' profession (Johnson, 1972) has meant that it has never possessed the power to exert a high level of occupational control; in Larson's terms, therefore, this has limited the extent to which social work could achieve professional status. However, there is no doubt that the search for this status has been a continuing preoccupation for social work throughout its existence, despite the dissenting voices cited earlier. The early attempts within the COS and the Settlement Movement to establish agreed systems of education and training for social workers were part of this. In addition, some parts of the occupation – notably hospital almoners and psychiatric social workers – were successful in gaining a substantial measure of control over their work. There is little doubt that the adoption of psychological theories in the 1950s was also part of the professionalisation process. In more contemporary times, the establishment of social work as an occupation for which one is required to possess a degree in order to enter (DoH, 2002d), combined with a process of registration of social workers and the social work title through the creation of a General Social Care Council (with its similarities to bodies already in existence in medicine, nursing and other health professions), can both be seen as elements of social work's continual striving for professional status.

However, social work has not been successful in establishing an undeniable, publicly accepted case for professional status (Lymbery, 1998a). The general public manifestly does not accept that social work should be considered as equivalent in status to medicine, while the occupation has never satisfactorily managed to articulate the complex and sophisticated professional judgements that underpin its practice. In addition, the development of policy in social welfare in the 1990s has helped to turn social work into a more routinised, even deprofessionalised activity than before (Hugman, 1998b). For a variety of reasons (Lymbery, 1998a), which are further explored in Chapter 6, social work with older people has been disproportionately affected by this.

The uncertain professional status of social work creates a particular problem in relation to the development of collaborative working, as such practice entails working with some occupations whose professional status has long been accepted (medicine) and others where the degree of public acceptability of their work is much higher than for social work, even though professional status has not been fully secured (nursing). While Meads (2003) has argued that 'professionalism' is a potentially unifying concept, his understanding of the relationship between professions significantly downplays the elements of power that can hinder inter-professional work. Effective collaboration depends on various occupations being able to work together in a structure predicated on a parity of respect and esteem between them. This has never existed between medicine and nursing; given that the historical relationship between medicine and social work is even less positive (Bywaters, 1986), this level of parity has been more of an aspiration than a reality. Therefore, the idea that the barriers between professions can be removed simply through greater access to each other – which seems to permeate Meads' analysis (2003) – would seem to be unfeasibly naïve. Indeed, in a paper in the same volume, Glendinning and Rummery (2003) highlight the importance of GPs' power in relation to other professional groups represented on Primary Care trusts. They also note that the GPs are the weak professional link in the collaborative chain, in part because their powerful position can serve to obstruct working as equals with representatives from other occupations.

Another important strand of analysis focuses on the boundaries between professions; the essence of this argument is the contention that: 'the development of the formal attributes of a profession is bound up with the pursuit of jurisdiction and the besting of rival professions' (Abbot, 1988: 30). In this analysis, Abbot has suggested that the development of any profession should not be examined in isolation from others that exist in the same general area of activity. With regard to practice with older people, therefore, the way in which social work has progressed should not be separated from the development of other related occupations – of which nursing, medicine, occupational therapy and physiotherapy are particularly important. Abbot's emphasis on the significance of boundaries is particularly pertinent in the context of inter-professional practice. If inter-professional rivalries and boundary disputes come to characterise collaborative practice (Miller and Freeman, 2003), there will automatically be problems around the quality and sustainability of such working. This is why it is vital for social work practitioners both to comprehend the nature of their own occupational role and also the legitimate roles of other occupations. Otherwise, it is inevitable that destructive conflicts will characterise inter-professional working, as is more fully explained in the following section.

SECTION SUMMARY

This section has engaged with the following issues:

- It has acknowledged the contested nature of social work's claims to professional status.
- It has argued that social work has been, and still is, engaged in an attempt to secure professional status.
- It has suggested that all professions seek to maximise their power, influence and control in relation to others.
- Both of these points have an obvious effect on inter-professional working – indeed the search for power and control could derail attempts to instigate a good quality of collaborative working between professions.

OBSTACLES TO COLLABORATIVE WORKING

As the previous section has argued, inter-professional rivalries may impact negatively on effective collaborative working. Hudson (2002) has observed that such rivalries are a key aspect of the substantial 'pessimistic' tradition of literature on the subject, which includes the following dimensions:

- Professional identity and territory;
- Relative status and power of professions;
- Different patterns of discretion and accountability between professions.

All of these derive directly from the sociological literature to which the previous section referred, much of which (see Dingwall, 1982 and Huntington, 1981 for classic accounts) focuses on difficulties and problems, emphasising particularly the inequalities of status and power between medicine and social work.

Given that the concepts of 'power' (Johnson, 1972) and 'boundaries' (Abbott, 1988) are at the heart of professional formation, medicine has been particularly effective in establishing its power over subordinate occupations (Freidson, 1970) and in delineating the work terrain of such occupations substantially in relation to medicine. In Brewer and Lait's terms (1980) the 'rule of medicine' has always been apparent in health-related social work, particularly in hospitals. While this was a particular problem in the early days of social work's involvement in health services (Bell, 1961), it also occurred in the post-war National Health Service era (Dedman, 1996) as medical social work was extended to a wider range of hospitals. While there are fewer reports, of such power differences having a negative effect in primary health care, Huntington's (1981) 'ideal-type' characterisations of general practitioners and social workers illustrate how ongoing difficulties between the two might come into being.

The outcomes of occupational boundary maintenance are evident within the relationship between social workers and doctors. Bywaters (1986: 663) commented on the 'widespread emasculation' of the social work role in hospitals as a consequence of this. The fact that contemporary writers see limited potential in hospital-based social work being able to transcend the bureaucratically and administratively defined nature of practice (Rachman, 1997) is further confirmation of this lack of occupational power. Social workers do not have anything to fall back on that is equivalent to doctors' 'clinical judgement'. Essentially, many of them operate in an environment where control of the nature and content of their work rests with managers or health professionals. While they retain the capacity to organise the conduct of their work – although even this is increasingly circumscribed (Harris, 1998) – this is outweighed by the other forms of control to which they are subject.

While this particularly applies to social workers in the hospital setting, similar issues will occur within primary health care, particularly if and when social work posts in such settings become more common. Huntington (1981) suggested that many of the disputes between doctors and social workers could be explained with reference to the differences that exist within the occupational cultures of the two, which led her to a somewhat pessimistic conclusion about the potential for genuinely collaborative work. However, Huntington does point out that the differences can also be productive, provided that they are both recognised and accepted. Of course, in establishing collaborative working for older people, a 'culture'-based analysis must also address the other occupational groups that will make up a part of this team. This increases the level of complexity that is required to make sense of cultural similarities and differences within inter-professional teams. For example, each occupation has its own sense of history, role and purposes, and techniques for carrying these out. A coming together of all of them into a team working towards an agreed end implies an acceptance of the legitimate distinctions between occupations and the forms of practice that will then arise. For example, a district nurse will organise her/his work in a different way from a social worker, as well as having additional managerial responsibilities to accommodate. Similarly, an occupational therapist has a distinctive approach to assessment, requiring service users to demonstrate their capabilities more than most social workers would do. In another example, a social worker may be more familiar with balancing the needs and wishes of a range of family members than of any of the other occupational groups. These differences can be a source of great strength; however, they could also be the cause of disagreement and conflict. The key is in how such cultural issues are managed. At least, there are fewer issues of structural power to consider when looking at the relationship between social work and other related professions, unlike the relationship between social work and medicine.

Despite these formidable obstacles, one should recognise that there is also a more optimistic academic tradition on which to draw (Hudson, 2002). For example, it has been suggested that fruitful alliances can be developed when inter-professional teams are established (Dalley, 1989). It has also been contended that effective inter-professional working can help to meet the goals of different organisations while providing better service delivery (Lymbery, 1998b). Indeed, there is considerable recent research that highlights successful inter-professional working, although these studies often emphasise improved collaborative processes rather than demonstrate improved outcomes for service users (see, for example, Lymbery and Millward, 2000). Finally, one must pay attention to the normative element in accounts of inter-professional working: simply put, closer collaboration can be seen as a 'good thing' (Hudson, 2002). Therefore, while it is important to be aware of the pessimistic tradition of inter-professional working, it is equally vital not to be constrained by it.

As this book seeks to suggest, there is room for cautious optimism about the development of collaboration towards the care of older people. However, it also recognises the potential pitfalls that may confront collaborative working. The following sub-sections explore the nature of these pitfalls, deploying an analysis drawn from Beattie (1994). The particular value of the model is that it draws attention to various dimensions that affect the collaborative enterprise. It brings an analytical clarity that is helpful in terms of understanding the range of factors that impact upon collaborative working; however, the interdependence between the different levels also needs to be recognised. For example, Johnson et al. (2003) emphasise the way in which structure and values inter-relate. In addition, the literature on professional socialisation (Clouder, 2003) reminds us of the way in which the process of 'becoming' a professional entails an interaction between the individual and the culture of the profession.

SECTION SUMMARY

This section has discussed the various obstacles that might obstruct
collaborative working in general terms. It has addressed the following:

- The potential impact of differences in status and power of professions
  working within health and social care.
- The fact that social workers – along with other professions – are
  particularly vulnerable to the 'rule of medicine'.
- The structural differences between doctors and social workers that might
  serve to explain conflict between the two.

STRUCTURAL/ORGANISATIONAL

The importance of considering structures and organisations is based on the
understanding that these bodies can either facilitate or obstruct collaborative
working through the ways in which they operate (Cameron and Lart, 2003). In
essence, effective work at this level can help to create the conditions for successful collaborative practice at the front-line, although it cannot ensure that
such practice actually takes place. One key element that predicts successful collaborative working in the future is a history of prior joint working (Cameron and
Lart, 2003; Lymbery, 1998b). For example, the perceived success of one form of
collaborative working in a particular locality (Lymbery and Millward, 2000,
2001) helped to lay the groundwork for other related developments (Torkington
et al., 2004). This is not to say that effective collaboration is impossible without
this advantage, but it does make the process easier.

The first pre-condition for effective collaboration is good planning (Gregson
et al., 1991). There are a number of factors to consider before professionals can
be enabled to work together successfully. For example, if there is an incompatibility of goals adopted by different organisations as their preferred outcomes of
collaboration this will inevitably have an impact on the perceived success of any
subsequent project, particularly if the mismatch is obscured by the rhetoric of
'collaboration' (Lymbery and Millward, 2001). It will therefore be important to
establish clear aims and objectives which are understood and accepted by the
agencies and individual professionals concerned (Cameron and Lart, 2003).

On a more practical level, different agencies will have their own mechanisms
for recording information and, deriving from this, may well use computer programs and systems that are incompatible with each other. Since various studies
have raised the important role that shared recording processes can have on the
quality of joint working (Gregson et al., 1991; Torkington et al., 2004), there will

be major consequences if it proves impossible to establish such procedures. This incompatibility has been a major obstacle in the implementation of the single assessment process for older people (McNally et al., 2003) and also hampers efforts to reduce the impact of delayed hospital discharges (Lymbery and Millward, 2004). If the drive towards greater collaboration is to be successful, this sort of obstacle needs to be resolved. Of course, this is easier said than done: computer systems represent a heavy investment for each organisation, which cannot simply be written off when a degree of incompatibility is uncovered.

Good planning also requires an effective preparation process for those staff who are to work in collaboration, in addition to those others whose work will be affected by the change. All parties need to be fully informed as to what will be expected of them and provided with opportunities to discuss the practical implications of change. Altering patterns of working that have become well-established will take time, as will the establishment of new ways of interaction within the inter-professional environment. If this is not well understood, structural change may run ahead of the capabilities of those staff who will be required to ensure that there are meaningful improvements to practice.

Another important element of planning refers to the provision of resources, including administrative support. Establishing structures to facilitate collaborative working will lead to considerable additional expense, at least in the early stages (Hardy et al., 1996). It is important that all the agencies involved in joint working accept and are able to act in accordance with this requirement. The issue of administrative support has been a continuing source of difficulty for social work within many hospital settings. Although the employment of hospital-based social work staff transferred to social service departments following the 1974 reorganisation within the NHS (Hugman, 1995), the position of administrative staff has become anomalous: although their work is for social services, they are employed by the hospital. Administrative support is also a critical factor when planning pilot or demonstration projects, which often act as the precursor to more fundamental changes in policy and practice. Sometimes, the administrative arrangements that are needed to support such projects are given insufficient attention, with the primary focus being on the inter-professional elements of the project.

The location of those people who are to engage in collaborative working is an important consideration. It is interesting, for example, that the majority of social workers based in hospitals are situated separately from the staff who provide health care. By contrast, 'co-location' of staff has been regarded as an important factor in the success of collaborative working within primary health care (Hardy et al., 1996; Lymbery and Millward, 2000). However, co-location is often a difficult goal to achieve, irrespective of setting. Many potential sites – for example, health centres, social services offices – are simply not capable of housing the additional numbers of people required, and conversion of such premises is often neither feasible nor desirable. Any capital building programme that seeks to include accommodation for the many professionals who need to work together for the better care of older people will inevitably be several years in development.

If major organisational change is to be achieved, strong leadership will be required. This is more than simply having a manager to 'champion' the shift, important as this can be. Rather, strong leadership will be required from the very top of the organisation, establishing clear aims and objectives to which collaborative working can contribute. This can help the organisation 'ride out' tensions and difficulties in the development of partnerships without its systems of collaborative working being subject to collapse. The direct management of collaborative working generates a number of issues. For example, the literature on inter-professional working emphasises the importance of good systems of management and support for disparate professional groups (see, for example, Cumella et al., 1996; Lymbery and Millward, 2000). There are two elements to this. The first of these is the issue of accountability, which is potentially problematic given the split nature of a practitioner's accountability – to her/his employer on the one hand, and to the inter-professional team on the other. The second concerns another linked dimension of management – professional supervision and support. In practice, social workers within multi-disciplinary teams will need to be able to take relatively quick decisions regarding their work, changing the nature of the relationship between practitioner and manager that has typified the work of social services departments (Lymbery, 2004b). A different conception of accountability and autonomy will therefore be required, with practitioners enabled to assume more responsibility for decision-making than hitherto. A model of enhanced professional accountability, akin to that hypothesised for workers within youth justice (Eadie and Canton, 2002), will need to be adopted to maximise the potential of social work practice with older people. A similar model already exists within community nursing, while doctors have always had a full measure of clinical responsibility for their decision-making. Of course, this would affect the professional status and activity of the social worker and will therefore also be addressed in the following sub-section.

SECTION SUMMARY

This section has examined the influence of a range of 'structural/organisational' factors on collaboration, including the following:

(Continued)

- The importance of good planning for the activity.
- The need for linked systems of information recording and retrieval.
- Preparation and development of staff involved in the collaborative activity.
- The importance of adequate resourcing, including administrative support.
- The benefits of co-location.
- The need for strong leadership and effective direct management.

PROFESSIONAL/CULTURAL

There is considerable literature that bears on this level of collaborative working, testimony to the fact that it has been the most studied. This literature has generated material that raises concerns about the feasibility of effective collaboration, focusing particularly on the relationships between the medical profession and social work. For example, in a classic account, Huntington (1981) itemised similarities and differences between doctors and social workers, arguing that the key differences between the two occupational groups (for example, in terms of status and income, training, ideology, location and distribution) predict major problems in working together as equal partners. However, since collaborative working in health and social care for older people involves a much wider range of professions than these two, it is interesting that there has been relatively little literature that has explored (for example) the similarities and differences between social workers and community nurses – although Torkington et al. (2003) identified more similarities than differences in their study of shared practice learning for district nursing and social work students. It is clear that the various professions involved in the provision of care for older people have different histories, cultures and work processes, all of which might impact negatively on their capacity to work together. This is particularly true if there are fundamental differences in values and ideology as Huntington (1981) detected with social workers and doctors (see also Dalley, 1989).

Indeed, following this line of argument Dingwall (1982) has suggested that the different professional groups within health and social care will tend to struggle for dominance, through a process of what he termed 'occupational boundary maintenance'. Since doctors are in the most structurally dominant position of these occupations, it is likely that they would be more successful in maintaining their position relative to the other groupings. Indeed, as Huntington (1986) has observed, this process has been a continued problem for social workers within health settings. The ideological differences between occupational groups can also be magnified by the difficulties of communication between the groups, given that each has developed its own language to describe its work (Rawson, 1994). The tempo of work of the different professions could also become problematic. Social workers are accustomed to function at a much slower pace than either doctors or community nurses: unless the reasons for this are properly understood, tensions and mistrust can easily develop. These differences can be of such an order that a planned programme of joint training and/or team-building may be required in order to create the conditions for effective collaboration (Cameron and Lart, 2003).

By contrast, Dalley (1989) has discussed the possibility that different professionals may develop similar perspectives on problems, regardless of the fact that they have disparate professional identities. She has suggested that this is a process of 'tribal allegiance', which can be contrasted with the variations constructed through separate and distinct 'professional ideologies'. This can create problems in two ways. First, it might potentially collapse the different perspectives necessary for good inter-professional work into one homogenised identity, thereby compromising the sense of difference that is important for effective collaboration. Secondly, it may potentially lead to the avoidance of conflict within the team, even where such disagreement would be a helpful feature of collaborative working.

Indeed, this can engender a fundamental confusion about roles and responsibilities within the team (Rawson, 1994). Good inter-professional working should have its starting point in the differences of perspective and expertise of the separate professional groups, as the acceptance of these leads to a greater degree of collective knowledge and understanding. Of course, this points to a tension that is at the heart of collaborative working – there is simultaneously a need for different professional groups to retain their identity while also developing a good understanding and appreciation of the contributions of others. The cause of inter-professional working is not best served by moving towards some form of professional merger between different professions, but by the way in which separate perspectives and orientations can be harnessed for the good of service users. Clearly, the presence of good communication of information between the various parties is essential (Hardy et al., 1996). Gregson et al. (1991) have identified a range of practices which would help to improve collaboration, including regular consultations and meetings, cross-referrals and writing notes in each other's records. This can help to build a sense of mutual understanding between professions of each other's roles and functions. Without this, there can be continued difficulties in seeking to reconcile the working practices of professional groups. Indeed, the fact that social workers have less capacity to make decisions without referral to others outside the inter-professional team can create a potential difficulty, highlighting core difference in relation to autonomy and accountability that could derail collaborative working (Cumella et al., 1996; Hardy et al., 1996).

The structural power and dominance of medicine within inter-professional teams is a source of potential difficulty for social workers, as well as for other professional groupings such as nursing. While doctors may be seen as the leaders of the inter-professional team that operates for older people – in that medical issues are likely to dictate the trajectory of any given set of professional responses – the way in which the team actually works must fully engage the insights and expertise of all its members. At a practical level, the experience, knowledge, skills and values of social workers should be welcomed by all other team members. While this may be readily possible in the relationships between, for example, social workers and community nurses (Lymbery and Millward, 2000), who have a similar sense of their own professional status in relation to doctors, and who share elements in common regarding their core competences (Torkington et al., 2003), this may be more difficult with regard to doctors. Two key points particularly affect this; the first is that the dominance of the medical model may cause other occupations to be seen as merely supplementary – a perception evident throughout Brewer and Lait's (1980) critique, and clearly expressed in Bywaters' (1986) warning against 'unconditional collaboration' with doctors. The second is more practical, that the nature of a doctor's work, where each consultation is strictly time-limited with a high volume of patients seen, is entirely different from the necessarily slower pace that a social worker has to deploy; a lack of understanding of this core difference can lead to frustration on both sides.

SECTION SUMMARY

This section has examined the impact of 'professional/cultural' issues on collaboration, highlighting the following:

- The ideological gap between different professional groupings working in health and social care.
- Communication difficulties that could stem from this ideological split.
- The danger that a homogenised identity could be the outcome of collaborative working, negating the unique characteristics and perspectives of a profession.
- The problems that could arise if systems of professional dominance apply in a given setting.

INTERPERSONAL

Many of the issues raised in the previous sections have an interpersonal dimension. For example, at the inter-professional level several writers refer to the range of ways in which an individual may seek to adapt to an unfamiliar environment, pointing to the temptation that a social worker could collude with the perspectives of doctors and potentially lose their professional identity (Dingwall, 1982). In addition, the existence of negative professional stereotypes within a team may generate attitudes which could militate against the development of good interpersonal and inter-professional working practices. That there is antipathy towards social work within the medical profession is apparent from Brewer and Lait's critique (1980). Were such attitudes to be carried into inter-professional working arrangements there would appear to be little chance of meaningful professional dialogue between the two – unless, of course, it was based on acceptance of the legitimacy of the 'rule of medicine' (Brewer and Lait, 1980: 204).

The fact that several writers point to the importance of the attitudes of team members to working within an inter-professional team reinforces the above points. For example, Engel (1994) has identified various characteristics and skills which should be developed by people involved in collaborative working, emphasising particularly participating in – and adapting to – change, managing self and others, and good communication. The willingness to extend such characteristics and skills is entirely dependent on the attitudes of staff engaged in collaborative activity. It may be that the attitudes of doctors are particularly significant, given that they often see themselves – and are seen by others – as 'team leaders' of a multi-disciplinary team. As Huntington (1986) has noted, doctors differ widely in the value they place on social work. To be effective, they must appreciate the role and function of the social worker, and must also be capable of engaging positively with social workers and other team members as individuals (Lymbery, 1998b). Gregson et al. (1991: ix) have noted that the existence of a 'friendly, informal relationship' with 'reciprocal use of first names' is associated with improved levels of collaboration. While the establishment of a congenial workplace might create a collateral problem, with colleagues from different professional disciplines reluctant to challenge others even where such challenge might be indicated, the professional advantages to be gained from such an approach are apparent. Certainly, the establishment of good interpersonal relationships has been assessed as aiding the development of effective inter-professional working (Lymbery and Millward, 2001).

The character and adaptability of the social worker are critical here, as more change is likely to be required of her/him than of any other party, given that the social worker is often located in health settings, particularly in primary health care (Hardy et al., 1996; Lymbery, 1998b). It is vital that any 'outposted' social worker must both be highly skilled in a professional sense and be personally mature and hence capable of functioning within a potentially challenging and problematic setting (Lymbery, 1998b). Therefore, the personal qualities of social workers operating in a collaborative environment are particularly significant factors. While the same could be said for all professionals placed into surroundings where the emphasis is on collaborative working, particular pressure will be placed on the individual who is working on 'foreign' territory. In addition, given the structural power of medicine as a profession, the personal qualities of the doctors involved in the team will also have a considerable bearing on its successful working. While excellent interpersonal relations cannot dissipate difficulties which are generated at the other levels, they can help to contain them, and provide a vehicle for their resolution.

SECTION SUMMARY

This section has explored the impact of interpersonal dynamics on collaboration, focusing on the following:

- The importance of an open approach to collaboration.
- The impact of the attitudes and values of all staff involved in collaborative working.
- Particular emphasis was placed on the need for the social worker to be both highly skilled and personally mature.

EFFECTIVE COLLABORATION: THE HOLY GRAIL?

The purpose of this section is to identify the features of effective collaboration, drawing on the main themes to have emerged from the above summary. While several other writers have addressed this issue in some depth (see, for example, Miller and Freeman, 2003), deploying a range of different conceptual and analytical frameworks in the process, the analysis in this section follows the three levels advanced earlier in the chapter. It is illustrated by a practice example that illustrates the various themes that are identified.

At the structural/organisational level, the following issues will need to be addressed, and a successful example of collaboration will need to resolve them in practice:

- The collaborative enterprise must be properly *planned*.
- There needs to be good *preparation*, both of staff directly engaged in the work as well as those staff whose work will be affected by it.
- *Effective administrative systems* also need to be established, including computer programs that allow different agencies to share information.
- There needs to be *strong leadership* at all levels of the organisations concerned, in order to ride out the difficulties that will inevitably occur.
- Careful thought should be given to the location of inter-professional teams – taking the fact into account that *co-location* has demonstrated advantages in practice over models of attachment.
- Effective structures for *managerial and professional support* also need to be considered, given that the literature on inter-professional working tends to highlight difficulties in this area of activity.

Practice Example 4.1

It was jointly agreed by the social services department and the primary care trust that three social workers should be attached to different primary health care settings, with the specific intention to improve the quality of collaborative working in respect of older people. This attachment was carefully planned, involving senior managers from both organisations. In this way, the core purpose, function and elements of the project could be agreed at the highest level in the organisations. To guarantee ongoing strong leadership, a steering group was established to guide the project; this group met regularly throughout the project and comprised managers from both organisations. This group organised a number of briefing and information sessions to ensure that all of those engaged in the project were given adequate preparation for its impact. Given the demonstrated benefits of co-location, the social workers were placed in a shared office with District Nurses, meaning that there were numerous people to be involved in this preparatory work. Systems of joint and shared recording were organised, to ensure that there were efficient administrative systems to support the project. In full awareness of the potential for the practitioners to be professionally isolated, managerial and professional support was provided, so that they had a reference point both for casework decisions and also for the professional components of their work.

At the second level there are a number of professional and cultural factors to consider. These include the following:

- That there are *key differences between the two occupational groups of social work and medicine* needs to be acknowledged.
- The *relationship between social work and occupations such as nursing* also needs to be explored, since members of these professions also work closely together in multi-disciplinary teams.
- The possibility that professions may struggle for *power and dominance* within the setting must be balanced against the potential for individuals to develop a sense of *tribal allegiance* that cuts across professional boundaries.
- In the light of this, it needs to be recognised that the *separate perspectives and orientations* of a range of professions can be harnessed for the good of service users.
- A range of *working practices* can help to improve collaboration; these will include regular consultations and meetings, cross-referrals and shared record-keeping.
- The *differences in working practices* between professions needs to be recognised, accepted and worked with.

Practice Example 4.2

As part of the planning and preparation of staff noted above, clarity was sought about the respective roles and responsibilities of the various parties involved in the project, particularly focusing on the social workers, district nurses and doctors. Through this it was agreed how the different parties could work together for the greater benefit of the project. Various forms of practical working arrangements were agreed between all parties, and it was also agreed that regular meetings would be held to check progress on the project and to iron out any practical or other difficulties. The arrangements for managerial and professional accountability and support were also discussed, with particular emphasis given to the position of the social workers, isolated from other social work colleagues and separate from the normal managerial arrangements that applied within the social services department.

The final set of prescriptions stem from the third level of analysis, which has focused on interpersonal issues. These include the following:

- The importance of *interpersonal relationships* within inter-professional working needs to be acknowledged as a factor of equal importance to the others.
- The *attitudes of different professionals* to the collaborative process are also significant, marrying issues at the 'professional/cultural' level as well as at the 'interpersonal' level.

- All practitioners successfully functioning in an inter-professional environ-ment need to have – or develop! – a good *range of interpersonal skills*, chief amongst which are effective communication skills (see Chapter 6 for more on communication skills within social work practice).
- In addition, all practitioners working in an inter-professional team must have a *high level of commitment* not just to their own goals but also to the wider aims and purposes of the team.
- Given their position of structural power and authority, *doctors have a key role in establishing the effective multi-disciplinary team*; they should model good practice through the way in which they relate to all other team members.

Practice Example 4.3

Having established the structural/organisational and professional/cultural basis for the project, careful monitoring of the project was needed to ensure that the interpersonal dynamics within the three settings did not conflict with the aims of the project. Initial attention was given to the selection both of project sites and of the social workers to be based in primary care settings, as people who are professionally capable, personally mature and with a high level of interpersonal skills were required to turn the projects into an effective reality. The character of the general practitioners within the settings was critical: they needed to be welcoming both of other perspectives on the work and of outside contributions to what many feel is *their* team. Particular emphasis was given to team development, to foster the establishment of good interpersonal relationships.

Given the preceding analysis, it is important to identify as clearly as possible what specific knowledge, skills and values that a social worker would contribute to a collaborative enterprise with older people. The following points represent an attempt to outline what such a contribution might look like.

- The values and ethical stance of social workers are a vital element of an inter-professional team, as these are areas in which there are key differences between social workers and other professionals (Herod and Lymbery, 2002). Through the expression of these values the social worker should be able to provide both critique and challenge within the multi-disciplinary team.
- In a related point, the fact that social workers work from a holistic perspec-tive – seeing the individual and/or group within a family, community and social context – provides an important contribution to the role of the team.
- The 'administrative' role of the social workers is particularly evident in the central, coordinating position that they occupy in relation to the establishment

and management of care packages. Because social work operates at the conjunction between the individual and society, practitioners mediate between each older person and the range of bodies – various parts of the health service, social security and other benefits agencies, voluntary organisations – with which that person may be involved. As such, social workers are particularly well placed to link and connect the various elements of a care plan. Indeed, it could be argued that 'social workers are the "glue" that holds care packages together' (Herod and Lymbery, 2002: 24).

- It may be that health care professionals particularly value the 'administrative' role of social work. However, experienced and skilled practitioners can potentially bring more to an inter-professional environment than simply this one-dimensional role. It will be a challenge for a social worker to forge a place within the team where other elements of knowledge and expertise are valued by other team members and therefore play a vital role in the overall work of the team.

- A core feature of this extended role within multi-disciplinary teams is the quality of relationship that social workers should establish with service users, carers and their families. One benefit of the nature of social work intervention, and the slower pace at which practitioners tend to operate (noted earlier in this chapter), is that it creates opportunities to establish a better quality of interpersonal relationship with the people with whom they work, despite the restrictions placed upon them within care management practice.

When taken together, it becomes evident that the role of the social worker with older people in a multi-disciplinary team is more than simply to coordinate care packages, even while one accepts that this has become the dominant mode of practice with older people. If a social worker is working effectively s/he will also contribute more widely to the multi-disciplinary team, as the above bullet points demonstrate.

CONCLUSION

It is important to note that the vast majority of studies that focus on collaboration concentrate on the processes of joint working rather than its outcomes, as Cameron and Lart (2003) point out in their 'systematic review'. Indeed, one substantial book which examines the development of inter-professional collaboration (Leathard, 2003) contains little evidence that better collaborative endeavour actually improves service outcomes. There are numerous reasons for this, chief amongst which is that it is much more straightforward to design research that provides good data about processes than outcomes. One of the few studies that have attempted to measure the impact of joint working was unable to reach any firm conclusions about the effectiveness of integrated team working for older people:

> The present research has not produced any findings which suggest that the integrated primary-care-based health and social care teams studied are more clinically effective than the traditional, non-integrated method of service delivery. (Brown et al., 2003: 93)

However, as noted in both Chapter 3 and at the start of this chapter, the 'new' Labour government is wedded to the idea that partnership working can radically improve the quality of services experienced by older people, as is evident from the *National Service Framework for Older People* (DoH, 2001a), in particular the priority given to the establishment of a single assessment process (DoH, 2002a). In this respect, the promotion of partnership and collaboration is progressing substantially ahead of research evidence that conclusively demonstrates that this will improve outcomes for service users. (As Chapter 9 indicates, a similar point can be made about intermediate care.)

As Whittington (2003) points out, it should not blithely be assumed that the development of closer collaborative working will necessarily, in and of itself, be a good thing – either for service users or for social workers. Gains in some respects may be balanced by losses elsewhere, and government policies are potentially 'double-edged' (Whittington, 2003: 28). A critical and analytical approach to partnership and collaboration is therefore needed to enable us to move beyond the glib rhetoric that informs policy. Inter-professional and multi-disciplinary structures have become essential to the provision of services for older people, and effective social work practice requires the ability to operate successfully within these structures. As Chapters 7, 8 and 9 will demonstrate, inter-professional collaboration is a central context for social work practice within the domains of assessment, care management and intermediate care. However, as this chapter has shown, making effective collaboration a reality will be a complex task.

CHAPTER SUMMARY

This chapter has examined the practice of collaborative working, and has addressed the following areas:

- Theoretical understandings about the nature of professions and their development, with particular reference to the concept of the 'professional project' and the boundaries between professions.

(Continued)

- A range of obstacles to collaborative working, focusing in turn on three levels of analysis – structural/organisational, professional/cultural, and inter-personal.
- A range of suggestions has been drawn from these three levels that can help to achieve the 'holy grail' of effective collaboration.

Social Work and Health
Care – Historical Connections

The problem for social work in health settings from its inception . . . is that doctors have frequently denied or rejected the diagnostic and therapeutic contribution of social workers. (Huntington, 1986: 1152)

Given that the concepts of partnership and collaboration are critical to the government's vision for the care for older people (as identified in Chapter 4), it is important to trace the historical relationship between health and social care. As I have earlier argued, developing a productive working relationship between the two is potentially problematic for political, organisational, professional and practical reasons. An exploration of the history of health-related social work provides some illumination on the causes of these difficulties. While there have been direct connections between social work and health care for over 100 years, the nature of the relationship between the two remains troubled, although it has been argued that social work has made a strong contribution over this time (Auslander, 2001) – a theme that will be explored in the conclusion of this chapter.

The chapter argues that there are several reasons why the relationship has been problematic. The first of these relates to the different levels of status and power that have attached to professional groups, particularly doctors and social workers, and the conflicts that have arisen from this (a flavour of such disagreement is captured in the quotation at the start of this chapter). This has tended to emphasise the comparative weakness of social work as a discipline in comparison to medicine, which has been evidenced throughout social work's history. This intersects with the traditional ability of medicine to dominate its territory; as Freidson (1970) has observed, professions – and professional authority – are central to the organisation of health care. Its history has therefore been characterised by the dominance of medicine over other professions, which are constituted as subordinate. This closely links to the second key problem, the fact that medically defined conceptions of need take precedence over more socially oriented explanations (which is also evident in the above quotation). Despite the evidence that ill-health is closely connected to a range of social factors – poverty, deprivation, poor diet, etc. (Townsend et al., 1992) – a social perspective has been lacking in both public policy and medical practice (Peckham and Exworthy, 2003). As a result, the potential contribution of social workers to a broader response to ill-health has been ignored. The third difficulty derives from a lack of clarity about the role, purpose and function of social work, which have always been imprecise – particularly when contrasted with the apparent certainties of medicine.

The chapter outlines how these different factors have combined to form a barrier to effective joint working. It takes a historical perspective, working on the assumption that the nature of present relationships between social work and health care has been heavily influenced by the past. It also examines the progress of health-related social work in both hospital and primary health care settings. The earliest developments all occurred within hospital settings, yet links with primary health care may provide a more profitable avenue in relation to future services for older people (Rummery and Glendinning, 2000). The chapter is written on the understanding that it is both impractical and unwise to consider the social care needs of older people in isolation from their health care needs, as recognised within the *National Service Framework for Older People* (DoH, 2001a). It also argues against assuming that the various obstacles to effective joint working necessarily obstruct any chance of good inter-professional arrangements, citing a number of counterbalancing factors. It is also suggested that specific policy developments – particularly around the single assessment process and intermediate care – in relation to the care of older people have helped to ensure more favourable conditions for the development of productive working relationships. The chapter concludes by arguing that an understanding both of the problems and the possibilities is needed before effective joint working between health and social care can be developed.

EARLY DAYS

The first formal link between social work and health care came with the appointment of Mary Stewart as 'lady almoner' at the Royal Free Hospital in London (Bell, 1961; Willmott, 1996). In line with much early social work, the practice undertaken had an avowedly administrative orientation. The outpatient departments of voluntary hospitals were being deluged by many people whose primary need was not medical; consequently, it was argued by the COS that the application of systematic principles of social work would help to resolve this problem (Bosanquet, 1914). Due to the perceived success of the first almoners, there was soon a rapid spread to other hospitals. In typically robust style, Bosanquet accounted this a great success, claiming that it was 'a striking manifestation of the growing recognition that a patient can seldom be treated apart from his home conditions and surroundings' (1914: 221–2). However, equally typically, Bosanquet did not engage with the numerous problems that attended both the initial establishment and subsequent spread of hospital almoners (see Bell, 1961).

The nature of some of these problems can be linked to the title that was given to the hospital-based social workers. As Bell (1961) observes, 'almoner' was a term that had its origins in the middle ages, referring to people whose duty it was to distribute alms to the poor. The particular reason it was adopted for the social work role derived from the fact that it was the 'title given to the Governors of the ancient Royal Hospitals of St Bartholomew and St Thomas, who undertook to receive all applications for admission to the hospital and accept or reject them' (Bell, 1961: 26). The sifting of outpatients into those for whom the hospital was appropriate and those for whom other agencies could better meet their needs constituted the basis of the early almoners' work. However, the title of 'almoner' retained the connotations of almsgiving, and Bell's (1961) comment that it did not carry pejorative implications in the early years of the twentieth century is somewhat disingenuous. It certainly associated social work with one aspect of its potential role, while implicitly drawing attention away from others.

In addition, the early almoners had to cope with a climate of suspicion and mistrust in all the hospitals where they were located. Bell (1961) describes the difficulties that Mary Stewart encountered at the Royal Free Hospital; these derived – in her view – from the fact that the medical staff could not easily coun-tenance delegating the responsibility for decision-making to an individual (a woman to boot!) who was outside their direct control. As Willmott puts it:

> It was an irony that although her appointment had been made with the main pur-pose of checking outpatient abuse, Miss Stewart's first two years proved difficult partly because the medical and surgical staff objected to the new system. (Willmott, 1996: 1)

There are alternative interpretations of this resistance, however. For Brewer and Lait (1980), the objections were not grounded in a failure to recognise the extent of the problems but in a preference for an alternative method of resolving them. Several hospitals had made what they considered to be satisfactory arrange-ments for managing the problems of over-crowded outpatients' departments by appointing people to investigate individual circumstances of applicants without the 'pretensions' of the almoners, and without posing a challenge to the accepted medical order. They also suggested that the utility of Mary Stewart's position was much less evident than Bell reported, pointing out the fact that the hospital initially refused to renew her appointment, only agreeing once the COS agreed to continue to pay half of her salary (Brewer and Lait, 1980). The inference is clear: taking a stance that is consistent with their general critique of social work,

Brewer and Lait (1980) suggested that the role of hospital almoner was less helpful in practice than sympathetic historians like Bell could accept.

A similar difference is observable when it was suggested that the role of almoner should be extended into work with expectant mothers and people with tuberculosis. Bell (1961) reports that this was not greeted positively, a stance which she found hard to credit. Again, Brewer and Lait (1980) took a different line, arguing that the objections were more a product of concern that the almoner was simply neither competent nor qualified to adopt this extended role. In this exchange lies the nub of the early debate about the role of social work within health care settings – to what extent did social workers have a mandate to become involved in the sorts of decisions that would hitherto have been the domain of doctors? Inability to resolve this central question could easily result in a failure to communicate and hence agree on a role for the social worker.

The nature of the almoners' work is particularly interesting in the light of the core concern of this book, social work with older people. As noted above, the origins of social work in health care were in the desire to control access to the outpatients' departments of charitable hospitals. At this stage the duties of the almoner – as defined in 1914 – were as follows:

- To check abuse of the outpatient departments.
- To ensure that all outpatients would benefit from their treatment by securing their cooperation with it.
- To serve as a connecting link between outpatient departments and outside charities. (Willmott, 1996: 4)

To use the distinctions made earlier, there is little doubt that the primary orientation of the social work practised within health care was administrative. The desire to manage unpredictable and uncontrollable levels of demand for hospital resources was the principal reason why social work developed in the hospital setting. As a result, there was relatively little orientation to a more preventive form of practice. At this time, social workers did not have a specific role in relation to what is now called primary health care. In addition, the almoner's role did not encompass work with older people to any great extent, even when it was expanded to include other tasks, which included work in respect of ante- and post-natal care, sexually transmitted diseases and tuberculosis, alongside more general ward-based work which required liaison with a range of outside bodies (Bell, 1961; Willmott, 1996). The focus on maternity and tuberculosis was reflective of the fact that high rates of infant mortality and tubercular disease were accepted as major social problems to be addressed within society. The role of the almoner in addressing social problems was also emphasised in the First World War, with vastly increased numbers of people with traumatic injuries coming to their attention; this period also increased the work around maternity care and sexually transmitted diseases.

However, perhaps the most significant shift in the balance of almoners' work occurred in the 1920s when they accepted the responsibility for assessing the needs of patients in respect of the charges laid on them by hospitals, initially in the charitable hospitals and – following the passage of the Poor Law Act of 1928 – in all the public infirmaries that transferred to local authorities. In some settings, as Bell (1961) has recorded, the almoner was also required to collect the payments and record all the transactions. While this practical function helped to reconcile the medical profession to the almoners' presence, thereby helping to secure their immediate future, it also presented another problem – that the practitioners were forced to spend 'as much time on *administrative* as on *medical* social work' (Bell, 1961: 122; emphasis added). One contemporary almoner was strongly opposed to what she considered was a wasteful use of time:

> . . . where the hospital is sufficiently progressive, the social service department is . . . ready with knowledge of the patient's environment and personal difficulties. This specialized work is undertaken by the Almoner, who all too often is wastefully used by her hospital in the assessment of patients' payments and even in the collection of money. (Manchée, 1944: 3)

In Manchée's view, the role of the almoner should have rested primarily in the application of casework principles to the social problems of the hospital patient; she believed that the preoccupation with the collection of money was a distraction from this aim. This view was also shared by Bell (1961: 122), who believed that the concentration on 'administrative' work was submerging the 'essential function' of the almoner (see also Willmott, 1996). Two central issues emerge that have particular relevance for this book:

- The dominance of an 'administrative' form of practice, although this was resented by almoners themselves.
- Very little involvement in meeting the needs of older people.

During the Second World War an increased emphasis was laid on the work of the almoner, with the need first to empty hospital beds to make them available for casualties, and the subsequent influx of people – military and civilian – with war-related injuries. Whether it was the chaos engendered throughout this period that enabled almoners to become more assertive about their condition is unclear, but several clear statements about their role emerged. For example, Helen Rees – an almoner working in Australia – had been commissioned to prepare a report on the role of the almoner on an international basis. While being generally positive about the impact of almoners within hospital settings, she also observed that there was 'widespread ignorance of their functions displayed not only by the general public but also by many doctors and health authorities who ought to have known better' (Rees, 1942, in Bell, 1961: 149).

In the same year, the Institute of Hospital Almoners inserted a statement about the 'primary function' of almoners into its Annual Report:

> An almoner's primary function is the social work that the patient's condition and treatment require, and the so-called 'administrative' functions of the department will, if the primary duty be rightly interpreted, fall into their appropriate *subordinate* place. (in Bell, 1961: 151; emphasis added)

Perhaps most significantly, the Royal College of Physicians stated in 1943 that the work of the almoner was 'an assessment of the patient's needs rather than of the patient's means' (in Bell, 1961: 151), and recommended that all hospitals should employ properly trained almoners (Dedman, 1996). This was the type of support that was needed to enable the consolidation of social work within health care settings, to which the passage of the National Health Service Act 1946 gave particular importance.

SECTION SUMMARY

This section has examined the early days of health-related social work, addressing the following themes:

- The resistance that almoners experienced when first taking up their posts in hospitals.
- The conflicting accounts that have been given to explain the causes of such resistance.
- The fact that almoners' work was primarily administrative in nature, only expanding to more recognisable social work themes at a later date.
- The work that almoners tended to carry out, which responded to needs that were socially defined; in addition, little work was undertaken with older people.
- The collective efforts of the almoners to establish a more clearly defined social work role in hospitals, which bore fruit in the period after the Second World War.

SOCIAL WORK IN THE CONTEXT OF THE NHS

For almoners, one of the key changes brought about by the passage of this Act was the fact that, in the creation of a national health service which was free at the point of delivery of services, the almoners' requirement to assess patients' means and collect their contributions to hospital care simply disappeared. This gave more scope for their casework aspirations to flourish. As Dedman (1996) recounts, almoners were employed by hospitals and were enabled to establish their own departments independent of control by doctors. Their 'professionalising' aspirations were reinforced by the increased clarity about the almoners' role which was conferred by circulars from the Ministry of Health in 1947 and 1948. The first of these specified that there were three basic elements of the job; a joint responsibility (alongside doctors) for the health of the patient, freedom from basic secretarial or administrative work (for which they would be furnished additional support), and involvement in the training of medical students in 'social medicine' (Bell, 1961: 154–5). The second circular specified the duties of the almoner, which would be those of a 'medical social worker', encompassing a social assessment of needs, action to minimise social problems during illness and home visiting following discharge to ensure that the value of the medical treatment was sustained (Dedman, 1996). These definitions coincided with the preferences of the almoners themselves. For example, Manchée (1944) had specified that the various tasks of the hospital almoner could be sub-divided into what she termed 'medico-social work', 'administrative' and 'general' responsibilities, with the first of the foregoing being most significant. At this point, therefore, the role and status of social work in hospitals seemed to be more settled than it had previously, and there certainly appeared to be a clear and accepted role for the hospital almoner. However, various issues remained problematic.

For example, it proved difficult to recruit sufficient qualified people to fill the posts that were required due to the expanded service (Dedman, 1996). The Institute of Almoners – which had responsibility for the education and training of the workforce at this time – tried various strategies to improve the situation, including reducing the length of the training course, but the problem proved difficult to resolve. At the same time, in an echo of past treatment, they were not always welcomed into new work settings and their work was sometimes less valued than they would have wished:

> Some consultants were very socially minded and greatly valued the extra dimension which social workers brought to the total care of patients; others were less easy to work with and were more likely to see social work input as a possible hindrance to the speedy discharge of patients. (Dedman, 1996: 29)

The modern day focus on the development of multi-disciplinary teams was some years away, and almoners had to ensure that they could simultaneously meet the needs of the hospital and also demonstrate an independence of professional judgement. Holding these two elements in balance was not a straightforward task. As Butrym (1967) observed, the problem of convincing doctors and nurses of the value of social work persisted into the 1960s.

A more serious difficulty derived from the emphasis on 'casework' as the dominant mode of practice (which was examined in more detail in Chapter 2). The idea of casework had taken a strong hold in British social work in the 1950s, and medical social workers – the title of 'almoner' was changed to this in 1964 – were by no means immune from its influence (as is clearly evident in Butrym, 1967). While there was relatively little debate about this shift at the time – the consensus within social work seemed to be that it offered an opportunity to demonstrate a more 'professional' approach – in retrospect there are numerous problems with the casework model applied to hospital work.

- The first is, to echo the point made by Lewis (1995), that it was clearly not possible to apply the casework model to all people seen by social workers in hospitals: sheer weight of numbers made this impracticable.
- The second problem was closely related to the first, and concerns the extent to which this would have been desirable, even if it had been possible. The fact remained that social workers had a number of practical, 'administrative' tasks to undertake – and often had to attend to these rapidly. To have practised psychodynamically informed casework without attending to these tasks would not have been in the best interests of the majority of patients. Also, the staffing problems noted above created a particular disincentive for in-depth casework.
- The third issue is that other hospital staff particularly valued the social worker's ability to gain access to resources rather than their casework skills, thereby putting them under external pressure to resolve practical problems and arrange for the provision of services. Although social workers sought to convince doctors and nurses that their contribution could potentially be broader in nature (Butrym, 1967), they continued to run up against the weight of expectation that favoured their administrative abilities.
- To make matters worse, there was often a lack of understanding of the complexity of the processes by which an individual and a service could be brought together (Butrym, 1967). The effect of this was that the time and effort required to undertake this task were often underestimated.

However, the rhetorical adoption of 'casework' as the unifying preference of social workers at this period does reflect both the professionalising impulse within the occupation, discussed in Chapter 4, and social work's insistence on its generic nature.

At the organisational level, the reform of the NHS in 1974 had a major impact on the delivery of social work services. With SSDs only having been established for a few years, the requirement to take over the hospital social work function created pressure on structures that were already struggling to respond to changed demands (Osborn, 1996). As a result, few departments were able to analyse carefully the way in which hospital-based social work could best link to community-based social work, with the two aspects of service existing more in parallel than in harmony.

The passing of community care legislation created additional pressures on hospital-based social work staff. Whereas prior to 1993, people who entered independent sector residential and nursing home care were not required to be assessed by social services, this position was radically altered, such that any person in receipt of state support for any type of social care first had to have her/his needs assessed. This increased the workload on hospital staff in partic- ular, as often hospitals had used residential and nursing homes in the indepen- dent sector as a means to hasten discharges in a way that the legislation no longer permitted (Manthorpe and Bradley, 2000). Therefore, while having been perceived as something of a backwater within social services (Osborn, 1996), hospital-based social work suddenly found itself at the cutting edge of practice – particularly in respect of the needs of older people. As far as practi- tioners were concerned, this had mixed consequences (Rachman, 1997). As well as the expected increase in the overall volume of referrals, there were also major changes to the nature of the work undertaken. Social workers in Rachman's survey (1997) expressed great unease about the increased level of administration that the work required, dominated by the procedural require- ments of community care (Lymbery, 2004a). In addition, practitioners were concerned about the fact that the pressures of assessment activity meant that they had little outlet for creativity in their practice (Rachman, 1997). While they maintained the importance of counselling skills to their work, the oppor- tunity to practise with these skills at the forefront was becoming increasingly circumscribed. By contrast, their practice was more in accordance with the bureaucratic priorities that characterise administratively dominated forms of practice (Manthorpe and Bradley, 2000).

It is interesting that, with rising anxieties about the impact of demography on health and social care (Sutherland Report, 1999), older people have become a major priority within health and social care, which was rarely the case in the past. Therefore, hospital-based social workers are required to spend a preponderance of their time in this area of activity. In an echo of earlier practice, social workers are once again expected to respond to an issue which is defined as a critical social problem – in much the same way that maternity and tuberculosis were defined at an earlier time. The strategic level of importance of work with older people was further emphasised when the delayed discharge of people from hospitals became a major policy issue in the early years of the twenty-first century (Glasby, 2003), leading to the passage of the Community Care (Delayed Discharges etc.) Act 2003.

The publication of the *NHS Plan* (DoH, 2000b) made the government's policy on health and social care explicit. The use of hospitals was a major feature of the plan, which was preoccupied with the political need to reduce hospital waiting times. The only realistic way of achieving this was by maximising the use of hospitals, by cutting the average length of stay in an inpatient bed and reducing unnecessary admissions. Given that older people constitute the bulk of hospital admissions, two important – and linked – policy trends can be traced back to this priority – the focus on delayed discharge (which is further explored in Chapter 7) and on intermediate care (see Chapter 9). There is of course a close connection between the two policy areas: intermediate care has been widely used to speed up discharge processes, for example. As Glasby (2003) suggests, there are numerous factors which have contributed to the problem of delayed discharge, chief amongst which are issues related to inter-professional and multi-disciplinary working.

While the impact of this policy is not addressed at this point (it is covered more fully in Chapter 7; see also Lymbery and Millward, 2004), some key points emerge that are critical to the debate in this chapter:

- It is underpinned by a sense that SSDs are responsible for the bulk of delays to discharge, ignoring the level of complexity of the subject (see Glasby, 2003).
- It has been seen as unnecessarily punitive in its effects, particularly given the strides that had already been taken to resolve the problem (see Valios, 2004).
- It has placed considerable pressure on practitioners to complete assessments within timescales which may be entirely unreasonable, but which are dictated by the medical decision concerning when an individual is ready for discharge.
- It can also be interpreted as an example of government policy that works against the development of collaborative working (Miller and Freeman, 2003).

As we have seen, the pressure on social workers had already been magnified under community care; the emphasis on delayed discharge has further intensified this. Once again, therefore, the social work role has been limited to the mobilisation of resources. This is not an emphasis with which all social workers are comfortable:

> Discharge planning has always been seen as essential and necessary in health social work, but it is only part of the task; yet, once again, social workers are being seen as 'disposal experts' or 'bed clearers'. (Rachman, 1997: 213)

To conclude this survey of hospital-based social work one must take issue with the optimistic perspective of Baraclough, expressed in the following quotation:

> Social work in hospitals was conceived as a remedy for an organisational problem – the overcrowding of the outpatient departments – and began as a response to social need and the efficient use of resources. It endured and remains of strategic importance in fostering good health and social well-being and in bringing patients' needs to the fore. (Baraclough, 1996: 98)

While the first part of the statement is undoubtedly true, the final sentence is more questionable. The evidence that the presence of social work has been, or is, a central element in fostering good health is thin – indeed, laudable aspiration that this aim is, it does not represent the reality of practice (see Rachman, 1997). Social work in hospitals tends towards a more reactive approach, characteristic of administratively dominated procedures. Even if practitioners desire to undertake in-depth casework, there is little scope and no mandate for such activity. Equally, there is no historical evidence that social workers have been a radicalising influence on practice within hospitals – indeed, the 'radical social work' literature was almost silent about the potential for such practice within health settings, with Simpkin (1989) being an isolated exception to this rule. While we can see that there have been many changes in the nature and scope of social work over its existence, a number of themes remain constant.

- Tension between social workers and doctors about the role of social work within these settings and the content of practice, leading to power struggles between the two.
- This has been despite – and in clear opposition to – the constant injunction to improve the nature and quality of collaborative working with health colleagues.
- Pressure on social work to pursue a more 'administrative' orientation than the profession was happy to accept.
- A requirement to address the major social problems of the time – whether tuberculosis or maternity care in the early years, or the needs of older people following community care.

The outcome of this leaves hospital-based social work in a crucial position in respect of government policy, if not in control of the purpose and content of its work. The future of hospital-based social work is perhaps less certain than has been the case in the past. Certainly, the development of collaborative working at the level of primary health care will be an important component of effective policy (Rummery and Glendinning, 2000), and will necessarily affect the delivery of services in hospitals as well. It is to this area of collaborative working that the chapter now turns.

SECTION SUMMARY

This section has examined the development of hospital-based social work from the Second World War to the present day. It has explored the following themes:

(Continued)

- The gradual professionalisation of this area of work in the immediate post-war years.
- The range of factors that remained problematic for hospital social workers, particularly their partial acceptance within hospital settings, and the requirement that remained on them to carry out a high proportion of administrative tasks.
- The relatively limited application of casework principles to hospital social work.
- The impact of community care legislation, which yet again privileged the administrative and 'bed-clearing' (Rachman, 1997) aspect of the role.

SOCIAL WORK AND PRIMARY HEALTH CARE

As noted in Chapter 3, hospital-based care has been dominant in the history of health provision in the UK (Ham, 1999). Chapter 4 pointed out the relative lack of coordination between different parts of the health and social care system. The development of social work within the context of primary health care has been much slower than in hospital care, as a direct result of a combination of these two factors. As previously noted, the first hospital-based almoner took up her post in 1895, but the first almoner to work within general practice was not appointed until 1948. Even then, further development was relatively patchy, with a small number of experimental projects being established in the 1950s and 1960s (Dedman, 1996). It still remains the case that relatively few social workers are based in primary care settings. However, there has been considerable literature on the subject, reflecting the fact that there is often more research undertaken in respect of new and innovative projects than on aspects of 'normal' practice. These writings have been produced in two periods:

- In the 1960s and 1970s, several monographs focused on individual projects (see, for example, Collins, 1965; Forman and Fairbairn, 1968; Goldberg and Neill, 1972); this period culminated in a major edited text produced in 1982 (Clare and Corney, 1982).
- There was then relatively little literature on the subject until community care reforms once again brought the issue into the policy (and hence academic) limelight (see, for example, Cumella et al., 1996; Hardy et al., 1996; Lymbery and Millward, 2000, 2001; Rummery and Glendinning, 2000).

This second wave was also helped by the emphasis that was placed from the mid-1990s on the concept of a 'primary care-led' NHS (Littlejohn and Victor, 1996). Although Peckham and Exworthy (2003) have suggested that the shift in power that this implies has been more *apparent* than *actual*, it is undeniable that considerable policy attention has been paid to the development of primary care by the 'new' Labour government, continuing a theme that was also evident under the previous Conservative administration (Peckham and Exworthy, 2003). Indeed, the establishment of Primary Care Trusts (DoH, 1997a), with a responsibility to integrate the provision of health care and act to commission its delivery, has been the major policy development in this area (Peckham and Exworthy, 2003). There are a number of reasons that have helped to create this situation:

- A perceived crisis in the funding and management of the health service in general, with particular emphasis on the needs of older people.
- A consequent increase in the extent of managerial and financial control within the health service, which has affected both the hospital and primary care sectors; this has encouraged the emphasis on the cost-effectiveness of all services.
- Increased importance to general practice and primary health care to the overall health system.
- Changing expectations of the service, from both patients and professionals.
- The emphasis – particularly strong in 'new' Labour policies – on services being provided on a locality and community basis.

The relatively slow and patchy development of social work in primary health care requires some explanation, particularly given the extremely positive tenor of much of the literature on the subject (Lymbery, 1998b). Part of the problem can be attributed to the difficulty of translating policy from an individual pilot project to a more generalised, mainstream service. This is particularly evident when additional resources have been ploughed into a pilot that cannot be made available on a wider basis. At the root of the difficulty is the fact that organisations within health and social care have to balance the needs and requirements of the entire population against the excellence of service that can be developed for a few.

Therefore, although the increased coordination of health and social care services in the community has been advocated in numerous official documents – for example, the National Health Service Act 1946, the Seebohm Report of 1968 and the Otton Report of 1974 all recommended the establishment of health centres to house doctors, community health and social care staff – there have only been limited developments. For example, despite the fact that the Seebohm Report recommended the 'attachment' of a social worker to all health centres and group practices (Seebohm Report, 1968), formal attachments of social workers to primary health care settings have been the exception rather than the rule (Lymbery, 1998b; Levin et al., 2002). The typical pattern of organisation within the community perpetuates a structure whereby there is a separation between health and social care rather than a unification of the two (Hugman, 1995). Indeed, this was intensified rather than resolved by the parallel reorganisations of local authority SSDs and the NHS in the 1970s (Hugman, 1995). While it was accepted that it was important to improve working relationships between doctors and other professions, including social workers (Jefferys and Sacks, 1983), there has only been a gradual change in such relationships.

However, as noted above, there has been a considerable body of literature on the links between social work and primary health care. The main reasons why social work was first established in primary health care included the lack of unity that characterised social services of the time, and the division between medical and social care. Collins (1965) reported how the location of a social worker within general practice can help to unify the fragmented organisational patterns of health and social care. Forman and Fairbairn (1968) concluded that the development of social work services within general practice could be more economical and effective than comparable investments in services which were isolated from primary health care. From the experience of social work attachments to general practice it was argued that the creation of multi-disciplinary health and social care teams would provide a coordinated response to need (Goldberg and Neill, 1972).

Indeed, the Seebohm Report (1968) recommended that considerable effort should be expended in improving the relationship between social workers and doctors, while acknowledging that this was starting from a poor base:

> Survey after survey has shown that many family doctors do not seek help from social workers nor use social services that are available: they often do not know about them, or do not understand or value them . . . Realistic attempts at prevention in the social field, whether in detecting early trouble or intervening at times of crisis . . . will often have to be based on family practice and organised as a joint effort of doctors and social workers. General practice today is in touch with a higher proportion of those who are in difficulties than any of the other social services and it needs the full support of them all. (Seebohm Report, 1968: para. 692)

Only a few years later, the Otton Report (1974) on social work support for the health service recommended that 'all new health centres will be designed to include accommodation for the use of social workers' (para. 45), as part of its call for the improvement of collaboration between health and social services in primary care. Although there was only sporadic and unsystematic development of the theme in the 1970s and 1980s (Osborn, 1996), it was rediscovered following the publication of the Community Care White Paper (DoH, 1989: para. 4.11–4.18), which called for closer cooperation between SSDs and GPs. This was further expanded in the subsequent Policy Guidance, which stated that 'GPs will wish to make a full contribution to assessment' (DoH, 1990: para. 3.47), in recognition of the close links between health and social care. Consequently, as noted above, there has been a resurgence of academic and professional interest in the subject.

There have also been changes within the social work world in recent years, with particular shifts in the social and economic climate, the public image of social work and the managerialist and performance-driven climate within which social work is practised (Lymbery, 2004b). This has engendered a major upheaval in the nature of social work practice with older people, with the introduction of care management having a particular impact on the experiences of practitioners (Postle, 2002). Indeed, this has more or less ensured that therapeutic case work by social workers within primary health care – previously identified as one of the four key functions of a social worker in general practice, alongside assessment, liaison and education (Ratoff, 1973; see also Jefferys and Sacks, 1983) – is no longer a prominent feature of such work.

However, even given the more restricted vision of social work that now exists, many writers have observed that there are marked advantages in this sort of organisation. For example, Hardy et al. (1996) concluded that it helped to improve professional collaboration and hence alleviate mutual suspicion. Similarly, Cumella et al. (1996) found that such arrangements improved the quality of cooperative working between the various parties. Lymbery and Millward (2000) also found that there were improvements in these areas, while also noting the increased level of accessibility of the social work services to people in the community – particularly people from ethnic minorities. A key limitation of the learning in all of these schemes is that they were well-resourced pilot projects; a consistent problem has been the fact that few have been able to transfer into mainstream services (Rummery and Glendinning, 2000). In addition, as Levin et al. (2002) concluded, there is relatively little evidence that the improvements that have been observed, which have to do with the organisation and process of work, have actually generated improved outcomes for service users (see also Brown et al., 2003).

However, as far as services for older people are concerned, with the primacy of policies concerning the single assessment process and intermediate care the potential attraction of establishing community-based multi-disciplinary teams for older people once again commends itself to policy-makers. Certainly, it is hard to see how the aims of government policy can be put into place without the closer integration of social work and a range of other health professionals at the community level. The majority of assessments that will fall under the auspices of the single assessment process will be carried out in the community. Similarly, it could be argued that the most effective form of intermediate care would also be community-based. However, given the range of factors that militate against successful social work within the health service, which were outlined in Chapter 4, it will be a matter of some complexity to establish such teams.

SECTION SUMMARY

This section has explored the development of social work within primary care settings, with particular reference to the following:

- The growing importance of the primary care sector within the delivery of health care in Britain.
- The various reasons that underpin the limited development of social work in primary health care.
- The consistent call for improved coordination between social services and primary health care.
- The potential benefits of this sort of organisation, as attested by numerous commentators following the implementation of community care.
- The ways in which the location of social work services in primary health care could meet the government's policy objectives.

THE IMPACT OF SOCIAL WORK ON HEALTH CARE

The ultimate purpose of this examination of the historical development of social work in health care is to consider whether the presence of social work has changed the nature of health care in any way, and, if so, to identify the ways in which this has been manifested. From this starting point, it is then possible to frame a view about the 'proper contribution' (Huntington, 1986) of social work to health care. One attempt to demonstrate the achievements of social work in health care was carried out by Auslander (2001). She surveyed 36 senior members of the social work profession – academics, practitioners and administrators – on an international basis, asking them to list the five key achievements of social work within health care. From this she was able to generate a list of the 20 most cited achievements, which are listed in order of the frequency by which they were cited by her respondents. The list provides an insight into what social work insiders see as the key contributions of social work within health care settings.

The first five accomplishments were those that were cited by most respondents – Auslander states that there was a 'very high level of agreement' to one and two, and a 'high level of agreement' to three, four and five.

1   Changing models of health and medical care.
2   Recognition.
3   Knowledge development.
4   Direct practice, psychosocial interventions.
5   Developing culturally specific, culturally appropriate and indigenous models
    of health and social services. (Auslander, 2001: 207)

While Auslander recognises that these achievements are of markedly different types, she suggests that their combination is equally significant:

> This group is interesting in itself, representing as it does four basic aspects of social work as a profession – theory ('changing models'), practice ('psychosocial interventions), organization ('recognition') and research ('knowledge develop-ment') – as well as one item ('developing culturally appropriate services') which crosses these divisions. (Auslander, 2001: 210)

Although the nature of Auslander's methodology leads towards a positive gloss on the achievements of social work in health care – senior members of the profession were perhaps unlikely to conclude little had been achieved in the hundred years of its existence! – the list is interesting on a number of levels. For example, it provides evidence to suggest that a significant achievement of social work has been to achieve a measure of professional recognition, lending weight to Larson's (1977) contention that social work and other comparable occupations have been engaged upon a process of professionalisation. Using this analysis, the development of health-related social work does accord with Larson's definition of a process of professionalisation. For example, almoners defined themselves as specialist social workers, and claimed a particular expertise – which was often contested by others. They created a professional association and devised their own forms of training, to which they controlled the access (Bell, 1961). In so doing, they did go some way to creating an occupation that was able to operate at least semi-autonomously within the confines of health care services. That two of the five most commonly cited achievements concerned professional recognition and the development of knowledge – key tasks in the process of constructing a profession (Freidson, 1986) – is testimony to the significance of this process.

However, any success in terms of professional formation also needs to be accompanied by a measurable impact upon health systems. It is therefore significant that the strongest measure of agreement within Auslander's sample (2001) regarded the ability of social work to change accepted models of health and social care. While numerous factors have influenced the gradual shift away from a purely bio-medical conception of health care, a point accepted by Auslander (2001), she has argued that since social workers have always espoused a broader conception of health their involvement in health care systems has therefore helped to shape this change. The fourth and fifth points may well be where most impact has been made in respect of changing models of health and social care – that is through the direct practice carried out by social workers and the value positions that social workers ought to espouse.

As this book has illustrated, the direct practice of social workers in health care settings has always been linked to the dominant models of practice within the profession as a whole. Therefore, the primacy of the casework approach in the 1950s and beyond was also reflected in health-related social work. On a more contemporary note, the bureaucratised and procedurally driven task-centred model that holds sway in many areas of social work (Lymbery, 2004b) is also clearly evident within health-related practice – more particularly in hospital settings (Manthorpe and Bradley, 2000) than in primary health care (Lymbery and Millward, 2000). However, the fact that direct practice was rated as highly important by Auslander's informants does indicate that – in the eyes of senior members of the social work profession at least – the day-to-day work of social work practitioners has achieved some measure of impact within health care.

The ability of social work to develop culturally specific models of practice is also highly rated within Auslander's survey. The value-led orientation of social work is well captured in the definition of the social work task outlined by the International Federation of Social Workers (2000):

> The social work profession promotes social change, problem solving in human relationships and the empowerment and liberation of people to enhance well-being. Utilising theories of human behaviour and social systems, social work intervenes at the points where people interact with their environments. Principles of human rights and social justice are fundamental to social work.

This implies a strong commitment to value-driven practice, which may well differentiate the social worker from other members of an inter-professional team (Torkington et al., 2004). It is possible that this may also have enabled social workers to have a strong influence on health care systems.

Given the limitations of Auslander's (2001) methodology, the fact that there is corroboration of some of her points from another source is important. Huntington (1986) has summarised the contribution of social workers to health settings, suggesting that there have been three ways in which social workers could make a specific contribution to health care:

1   Direct work with individuals and their families.
2   Influence on the processes and policies of health care.
3   Service planning and development.

Although these points are not identical to those generated by Auslander's survey, there are areas where the lists overlap. For example, the second and third could contribute to the process whereby models of health and medical care can be changed. In addition, the significance that Huntington (1986) placed on direct work is echoed in Auslander's later survey (2001). The key difference between the two comes from Huntington's recognition that 'social workers' freedom to make the kind of contributions they deem proper remains dependent upon doctors and the importance they attach to psycho-social factors in illness' (Huntington, 1986: 1152). In her view social workers in health settings have always had to struggle against the prejudices of doctors, who have had the ability to deny or reject the contributions of social workers. In the light of this, her contention was that social workers have always been particularly valued by doctors for the way in which they have been able to access resources (see Brewer and Lait, 1980, for confirmation of this perspective), a contribution to health care that is strikingly absent from the achievements that social workers themselves describe (Huntington, 1986).

This dichotomy is significant in that, as is evident from an understanding of the history of social work within health care, social workers have always had to fight hard to demonstrate their usefulness in health care settings. As a result, they have often accepted work that was of limited occupational potential (the almoners' role in assessing the ability of patients to contribute to their hospital care from the 1920s being a good case in point) in order to justify their existence. Because this pattern is unlikely to be immediately disturbed social workers will still be required to carry out a range of administratively oriented tasks. The challenge for social workers – and the organisations within which they are employed – is to ensure that these tasks do not become the only thing that social workers contribute to health settings.

SECTION SUMMARY

This section has sought to evaluate the impact of social work on the delivery of health care, concluding the following:

- Following Auslander (2001) it is suggested that there have been five specific areas where social work has impacted upon health care – changing models of health and medical care; recognition; knowledge development; direct practice; developing culturally specific and appropriate models of health and social services.
- It is also acknowledged that social work has always had to struggle to justify its existence within health settings.

CONCLUSION

Having surveyed the history of social work's involvement with health care in Britain, the final section will attempt to clarify the key elements that social work can contribute to a multi-disciplinary environment. In so doing, it draws on previous research (Herod and Lymbery, 2002) on a similar theme, as well as the work of Auslander (2001) and Huntington (1986), outlined in the previous section. The list seeks to elaborate on the broad vision of social work set out in Chapter 2, encompassing a range of functions from administrative, through individual work to a social action perspective. It is not presented in order of priority – but an essential consideration is that a social worker's success in the first four areas of activity render it more likely that s/he would be able to have a meaningful impact on models of health and medical care.

1   *Practising from a clearly defined value base, placing the individual at the forefront of all work.* Social workers approach their work in a different way from other occupations, as has been recognised and valued by health professionals (Herod and Lymbery, 2002). Provided that this stance is recognised, it does bring a particular strength to the multi-disciplinary team. While there is little in the way of hard evidence to support this contention, other small-scale research has noted the beneficial impact of the value position of a social work student upon a district nursing student (Torkington et al., 2004). Certainly, social workers have more of a commitment to the values of emancipatory practice than other professionals, even if this commitment is not always easy to put into practice (Jordan, 2004).

2   *Direct work with individuals and families.* While the importance of this direct work has been underplayed in recent community care policy, health professionals have acknowledged that: 'social workers typically establish a quality of relationship with clients and families which is essential for effective intervention' (Herod and Lymbery, 2002: 26). Here, the different pace at which social workers operate – which can be the source of tension within a team (Huntington, 1981) – can provide a valuable resource to the multi-disciplinary setting. It also recognises that people with the sorts of need that require health and social care responses will often benefit greatly from some assistance to help them adjust to the changes that have occurred.

3   *Coordinating and organising services and resources.* As this chapter has amply demonstrated, social workers within health care have generally had to take on this responsibility, albeit often unwillingly. For social work with older people, the 'administrative' side of practice has become particularly firmly entrenched, with the focus on delayed discharges from hospital a particular manifestation of this trend. However, it has ensured that social workers have become familiar with the demands and requirements of care management,

which should make them particularly useful to the coordinated approach required by the single assessment process. It should also stand them in good stead as an integral part of intermediate care teams, which will also depend upon the effective coordination of resources for their effectiveness.

4   *Liaison functions between other occupations and providers.* As well as coordinating resources and services, social workers also have a particular role to play in ensuring the smooth workings of multi-disciplinary teams. Because they are required to see things holistically, social workers should bring a different perspective to the multi-disciplinary team, without which a team would be the weaker: 'Health care professionals valued the viewpoint that social workers brought to the multi-disciplinary team, and claimed that the work of the team would be compromised if that perspective were absent' (Herod and Lymbery, 2002: 26).

5   *Working to change models of health and medical care.* If a social worker is able to be effective in the other four functions, then s/he has more of an opportunity to affect the way services respond to individual, family and community needs. Essentially, the building up of a credible professional profile is vital for social workers in health settings; credibility in terms of the nuts and bolts of social work practice provides a practitioner with some licence to change the working practices of the teams within which they are based: 'The ability of social workers to have a powerful organisational and strategic role in multi disciplinary teams was also identified as significant . . . This was attributed to social workers' ability to work with systems as well as individuals, combined with their strong ethical and value-based perspective' (Herod and Lymbery, 2002: 25).

In matter-of-fact terms, a social worker must first ensure that s/he is respected for her/his practice abilities. If this is managed successfully, the social worker may then be given sufficient credibility to work more broadly on changing the way in which the team operates. While this is not an ideal situation – after all, professionals in other fields are not expected to prove their individual competence before being able to influence policy and practice – it recognises the imbalances of power which confront social workers in health settings. A key message for social workers from the history of social work in health care is that they must expect to *struggle* to carve out a role within health settings. Given that there are many reasons to assume that services for older people will be increasingly delivered in multi-disciplinary teams (see Chapter 6), this represents an important message for social work practitioners. The role that they can fulfil within health settings is essential to the well-being of older people and should help services to function more effectively and humanely. This is clearly an important task for the social work profession.

CHAPTER SUMMARY

This chapter has engaged with the history of the relationship of social work to health care. In so doing, it has highlighted some observations that are important when considering the connections between social work and health care in the early years of the twenty-first century:

- The place of social work within health care settings has always been contested.
- As a result, social workers have had to take on various tasks – for example, before the establishment of the NHS, the assessment of the contribution of people to their hospital stay (in some cases, even the collection of this contribution) – that they would rather not have undertaken.
- Submission to the 'rule of medicine' has been a consistent feature of social work's experience within health care settings.
- While the development of 'casework' was the predominant form of social work in the years immediately following the creation of the NHS, hospital-based social workers were unable to put casework principles into effect in the vast majority of cases.
- In fact, the practice of social workers has had an increasingly administrative orientation, particularly since the implementation of community care.
- While there has been considerable literature promoting the potential benefits of closer links between social work and primary health care, relatively few social workers with older people are actually based in such settings.

PART III
Practice

The Developing Social Work Role
with Older People

What social workers can do is open up rather than foreclose possibilities because social workers are structurally located to witness the inequities of people's lives on a daily basis. (Neysmith and MacAdam, 1999: 22)

This chapter examines the development of the social work role with older people. Drawing on the insights of previous chapters, it suggests that this has been dominated by practice deriving from its *administrative* roots, with little evidence of practice that derives either from the *collectivist* or *individualist-therapeutic* traditions. Specifically, it notes that there was little interest in the development of individualist-therapeutic work with older people during the periods when 'casework' was in the ascendant during the 1950s and 1960s. Similarly, it notes the relative absence of social work with older people from the more collectivist social work discourse of the 1970s and 1980s. Instead, practice with older people has been dominated by administrative priorities; indeed, for much of social work's history a qualification has not been deemed to be a requirement for such practice.

Although the passage of community care legislation boosted the profile of social work with older people, this has had mixed consequences. In particular, the chapter suggests that practice has become even more dominated by financial and bureaucratic priorities, despite the focus on the needs of the service user suggested in community care policy and practice guidance. It suggests that the restricted forms of practice that have been developed reflect an ageist view of the potential of older people and argues that this has compromised the abilities of social workers to achieve empowering forms of practice, which is neither in the interests of older people themselves nor conducive to a satisfying professional role for practitioners. It then seeks to identify the main ways in which a social worker can contribute to work with older people, focusing in general terms on the core aspects of practice that distinguish social work activity. The chapter then identifies the main issues for social work that arise from the *National Service Framework for Older People* (DoH, 2001a), arguing that it contains the potential to enable the establishment of more creative forms of social work – in particular, through its emphasis on combating age-related discrimination. It also briefly comments on the possibilities and problems that are heralded by the Green Paper on the future of social care for adults (DoH, 2005). The chapter concludes by suggesting that there are three general areas of activity where it can be argued there is a specific role for social work; these themes – which focus in turn on assessment, care management and intermediate care – are expanded upon within the concluding three chapters.

LIMITED OCCUPATIONAL POTENTIAL? THE PLACE OF OLDER PEOPLE IN SOCIAL WORK

This section summarises the development of social work with older people, focusing particularly on the post-war years. At a time when the social work profession was preoccupied with the potential of therapeutically-oriented casework (Morris, 1955), practice with older people was not seen as having the same occupational potential as other, more favoured areas of specialisation. While there are a number of reasons for this, it is hard to resist the conclusion that the fact that the practical orientation of most work with older people (Younghusband, 1978), was less about the inherent nature of older people's needs and more about deeply ingrained ageist attitudes – within society and within social work itself – which held that those needs could be resolved by the application of straightforward, administratively focused actions. Little formal training was required for practitioners, unlike in other specialist areas. The practice that developed drew extensively on administrative models and social work with older people was not a popular area for specialisation.

With the creation of unified SSDs and the development of a generic form of social work training, it could have been expected that there would be some change in the patterns of response to older people's needs. However, their low status within the social work world did not vary greatly during the 1970s. For example, research found that social work with older people was still perceived as having low status, with most social worker time being devoted to child care work and with most social work students seeing their future in this area of activity (DHSS, 1978). The content of generic forms of training included little on the needs of older people, being more oriented towards other forms of practice.

While the 1970s also saw the development of forms of 'radical social work', established in opposition to the prevailing orthodoxy of casework, there was relatively little focus within the movement on social work with older people. It may have been that radicals were not drawn to this area of work, or alternatively that they saw little radical potential in it; whatever the reason, the paper by Phillipson (1989) is a relatively isolated example of an attempt to define and promote radical social work alternatives for older people. However, the sorts of practice that Phillipson advocates – drawing on aspects of anti-ageism, feminism and community action – will have provided little guidance for those few practitioners engaged in social work with older people, particularly in the context of the changes wrought by community care policies.

From the 1980s onwards, a number of attempts have been made to increase the profile of social work with older people (see, for example, Hughes, 1995; Marshall and Dixon, 1996; Rowlings, 1981; Thompson, 1995). They draw on the growing literature of social gerontology (Bond et al., 1993a) in presenting ageing in a more rounded sense, and seek to present social work with older people in a more positive and optimistic light than hitherto. However, a somewhat defensive tone is common, as if the authors believe that readers needed to be *convinced* about the value of social work with older people. The following quotation acknowledges the legacy of neglect of this area of work: 'social work with old people has been seen as having limited scope and challenge and as being bound up with the arranging of practical services for those needing help' (Marshall and Dixon 1996: 1). The relatively low status of working with older people is also not unique to social work; it has been suggested that the intellectual and interpersonal skills required to work with older people have been consistently undervalued in a range of occupations (Nolan et al., 2001b).

As Chapter 3 addressed in more depth, community care policy sprang from a range of factors, particularly the uncontrolled growth of social security expenditure and the poorly coordinated pattern of services for adults on the boundaries between health and social care. SSDs were given the lead responsibility to manage community care, with a particular emphasis on the assessment of need and the creation of care packages. The terms 'social work' or 'social worker' do not figure in the official literature of the time (DoH, 1989; DoH/SSI, 1991a, 1991b); instead it was suggested that the newly created function of 'care management' (DoH/SSI, 1991a, 1991b) would ensure effective coordination and management of services. While this theme is expanded further in Chapter 8, it is worthy of some further discussion in this chapter because of its centrality to the development of social work in the 1990s and beyond. The following section explores the outline implications of community care policy for social work, with particular attention paid to care management.

SECTION SUMMARY

This section has outlined the history and development of social work with older people, and has concluded the following:

- It has had relatively little professional development, particularly when compared with other areas of practice.
- There has been limited development either of 'individualist-therapeutic' or 'collectivist' approaches to work with older people.
- By contrast, 'administrative' forms of practice have always dominated.
- The implementation of community care policies has confirmed the overwhelmingly administrative nature of practice with older people.

COMMUNITY CARE – A REVOLUTION IN PRACTICE?

The central requirement of community care has been that all people who may want the assistance of social services must have their needs assessed as a pre-requisite of receiving any services. This policy has substantially increased the numbers of assessments that must be carried out. In order to allocate resources equitably, all SSDs have had to draw up sets of criteria against which an individual's eligibility to receive services can be measured. This has been particularly important due to the overriding importance given to cost considerations in the development of policy (Lewis and Glennerster, 1996), as outlined in Chapter 3. Thus two sets of requirements were established that operated in conflict with each other:

- The first, enshrined in the policy guidance for community care (DoH, 1990), was that there must be a thorough assessment of needs before services can be provided.
- The second was that assessments have to take place within the framework of eligibility criteria, the application of which determines what services an individual can be offered.

While it was always suggested that the assessment of *needs* should not be contaminated by the assessment for *services* (DoH/SSI, 1991a, 1991b), the fact that there was such a close relationship between the two meant that, in practice, links have inevitably been made between needs and resources throughout the assessment process. This has been exacerbated by the extent to which priority has had to be given to the rationing of scarce resources, leaving a substantial unresolved residue of 'unmet need' (Cordingley et al., 2001; Godfrey and Callaghan, 2000). As will be discussed in Chapter 7, numerous practice dilemmas are created as a result of this inherently compromised position.

While the assessment process draws on the sorts of skills and approaches that have been common throughout social work's history, community care also brought a new role into existence, that of 'care manager'. As Payne (2000) notes, the model of care management that has developed in services for older people – which he terms 'social care entrepreneurship' – has been applied in an environment where the availability of services is tightly constrained by costs. Therefore, as Sturges (1996) has indicated, practice has become tightly bound up with the bureaucratic requirement to ration services and cut costs. The consequences of this for practitioners are unwelcome, with practice increasingly dominated by routines and procedures (Carey, 2003; Postle, 2002). One result of this is that social workers have found it difficult to retain some of the core aspects of their role – in particular, responding positively to an individual's feelings and emotions and engaging with her/his social world (Phillips and Waterson, 2002) – in the face of these requirements. Therefore, it can be argued that practice with older people has become suffocated by the straitjacket of care management, and therefore offers even less occupational potential than before (Carey, 2003).

The chequered history of this area of activity renders it difficult to assert the social work role with a degree of confidence. The focus on the administrative components of practice has reduced the opportunity for social workers to engage in therapeutically oriented work, and has also meant that there has been little development of collectivist alternatives. The way in which the social work role has been constrained by the organisational contexts within which practitioners operate (Lymbery, 2004b) has made it difficult to claim that practice with older people can be more than simply a treadmill of routinised assessments leading to unimaginative packages of care. Without some will to reconstruct social work the following suggestions towards a more proactive role may fall upon deaf ears. However, while there are apparent threats to the social work identity through the creation of multi-disciplinary teams, there is also a potential opportunity to create a more central role for social work in the response to older people's needs. Indeed, the role for social workers outlined in the Green Paper highlights the potential for practitioners to engage in 'constructive relationships and specific therapeutic interventions' (DoH, 2005), implying a move away from assessment-dominated practice. The following section will introduce the core aspects of what should constitute the main aspects of a social work role with older people, seeking to identify ways in which more individualist-therapeutic and collectivist perspectives can help to improve the quality of older people's lives.

SECTION SUMMARY

This section has examined the nature of social work practice in community care, highlighting the following:

- The fact that practice is carried out in an environment dominated by cost constraints.
- The consequent priority given to rationing of scarce resources, leading to sterile and unimaginative forms of practice.
- The difficulty for practitioners to transcend the barriers to more creative forms of practice, particularly those drawing on social work's 'individualist-therapeutic' and 'collectivist' traditions.

GENERAL ASPECTS OF SOCIAL WORK WITH OLDER PEOPLE

As indicated in Chapter 1, older people are likely to encounter a range of circumstances that will create specific needs for health and social care interventions. There is often a definable role for a social worker, even if this has been historically little in evidence. The purpose of this section is to break down the social work role into a set of values and skills that should inform the practitioner. Drawing on the insights from Chapter 2, the section seeks particularly to integrate the different orientations to social work, with particular emphasis on its neglected individualist-therapeutic and collectivist elements.

VALUES AND ORIENTATION

Social work's commitment to anti-oppressive practice is a feature that distinguishes it from other occupations working within the field of health and social care. It is vital that practical expressions of this commitment are found, as social work has been arguably more effective at the level of rhetoric than reality in the expression of anti-oppressive practice. As Phillipson (1989) has suggested, in practice with older people this needs to start with an understanding of the ways in which ageism operates within society in general, and within systems of health and social care in particular. As was pointed out in Chapter 1, older people experience many forms of oppression, a number of which are actually built into the structures and organisations within which social workers operate. For example, there would be no need to root out age discrimination – the first standard within the *National Service Framework for Older People* (DoH, 2001a) – were it not for its existence in the first place. Chapter 1 identified a number of ways in which ageism can be seen to operate in respect of health and social care services for older people:

- In the policies of government, both at national and local levels.
- In the way in which services for older people are organised and staffed.
- In the differential development of understandings about the abuse of older people as opposed to the abuse of other groups, particularly children.
- In the attitudes and values of those staff employed to work with older people.
- In the language deployed to describe older people.

Put simply, social workers must seek to ensure that older people do not experience second-rate treatment as a consequence of these various forms of ageism.

In addition, it should not be assumed that older people will only experience discrimination on the basis of age; as Thompson (1995) has observed, older people may be subjected to the other forms of discrimination that can affect all adults – on the grounds of race, gender, class, sexual orientation, etc. Often, the different forms of discrimination will interact to multiply the forms of disadvantage that derive from them. Therefore, a social worker should expect that any given older person may have experienced or be experiencing multiple forms of oppression, which itself could affect the way in which s/he responds to the social worker's approach, or the attitude towards authority that s/he has.

The principle of empowerment of service users and carers is also one to which social workers should adhere. Because empowerment is a contested concept (Means et al., 2003), it is important to be clear about how the term is deployed here. After all, there is a world of difference between the consumerist vision of empowerment within which community care was framed and the more radical approaches advocated by the disability movement (Cooke and Ellis, 2004). The central weakness of the consumerist perspective is that it fails to recognise an essential point: that for many older people the ability to exercise choice is severely circumscribed by factors such as their health, marginalised social position, social class, etc. (Lymbery, 2000). Therefore, their ability to 'exit' from services is constrained. As a result, social workers must have a broader conception of how empowerment can be achieved than simply relying on the consumerist vision that informed community care policy. Means et al. (2003) have suggested that there are alternative ways of conceptualising the process of empowerment. One of these is the notion of 'voice', where service users have the opportunity to change their circumstances by speaking out about them. While 'voice' is an important element of empowerment, it remains relatively weak; indeed, less scrupulous service providers can easily ensure that users and carers are given a voice, while ensuring that what they have to say does not affect the delivery of services in any way. Therefore, while the development of empowerment based on conceptions of 'exit' and 'voice' is useful, it is inadequate to address the genuine imbalances of power that have historically existed between service users and service providers.

Stronger conceptions of empowerment can be found in the other potential strategies outlined by Means et al. (2003) – empowerment through 'rights' and 'struggle'. Implicit in both of these conceptions is a limitation of the role and responsibility of the social worker. As an educator, it is by no means uncommon to read the work of students who claim to 'have empowered X by Y'! In reality, empowerment is not a commodity that a social worker can transfer to a service user, but rather a condition that a service user is able to achieve (Neysmith and MacAdam, 1999). A social worker can assist in this process, and should help to create the environment within which empowerment could become a possibility. However, if one looks at the language of 'rights' and 'struggle' the fact that a social worker cannot simply empower others becomes manifest. The conception of 'rights' – most clearly embodied in the Human Rights Act 1998 – rests on the contention that there are universal entitlements to which each individual should have access. However, in the context of community care, service users have few if any absolute rights or entitlements to a service (Mandelstam, 1999), and what rights they do have are both fragile and often conditional (Dean, 2002). In the context of care services this can be attributed to the central fact that the more rights people possess the greater the required budgetary expense to support those rights – a position that would run counter to the primary purpose of the legislation, that of achieving budgetary control over social care expenditure (Lewis and Glennerster, 1996).

Therefore, the recognition that empowerment for service users and carers will not be achieved without a 'struggle' is vital here. A social worker's capacity to act on behalf of service users may sometimes be constrained by legislation or agency policies and procedures. Social workers need to work within these constraints to maximise the benefits for service users. However, learning from the example of the disability movement, they must recognise that any improvements in the status of people with disabilities in society has not come about through the goodwill of professionals, but has been an expression of the ability of disabled people working together to affect change (Oliver, 2004). Collective action can achieve change that would be impossible at the individual level. Although older people have been relatively little involved in collective action regarding social care, its potential to bring about benefits in a range of ways is apparent (Phillipson, 1989). While a social worker can be instrumental in supporting the struggle of others to achieve empowerment, s/he also has the capacity to be obstructive. Each social worker therefore has a choice concerning how s/he is positioned in relation to the concept of empowerment through 'struggle'.

Another key element of a social worker's orientation to the role should be located in her/his ability to see each individual older person within a family and social context. One of the distinctive contributions of social work is in its focus on wider social dimensions; without this, the fact that doctors, nurses and therapists have a predominantly functional approach can ensure that insufficient attention is given to the individual older person's strengths and preferences, as well as those of her/his family or carers (Caldock, 1996). In addition, a social worker ought to place the individual older person at the centre of practice, involving her/him fully in decision-making, responding appropriately to her/his concerns and building on her/his perceptions of strengths and limitations. Indeed, it is precisely such forms of practice that are recommended in the government's Green Paper on the future of social care for adults (DoH, 2005). While such an approach should pay dividends in many ways, it should also be acknowledged that it requires time – one of the most valuable commodities in hard-pressed social services organisations. Typically, due to the managerialist imperatives which have placed organisational requirements above the needs of older people (Lymbery, 2004a), social workers have been given too little time to develop the more person-focused aspects of their job. This is, of course, a key reason why some aspects of a more therapeutically oriented social work have fallen into disuse – but, as Hardiker and Barker (1999) have concluded, social workers' practice in community care must involve this wider engagement with 'psychosocial' issues to be successful.

Finally, the social worker must place the individual at the heart of any practice that is undertaken. Person-centred practice is a core theme of much government policy in social care, ranging from the single assessment process for older people (DoH, 2002a) to much work deriving from the White Paper *Valuing People* (DoH, 2001d) for people with learning disabilities, and is the core of the professional role in relation to future social care for adults (DoH, 2005). Nowhere is this better exemplified than in modern developments relating to the care of people with dementia, which have been heavily influenced by the writing of Tom Kitwood (Kitwood, 1997). The critical impact that Kitwood made was to reclaim the 'personhood' of the individual with dementia, seeking to ensure that care responses were constructed in accordance with individual experiences of dementia, moving beyond the bio-medical understandings that had previously dominated practice. Although there were flaws in Kitwood's methodology on the basis of his published work (Adams and Bartlett, 2003), his ideas have received a favourable response amongst professionals in the field. In particular, his insistence on the importance of the inner life of the person with dementia is attractive to a social worker and should chime with the values and orientation of the practitioner, as noted throughout this section.

THEORY

It is, of course, important for both practitioners and students to be clear that social work practice is not theory-free, just as it is not value-free. As Hughes (1995) has pointed out, social workers with older people potentially have the opportunity to use any theory that could be applicable to any service user group. At the same time they also require a range of theoretical knowledge and understanding that is specific to the needs of older people. While this sub-section is necessarily brief – a book of this nature does not lend itself to a detailed explication of any of the theoretical approaches that are cited – the reader is encouraged to read further in more general theory-based texts. In passing, however, the reader might wish to note how seldom practice examples focus specifically on the needs of older people in such texts (although Braye and Preston-Shoot, 1995, is an honourable exception to this rule).

As far as social work theories are concerned, a number lend themselves particularly to work with older people – although this can be a problematic relationship. For example, Sheppard (1995) has identified the close links between care management and *task-centred theory and practice*. However, he does not see this necessarily as a benign interaction, pointing out that the theory is often used reductively without analytical rigour. He has also pointed out the emphasis within task-centred practice on the individual service user as a purposive actor, capable of making decisions regarding the most appropriate courses of action to follow. In this respect, therefore, the theoretical understanding links directly to both values and orientation.

Systems-based thinking (Evans and Kearney, 1996) is also of great use to a practitioner working with older people on two counts. First, it promotes a view of the older person within a family and social context, enabling a broader, context-specific understanding of that person. Secondly, it helps in understanding the various professional systems that are in place regarding an older person. For example, any analysis of hospital discharge (see Chapter 7) needs to understand how the different systems and processes that characterise such a large and complex institution interact: systems-based thinking can be particularly helpful in such a context.

Social workers with older people will also need an understanding of *crisis intervention theory* (Golan, 1978), as it is often a 'crisis' that has brought about the need for social work support. As with task centred theory, crisis intervention work is generally of relatively short duration and responds to problems and crises in individuals' lives. However, it differs in one key respect: since a critical focus is on helping to enhance individuals' capacity to respond productively to situations of crisis, it engages much more with their emotional response to issues and the unconscious or possibly irrational behaviours that could result (Payne, 1997).

A number of theoretical approaches are likely to be less commonly used, although there may be circumstances where they are directly applicable. For example, *cognitive behavioural therapies* have become heavily used in certain sectors of social work and related activity (Payne, 1997). The work of probation officers is particularly dominated by this approach, which has been widely verified as successful in numerous settings, including mental health and learning disability (MacDonald et al., 1992). However, for many older people it would not seem to be appropriate, particularly where the behaviour of the older person is not the primary cause for concern. Even where the behaviour may be problematic – as in the case of an older person with dementia – it is questionable whether cognitive therapies would be appropriately applied, given the cognitive deficits caused by dementia. Similarly, while insights derived from *psychodynamic theory* underpin both loss work and crisis intervention, it is not likely that social workers would spend much time in explicitly psychodynamic practice with older people.

RISK, UNCERTAINTY, PROTECTION AND INDEPENDENCE

These four concepts are linked together because they are interdependent. For example, an assessment of risk will have potential consequences for an older person's autonomy and independence. Similarly, it is impossible to protect an individual against all hazards without that level of protection leading to some compromise of independence. The concept of 'risk' has become omnipresent in British social policy (Kemshall, 2002), and the assessment and management of risk has become a similarly unavoidable topic in social work (Parsloe, 1999). In respect of older people, a primary focus on risk runs the risk of over-protecting an individual, assuming that s/he is incapable of making judgements about the levels of risk that s/he is prepared to tolerate. Typically, many admissions to residential care have come about because families are unwilling to accept the level of risk that inevitably must attend a vulnerable older person's maintenance of independence in the community.

As Stevenson (1999) has suggested, the examination of risk in the context of older people involves judgements about 'capacity'. If an individual has the full capacity to make decisions about her/his own life, and the risks that may be part of it, then it is more likely that there will be a greater professional toleration of the possibility that significant harm may befall her/him. The more that capacity is reduced – for example, though progressive dementia – the more likely it is that decisions will be taken that potentially compromise the person's independence. In practice, it is also important to remember that the predominant model of risk is individualised, which can serve to obscure the fact that risks can derive from the failure of society to adapt the environment so that it is more appropriate to the needs of frail older people. For example, the fact that the very oldest people are more likely than other groups to live in accommodation that is not centrally heated (ONS, 2001) increases the possibility of hypothermia. The relative poverty of many older people (ONS, 2001) can compound this risk, rendering it more difficult for them to purchase the fuel needed for comfort in the winter. It is inadequate, therefore, for a social worker to focus on risk exclusively as an individualised problem.

However, some issues can only be addressed through a focus on the individual circumstances of service users. For example, in making judgements about a person's capability of benefiting from a regime of intermediate care, a social worker must consider the genuine areas of risk that might accompany the maintenance of independence (see Chapter 9 for more on this theme). For example:

- Will the person be capable of maintaining the levels of nutrition that are vital for the maintenance of good health (Copeman and Hyland, 2000)?
- If the person has fallen in the past – having fallen once is a good predictor of future falls – what constitutes an acceptable level of risk in the future?
- Can the potentially contradictory views of the service user and her/his family be reconciled?

A core criticism of the focus on risk is that it is inherently reductive: life is risky, and it is neither possible (nor, in fact, desirable) to eliminate all aspects of life that might carry some level of hazard. This perception runs counter to managerialist thinking that proceeds as if all problems are amenable to technical solutions. Schön (1991) has identified that a search for 'technical rationality' is under way within human service professions; unconvinced by the thinking that underpins such a shift, he has suggested that, in reality, the problems that confront workers in such occupations are often messy, uncertain, and not amenable to straightforward technical solutions. By implication, therefore, social workers (and their managers) should accept that their work often requires the exercise of complex judgements, the outcomes of which cannot always be predicted in advance. That is not to suggest that risk assessment is not an essential part of the overall assessment process, but rather to assert that it should be located within a context which is characterised by uncertainty. Support for this position can be found in the Green Paper on the future of social care for adults, which appears to recognise the complexity of balancing the twin elements of risk and protection (DoH, 2005: 27–28, 4.3–4.6).

Indeed, one of the central dilemmas for a social worker in practice with older people is to hold the principles of autonomy and protection in balance (Stevenson, 1999), and to make decisions that, as far as possible, enhance the older person's independence. This has always been a complex and challenging task, not helped by the difficulty of establishing what autonomy actually is and how it can be enhanced (Neysmith and MacAdam, 1999). In addition, there is a historical legacy that runs counter to the above goals: as we have seen in Chapter 3, for many older people the period before community care represented a time when decisions were taken paternalistically, with scant recognition of their need to retain a sense of autonomy and independence. Issues concerning the protection of older people (amongst other vulnerable adults) have been given much greater prominence with the publication of *No Secrets*

(DoH, 2000a), which clarifies the role of SSDs and social workers in cases of abuse. While the abuse of older people was accepted as a significant social problem later than in respect of children, its nature and dimensions are now well understood (Bennett et al., 1997), although there is little agreement about its extent.

Of course, the desire to ensure that older people are adequately protected can run counter to the principle of maintaining independence. Although decisions can be taken solely on the basis of risk, such decisions would override the individual's desire to balance risk and autonomy. While there are a number of ways in which an older person can be protected from abuse, there are other potential risk factors against which there is no easy level of protection. At this point delicate judgements have to made, balancing the needs of the individual, the risks in any particular course of action, the person's capacity to make informed judgements about risk, the desire to protect the individual and the understandable anxieties of family members or carers. There are no straightforward formulae that can make such decision-making easy: it relies on an interlocking series of judgements about all the above. The final decisions that are arrived at will necessitate professional skills of a high order, in order to reach a conclusion that satisfies the service user while accommodating the range of other concerns that are raised. Each individual set of circumstances will be different; having satisfactorily resolved similar issues in the past will be helpful to the worker's confidence, but will not provide a ready blueprint for action in the future.

In all considerations of the balance between risk, protection and independence, the element of uncertainty will remain. Social workers have to facilitate decisions which are often difficult and painful. This is particularly so because social workers are generally involved only at the point at which maintaining an individual's independence may no longer be possible. As was explored in Chapter 1, people are likely to experience strong feelings and emotions at such a time in their lives. It is precisely for this reason that social workers need to be skilled at working with older people in periods of turmoil caused by multiple losses (a theme explored in more detail in the following section).

If the maintenance of an older person's independence is the primary task for a social worker, it will be vital that the practitioner has a sense of what independence actually means in practice. There is a tendency for the term to be used unreflectively, assuming that independence is a state within which an individual has the capacity directly to undertake all aspects of living. A key element of learning from the disabled people's movement, however, is that independence means the control over decisions that affect one's own life, a goal to which most older people can aspire, rather than the physical capability to undertake all daily tasks of living, which may be beyond many of them (Mercer, 2004). In the past, much care and support for older people has not reflected the need to enhance independence. Instead, the services provided often worked in opposition to the desire to maintain independence (MacFarlane, 2004). They also often contradicted the expressed wishes of many older people, who would prefer services to be offered as 'assistance' rather than 'care' (Clark et al., 1998).

The weakness of much of the service that has been available has been obscured by the apparent 'gratitude' of many older people, linked to their unwillingness to express concerns and criticism and their relative lack of a collective voice. Ultimately, the best way of ensuring that older people are enabled to live in ways that they choose will be the development of groups that are more able to speak and act on their behalf. While this will not represent the major part of a social worker's professional activity, it is important that s/he is aware of the need for collective action – a reminder of aspects of social work's more radical history – and acts so as to facilitate it. However, in day-to-day practice, collective action is unlikely to resolve the issues with which an older person is confronted; it is here that the skills of the social worker in helping to manage complex and emotionally challenging sets of circumstance will be required.

SECTION SUMMARY

This section has explored a number of general aspects of social work with older people, with a particular focus on the following:

- The values and orientation of social work practitioners.
- The place of theory in social work practice.
- The interconnected issues of risk, uncertainty, protection and autonomy.

SKILLS REQUIRED IN SOCIAL WORK WITH OLDER PEOPLE

In line with the analysis of Chapter 2, this section proposes that social workers require skills in all three core aspects of social work's identity, enabling a promotion of the individualist-therapeutic, administrative and collectivist elements of the social work role. It follows the point made by Hughes (1995) that social workers with older people need to be able to apply an equivalent level of skill that would be expected of practitioners with other service user groups, while being able to comprehend the uniqueness of an older person's experiences. Although particular skills tend to promote certain forms of social work action – effective therapeutically oriented action is simply inconceivable without a high level of interpersonal skill performance, for example – the contention of this section is that they are inevitably inter-related. Therefore, interpersonal skills also help to facilitate social work in its more administrative or collectivist orientations. Similarly, skills of planning will assist social workers to carry out both individualist-therapeutic and collectivist objectives.

INTERPERSONAL SKILLS

There are a range of interpersonal skills that will contribute to good quality social work, as is suggested in the following paragraphs.

Counselling skills

As noted in Chapter 2, the Barclay Report (1982) identified 'counselling' as one of the two main areas of social work, alongside 'social care planning'. Of course, in the contemporary world we have to acknowledge that the majority of social workers are not counsellors, nor should they consider themselves as such. However, the commission of their legal and statutory duties requires the exercise of many counselling skills. For example, as noted earlier, older people and their families are almost certain to be experiencing high levels of stress when they require assistance from social workers; to be successful, any tensions in the family need to be sensitively addressed, an act that will require a good level of counselling skill. We can therefore agree with Brearley (1995), who has suggested that counselling skills underpin all social work tasks and that they represent a significant function in themselves, practised alongside other approaches. However, the high volume and low intensity of much social work with older people militates against activities that might create a longer-term involvement with service users, and the exercise of counselling skills will generally ensure that the work proceeds at a slower pace than organisations would prefer. As Howe (1996) has put it, the employing organisations within which social workers are located have an inbuilt preference for 'surface' explanations, as these will lead to more straightforward responses than any search for 'depth' by the social worker. The dilemmas that this creates will be addressed in Chapters 7–9.

Communication skills

Successful communication is also central to good social work practice. As Thompson (2003) has reminded us, these skills apply equally to verbal, non-verbal and written aspects of communication. Indeed, if only one aspect of communication (for example, the verbal) is addressed, there could be significant limitations in the quality of practice. Of course, much face-to-face communication with service users is carried out at the verbal level, as social workers usually use these skills as a central element of their work in assessing, planning and coordinating care. Despite its centrality to practice, communication is often a taken-for-granted accomplishment, although different individuals self-evidently possess this facility in differing degrees. Clearly, therefore, communication skills can be honed, developed and improved.

There are a number of different facets of verbal communication, which identify it as more than simply a one-way process. For example, how a social worker *listens* is every bit as important as how s/he speaks. Communication depends on two aspects: what is put across and how it is received. The ability of social workers to demonstrate active listening skills is important to the establishment of a trusting relationship, as this can reassure the service user that the content and meaning of what s/he wishes to communicate is accurately received by the social worker. As Goldsmith (1996) has indicated, such skills are particularly vital in establishing a relationship with a person with dementia. Similarly, aspects of communication that Thompson (2003) terms 'paralanguage' – tone of voice, speed of language, intonation and inflection, etc. – can have a vital impact on the effectiveness of communication. For example, words that appear to be gentle and caring can be undercut if delivered in a harsh tone; this can create a sense of confusion (or worse) in the listener.

In encounters with service users, non-verbal communication – facial expression, eye contact, distance and proximity, posture, etc. – can be important, as such forms of communication can either serve to confirm or confound the verbal messages. In some cases, indeed, non-verbal communication can become more important than verbal communication. For example, if an older person suffers from dementia or an equivalent cognitive impairment, a social worker will need to be capable of supplementing verbal communication with other possible forms of non-verbal communication – touch, expression, etc. – that communicate empathy and respect. The development of a trusting relationship that can enable the delivery of good social work practice for people with dementia (Marshall, 1990) will therefore be dependent on a repertoire of other communication skills.

In addition, social workers must be skilled at communicating in writing – the nature of social work is such that the outcomes of practice are usually codified in written form, as assessments, care plans, reports, etc. In fact, what a social worker writes about her/his work is often taken as a proxy for the quality of practice itself (Pithouse, 1998). As a result, irrespective of the quality of interpersonal communication, the effectiveness of a social worker will be compromised if her/his written work is poor. At a basic level, a well constructed, literate care plan is more likely to be supported by managers than a plan that is shoddily put together. In addition, the way in which a social worker communicates in writing with service users is an important element of practice. It is important to keep in mind that all written communication must be capable of being understood by the people who are its object: a care plan therefore should be written in plain language. In addition, in general terms, the excessive use of jargon should be avoided. While one person's jargon is another's technical language, capable of adding clarity to a written account, one of the problems with jargon is that it can mystify the meaning of a written communication for those who are not initiated into its complexity, and can therefore be actively unhelpful. Precision is important, however, and ensuring that a piece of writing is accurately punctuated and grammatically correct can help in this respect.

Practitioners also need to understand that communication does not occur in an interpersonal vacuum. It is affected by a range of social, environmental, cultural and psychological factors. For example, any social worker has to recognise that s/he occupies a powerful position in relation to a service user because of her/his official status and the fact that s/he has access to resources that may be essential for the maintenance of independence and quality of life. As Hughes (1995) has observed, communication can be obstructed in one of three ways:

- The difference in expectations between the older person and the practitioner can create a particular problem.
- The fact that the professional agenda can tend to dominate the personal can also skew the content of communication.
- A tendency on the part of practitioners to see problems in a superficial way can lead to her/him ignoring the fact that there may be deeper issues under the surface (see also Howe, 1996).

Any form of communication is also affected by other inequalities; for older people, the internalisation of ageist attitudes may reduce self-esteem, which could render that person overly acquiescent. The race and gender of the social worker and service user will also affect the way in which the communication takes place, both in terms of how it is transmitted and received. Without a conscious act of 'linguistic sensitivity' (Thompson, 2003) the language of communication can serve unconsciously to oppress individuals or groups.

The other power dynamic of which a social worker needs to be aware comes when s/he communicates with senior managers within her/his employing organisation. Here the location of power changes, with the social worker in the less powerful position; many social workers find it as difficult to communicate effectively with senior managers as with service users (Thompson, 2003), yet being able to wield some form of direct influence over those people who create policy and control resources is self-evidently vital for a practitioner. Another aspect of effective communication comes in the need for social workers to interact with other professionals, since collaborative practice will be a dominant theme in the foreseeable future. As discussed in Chapters 4 and 5, power dynamics can come into play in such forms of communication, particularly between social workers and doctors.

Networking, negotiation and mediation skills

These skills constitute a sub-set of communication skills, from which they derive. The needs of services users will only be partly met if there is inadequate coordination between professionals and agencies – and social workers will be at the heart of this, particularly in their role as care managers. This will require extensive *networking*: there will be a number of dimensions to this process, depending upon the role of the social workers at different stages of assessment and care management. For example, in carrying out assessments, social workers will need to have access to the views of a range of professionals – doctors, nurses, occupational therapists and physiotherapists, for example. This require-ment will be increased with the gradual introduction of the Single Assessment Process. It is best if the social worker has a profile with these individuals and organisations in advance of carrying out specific assessment-related work; if a level of trust has already been established in general terms it will prove easier to relate on an individual 'case' basis. In setting up care plans and establishing care packages, the range of people and agencies to which social workers need to have access will be increased, as providers of services will also be heavily involved. Again, it will be useful for a social worker to have become familiar with the range of service providers within the locality, which could entail networking with residential, home care and day care service providers. As well as the net-work of formal service providers, social workers also need to develop and then maintain a network of other people and organisations actively involved with older people. These can include a range of national voluntary sector organisa-tions such as Age Concern, Help the Aged and the Alzheimer's Disease Society, alongside smaller scale organisations that may exist in the locality – carers' support groups and the like.

The maintenance of effective networking with organisations and individuals of this nature will be an important consideration for practice development, as it emphasises the fact that social workers do not operate independently from other bodies involved with older people. The networking that is required to manage these relationships is best undertaken on a general level, and should be separate from – although obviously linked to – discussions that may need to be held regarding any individual. On this level, social workers will become heavily involved in detailed *negotiation* over the precise elements of service to be provided. However, such actions will need to involve more than the range of professionals and organisations noted above; perhaps the major element of negotiation will involve the service user and her/his family, friends and carers. As one of the key purposes of negotiation could be to secure justice for an individual (Coulshed and Orme, 1998), it can also be used in a challenging sense, particularly within the practitioner's employing organisation, as well as in the sense of ensuring the provision of appropriate services. When seeking to coordinate an assessment or a package of care services, a social worker will have to negotiate with at least five different groups of people:

1   Since the service user will be the focus of the assessment, negotiation with her/him about needs and the appropriate response to them will be the starting point.
2   At the second level the social worker will need to engage with family, friends and other informal carers. At this point, the negotiation process becomes potentially more complex, as each member of an extended family may perceive a problem in different (and possibly mutually exclusive) ways: achieving a 'solution' that is acceptable to this group of people may therefore be highly complex, particularly given the fact that the service user may have different priorities and wishes from all of them.
3   The range of professionals who will contribute to the assessment process constitute the next layer of negotiation, which will continue in the case of those professionals who may have an ongoing involvement in the provision of services.
4   In addition, this level is where negotiations should be instituted with other potential service providers – residential and nursing homes, home care agencies, etc.
5   Underpinning all the external aspects of negotiation, a social worker also needs to be mindful of the need for negotiation within the context of her/his employing organisation – potentially involving resource panels, specialist adult protection workers, specialist services for people with visual or sensory impairments, finance departments, and so on.

As the above summary indicates, there are many different types of negotiation, and locations within which it may be carried out. Given the potential complexity of these processes, it will be of paramount importance for the social worker to carry out the negotiation process in an open and ethical manner. This could include informing a service user that resource constraints may limit the services that can be offered, or informing a service user about her/his right to use the complaints procedures if unhappy about any aspect of the services provided. A service user may well be disappointed that her/his 'ideal' service could not be made available, but withholding such information would clearly be wrong. Genuine partnership with service users can only be based on the honesty of the social worker: indeed, honesty is central to the development of trust in all relationships, particularly where there are inequalities in power between the parties involved. If a practitioner is able to share her/his assessment, the basis on which judgements were made and an outline plan based on the assessment's outcomes, the service user and other family members have a full understanding of the thought processes that have contributed to the assessment. It is still possible that all parties will not necessarily agree with the proposals, but at least any disagreement will be based on accurate information. At the same time, a social worker might have to carry out other forms of negotiation – perhaps to overcome forms of resistance within the organisation – which are more likely to occur when creative alternatives are being explored.

Mediation is a particular form of negotiation, where a social worker arbitrates between various parties involved in the care of an older person where their interests and desires might clash. An immediate attraction of this approach for a social worker with older people is that the principles underpinning mediation operate to a standard of adult behaviour that is characterised by fairness, mutual respect and equity (Roberts, 1997), surely appropriate principles to guide all practice. In addition, as Bush and Folger (1994) have pointed out, effective mediation has the capacity to act in a profoundly empowering way by transforming the circumstances within which the parties have previously existed. Given that much work with older people is characterised by attempts to resolve intra-familial disputes – often both long-standing and intractable – then the attractions of mediation become evident.

A repertoire of skills and qualities will be required to manage negotiation and mediation processes successfully. This will include the following:

- As noted above, *honesty* is a prerequisite for successful practice, whether with service users, family members, other professionals or within the social worker's employing organisation.
- Allied to this, social workers need to demonstrate *determination* in the negotiating process. There will be many occasions when the perceptions of the practitioner are challenged; in such circumstances s/he must be able to recognise where there are points of principle that cannot be conceded. In addition, the social worker may encounter obstacles in the negotiation process, which will often require a determined opposition to overcome them.
- At the same time, a social worker needs to demonstrate *flexibility* in negotiations – there will be some occasions when alternative perceptions of a situation might cause a social worker to amend her/his intentions. It is important to recognise where these situations occur and accommodate them appropriately.

Advocacy

Effective negotiation may also require the social worker to demonstrate skills of advocacy, a concept that has been well developed in services for people with disabilities (Brandon et al., 1995), but which has had significantly less purchase on practice with older people (Aronson, 1999). As Braye and Preston-Shoot (1995) have noted, there are a number of distinctions to be drawn between types of advocacy. One of these is between 'case' advocacy, drawing on its origins in legal work, where an advocate is seeking to enhance an individual's access to the services, and 'issue' advocacy, which seeks to promote social change for groups. Another distinction can be drawn between paid advocacy – which is essentially what a social worker would undertake – lay advocacy and self-advocacy (Adams, 2003). In applying the various dimensions of advocacy on behalf of older people, the distinction between 'case' and 'issue' advocacy can be seen in the following. A clear example of 'case' advocacy would relate to the direct provision of services, where a social worker would seek to secure the best and most appropriate range of services. Examples of 'issue' advocacy are less tangible, but equally important: this could entail forming political alliances with organisations that can act on behalf of older people more generally (Hughes and Mtezuka, 1992), and in so doing to 'stand alongside' (Aronson, 1999) older people. Both dimensions of advocacy require skills of a slightly different order, but can contribute significantly to the general well-being of older people. Significantly, the second also potentially enables social workers to exercise some of the more collectivist dimensions of practice, as defined in Chapter 2, which have tended to be squeezed out of the picture as far as work with older people is concerned.

ADMINISTRATIVELY ORIENTED SKILLS

Social workers with older people also have to ensure that they develop a range of administrative skills that are essential in the world of care management. The fact that emphasis must be placed on issues such as budgeting and financial management may be uncomfortable for many practitioners, but as Chapter 5 made clear, this is far from the first time that social workers have had to address issues relating to money as a central element of their work roles. Hospital almoners were obliged to carry out financial assessments and even to collect money from patients (Bell, 1961), a task that was unpopular with many, even though it helped to legitimise the presence of the almoner within hospital settings.

However, under community care policy, there has been a renewed preoccupation with financial matters, with care managers at the forefront of this (see Chapters 3, 7 and 8). While the policy itself ensured the capping of the out-of-control social security budget, this created a core problem of balancing apparently infinite levels of need with finite resources. Much of social services' policy apparatus has been designed to keep a check on budgetary expenditure. For example, eligibility criteria function as devices that enable resources to be rationed. Resource allocation panels interpose a degree of scrutiny over the decisions of care managers that had not previously existed. Most organisations also closely monitor the cost of individual care packages, prepared – if necessary – to cap their total expenditure. In some localities, financial management and budgetary responsibility have been devolved to care managers, in line with the suggestions in early case management pilot projects (Challis and Davies, 1986). Care managers are at the centre of all of these mechanisms:

- They have to assess with the eligibility criteria explicitly in mind.
- They have to be prepared for challenge on all of their assessment decisions, particularly when they involve considerable financial outlay.
- As a matter of course they will be expected to monitor, review and amend care packages; they may also have the same responsibilities for the budgets that support them.

Budgeting and financial management

Social workers will need to have skills in both of these areas, as the above points make clear. They need to be able to calculate the cost of a care package, balancing its different elements and being able to justify when particular aspects of the package are more costly than packages developed for other service users. There is an important issue of equity at stake here; while an individual social worker may feel justified in arguing for the maximum expenditure on people with whom s/he works, there needs to be some parity of expenditure on people with broadly similar needs. As a result, practitioners must be particularly careful to ensure the accuracy and viability of financial data provided as a result of turning an assessment into a care package. In addition, in some localities social workers are expected to contribute to the assessments of people's financial contributions to the costs of care services, putting a premium on their abilities in this area of activity. While I would not suggest that such skills are the first that need to be learned by social workers with older people, the development of care management has meant that they can no longer be ignored.

Organisational and planning skills

On a more general level, a social worker needs to demonstrate excellence in these respects to function effectively as a practitioner with older people. It is likely that s/he will carry a heavy workload – on a *per capita* basis, it will probably be heavier than colleagues working with other service user groups. Amongst the essential *organisational* skills that will therefore be required are time management and the ability to prioritise, alongside more general management skills – management of resources and people, problem-solving, decision-making, etc. Although not usually conceptualised as 'managers' within the social services context, social workers who operate effectively with older people will certainly need to have well-developed managerial skills.

The requirement for excellent *planning* skills is possibly self-evident, as a major role of the social worker will be to construct and implement care plans. However the theme of planning does not only refer to the process of individual care planning, but should relate to all aspects of practice. For example, on a micro level, the quality of each separate contact with service users will be enhanced if it takes place within the context of a planned and organised approach (Marshall and Dixon, 1996). While this can help to save time, it also will contribute to each encounter being purposeful and hence useful for the service user. On a broader level, social workers should use their knowledge of services – and service deficits – to inform the planning process within their employing organisations. The fact that social workers have considerable direct contact with service users, their families and carers, gives them information that is vital to effective planning, even if it is currently under-used. Again, this can help to ensure the improvement of services at the collective level as well as the individual. On a daily basis, however, social workers are particularly aware of the issue of planning in the context of 'care planning' – the act of transforming the detail of an assessment into a plan of action that addresses the needs identified. Here, the social worker will have developed a clear idea of the sorts of needs to be addressed, and the strengths and capabilities within the life of the older person that can help them to be met. Having established this basic profile of the older person, the social worker has to propose actions that can address the issues s/he has identified, along with the necessary resources to put these actions into effect. In addition, s/he has to establish a framework by which the plan can be monitored and reviewed.

Accessing resources: The process of care planning involves another core task for social workers with older people: gaining access to a range of resources. As noted in Chapter 2, some commentators (Brewer and Lait, 1980; Wootton, 1959) have suggested that this should be the major task of social work. As the foregoing makes clear, the roles of social workers are much broader than this, and therefore practitioners will require a wider range of skills. However, the ability to locate and mobilise appropriate resources remains a core element of social work, particularly in respect of practice with older people. The more knowledge a social worker has about the resources that exist within a locality, the more effective s/he will be in this aspect of the job.

SECTION SUMMARY

This section has explored the range of skills that are required to work with older people, as follows:

- Under the general heading of interpersonal skills, the section has discussed the importance of counselling, communication, networking, negotiation and mediation, and advocacy.
- Under the general heading of administratively oriented skills, the section has examined budgeting and financial management, organisational and planning skills, and the skills of linking people to resources.

CONCLUSION

While there have been a number of positive developments in the way in which older people are perceived, the impact of these shifts should not be over-estimated. The various steps forward – in the areas of independence, empowerment, participation and involvement, the capturing of people's 'real' experiences (Nolan et al., 2001b) – are evident in the *National Service Framework* (DoH, 2001a), but as yet any progress has been patchy and inconsistent. There is a danger that the rhetoric of progress can obscure the reality. Certainly, as Grimley Evans and Tallis (2001) have argued, the promotion of the values of independence and rehabilitation – welcome as they are in general terms – carries with it the potential to bring about other forms of disadvantage for older people. That social workers need to be alert to such possibilities is clear.

The chapter was written within the framework outlined in Chapter 2, where different aspects of social work – 'individualist-therapeutic', 'administrative' and 'collectivist' – were identified, suggesting that all of these perspectives were appropriate responses to different sets of circumstance. As the above account makes clear, there have been relatively few opportunities under community care for practice to be anything other than administratively focused. However, if practice does not contain some element of individualist-therapeutic work, the psychological needs that older people will experience – identified in Chapter 1 – will not be met. Similarly, if it does not entail more collective responses to the situation of older people, challenging the fabric of ageist oppression within which they exist, then these circumstances will not change and the practices to which older people will be exposed will simply confirm their second class status.

In essence, therefore, good social work should involve a combination of all of the above. There will inevitably be an emphasis on specific aspects of the task at different times, but it is vital to retain the sense that social work entails more than simply the linking of people to resources, important as this task is. It is the balance and combination of roles, orientation, values, tasks and skills that distinguishes a social worker from a member of another occupation. Taken in isolation, there are few of the various tasks that social workers undertake that could not be accomplished by other professionals or even by staff without a formal qualification of any sort. In the field of intermediate care, Nancarrow (2004) has labelled these processes 'horizontal substitution' and 'vertical substitution' respectively. In the current conditions of inter-professional collaboration, the roles and tasks of a number of occupations will come under scrutiny in an attempt to clarify what is unique about each one. Social work must be prepared to engage with this debate, not in a spirit of professional defensiveness, but by asserting its continued relevance to the needs of older people, in order to clarify its current and future role.

CHAPTER SUMMARY

This chapter has addressed a range of issues that affect the practice of social work with older people. In particular, it has covered the following issues:

- The historically low status of social work with older people compared with other areas of specialism within the occupation.
- The impact that community care had on social work with older people – simultaneously raising its profile while providing numerous obstacles in the path of its development within the context of social services departments.
- A number of key issues that underpin social work practice, focusing particularly on the values and orientation of the practitioner, alongside social work's need to balance complex issues of risk, uncertainty, protection and autonomy.
- The core interpersonal skills that social workers have to demonstrate in order to practise effectively, including counselling skills, communication skills as well as skills in negotiation and advocacy.
- A number of administratively oriented skills that social workers require have also been identified, including budgeting and financial management, planning, and resource allocation.

The Social Work Role in Assessment of Older People

It is rarely possible to have a single purpose when dealing with families in trouble. Their real-life situations involve the assessing social worker in attempts to achieve a satisfactory balance between diverse needs, recognised risks and restricted resource provision. (Milner and O'Byrne, 2002: 23)

For all areas of social work practice effective assessment of need provides the basis for subsequent service provision; indeed, if comprehensive assessments of older people's needs are not available their quality of life and even safety could be compromised (Nolan et al., 2001b). As far as social work services for adults are concerned, assessment was particularly emphasised in community care policy and practice guidance (DoH, 1990; DoH/SSI, 1991a), and it has become the single dominant element of a social worker's role with older people. This chapter examines assessment practice, taking into account specific developments – notably the policy on delayed discharge (DoH, 2003a) and the single assessment process (DoH, 2002a, 2002b) – that are changing its nature. It suggests that since social work with older people has become a high volume activity characterised by large numbers of assessments, practitioners have tended to ignore the complexity inherent within many older people's lives and social circumstances.

The chapter starts by reviewing the general literature on assessment, before considering the impact of community care policy on assessment practice, arguing that this has brought about a procedural dominance. It then examines the introduction of policy – developed following the passage of the Community Care (Delayed Discharges etc.) Act 2003 (DoH, 2003a) – to reduce the impact on the health and social care system of delayed discharges of people from hospitals. The chapter suggests that one of the consequences of this policy, certainly as far as hospital-based social work is concerned, has been to confirm the need for speed rather than depth in assessment practice. The chapter then discusses the establishment of a single assessment process for older people, arguing that this cannot fully be put into place unless there is widespread creation of multi-disciplinary teams where members of different professional disciplines work alongside each other. For community-based social work, it is suggested that primary health care settings would be a more suitable location for such teams than separate social services offices. The need for effective inter-professional working is illustrated through a practice scenario that depicts how members of different occupational groups can work together to produce an excellent multi-disciplinary assessment. The chapter concludes by reviewing the contradictory directions for practice that appear to result from the emphasis on delayed discharge and the single assessment process, with the former appearing to set agencies against each other, while the latter emphasises the importance of multi-disciplinary working. It also notes that the grander aspirations of the single assessment process cannot be met unless additional resources are forthcoming; if they are not, practitioners will remain caught between the needs of individual older people on the one hand and the compelling requirement to ration services to restrict expenditure on the other (Parry-Jones and Soulsby, 2001).

ASSESSMENT: THE CORE OF SOCIAL WORK

In any form of social work practice, the act of assessment is critical. Informed action cannot be taken unless there is a clear understanding of the situation under consideration. Care plans cannot be created unless there is clarity about the service user's needs, her/his strengths, the capabilities of the family, the desires and preferences of the service user and her/his family, and the availability of services and resources. All of these factors have to be considered, weighed in the balance, and outcomes agreed – the essence of the assessment process (Middleton, 1997). Despite the centrality of assessment within social work, it has been relatively neglected in the literature (Milner and O'Byrne, 2002). When assessment has featured in general texts, it has tended to be reductionist in nature, presenting it as an apparently logical, value-free activity, favouring individualised interpretations of need. Milner and O'Byrne (2002) suggest that this ignores some essential elements of assessment, particularly its interactive nature and the need for practitioners to go beyond purely individual to more social considerations. The individualist conception of assessment that underpins much practice can be related to the occupational preference for models of 'casework' that have dominated social work for much of its history (examined in more detail in Chapter 2).

Under community care, as the following section will explore, assessment has been heavily dictated by procedural requirements, where the single act that most determines the course of an assessment is the decision about the range of services for which a service user could be eligible (Middleton, 1997). This relates particularly to the balance between legal and statutory obligations of social services departments, and the resources that are available to meet those obligations. The requirement for assessments to be carried out for all people who appear to be in need of community care services (s.47 of the National Health Service and Community Care Act 1990) is the legal basis for action. However, the effect of this requirement is vitiated by limitations on the resources available to social services departments. As a result, the priority in assessment is inherently 'administrative', linking to the underpinning theme outlined in more detail in Chapter 2. By contrast, a broader conception of assessment would transcend the individualist and administrative orientations by tapping into a more radical conception – being based as much on the strengths of individuals as it is on their limitations, and drawing on a broader, socially based understanding of an individual's circumstances.

To be successful, such an approach must be predicated on the establishment of a different sort of relationship between social worker and service user (Lymbery, 2001). The nature of this relationship will need to be negotiated in the light of the specific sets of circumstance confronting the service user – including individual, family, community and social issues. In the context of assessment, the social worker must seek to provide clarity about the nature of her/his role, what s/he is seeking to achieve and have a clear idea how the assessment can be managed in such a way as to maximise the involvement and participation of the service user.

This process can be assisted by the social worker's orientation to the assessment process. Smale et al. (1993) have suggested that three general approaches can be identified. These are as follows:

- *Questioning Approach*: Here the assessor seeks to elicit information from the service user. This model is based on the professional expertise of the practitioner, who interprets the material provided through the questioning process and proposes a course of action based on this interpretation.
- *Procedural Approach*: In this approach, the assessment is primarily governed by the agency function; the assessor's approach is therefore governed by the priority of determining an individual's eligibility for services. As the following section will indicate, the procedural model has come to dominate within community care.
- *Exchange Approach*: Here the service user is perceived both as having expert knowledge about her/his own circumstances and as having abilities and strengths on which to draw. The assessment process should be characterised by a relationship which is much more equal than either of the other two approaches; there should be an exchange of information where social worker and service user jointly identify the nature of the problem, the range of resources – both internal and external – that can be brought to bear on the problem, and use that information to develop a plan that aims to meet goals that the service user has identified.

The exchange approach ought to be responsive to the concerns of service users, while offering them more control over both the ends and means of the proposed intervention. The skills of the social worker in relationship building and communication, summarised in Chapter 6, will be particularly important here. Of course, assessments that are in line with the exchange approach will tend to take longer to carry out, which could be problematic given the resource driven nature of community care; however, there is more likelihood of their producing outcomes that are fully acceptable to service users and which are therefore more likely to be robust (Lymbery, 2004a).

Hughes (1995) has suggested that successful assessments depend upon a range of ingredients, including accurate factual detail, sufficient knowledge and grasp of theory to be able to make sense of the information, a wide range of interpersonal skills and the capacity to make well-informed professional judgements. This final point is vital because there is no direct causal link between the information collected and the conclusions of the assessment process. All of the separate ingredients are grounded in the attitudes and values of the practitioner, which are critical in making an exchange approach to assessment a reality. These ingredients can be readily incorporated into the five discrete stages of the assessment process, identified by Milner and O'Byrne, 2002: 61–4). These are:

1   *Preparation*: This involves clarity about what information needs to be discovered, the range of sources of this information and the processes through which the information will be collected.
2   *Data collection*: This involves not only the actual collection of data through interviews, letters, telephone conversations etc. but also how the data is stored and retrieved, how its reliability is checked and what gaps there are within it.
3   *Weighing the data*: This entails making judgements about the nature and seriousness of the situation under investigation, including themes and patterns in the data.
4   *Analysing the data*: This involves the development of hypotheses, drawing on a range of theoretical perspectives, which might help in the interpretation of the data collected. Any conclusions drawn at this stage are tentative, needing to be checked out with the key informants to the process – particularly the service user.
5   *Utilising the analysis*: Having checked the initial data analysis against the views of other key parties to the assessment, this stage involves the development of a plan that can address issues raised through the assessment process, including ways in which progress and outcomes can be monitored. As before, it is essential that feedback is gathered so that the plan can be amended if necessary before putting it into action.

When placed in conjunction with the exchange model, this staged approach should guarantee that the individual is placed at the forefront of the assessment process, with the skills and abilities of the coordinating assessor placed at her/his disposal. However, Milner and O'Byrne's framework does have one clear disadvantage. Because it requires thorough and painstaking work at all the different stages, it is difficult to carry out with the rapidity often required in community care assessments. Some of the dilemmas that this creates in practice will be discussed in the following section.

SECTION SUMMARY

This section has explored the centrality of assessment within social work, addressing the following issues:

- The fact that the act of assessment has received relatively little attention in the literature.
- The need to create a different sort of relationship between social worker and service user in order to construct more emancipatory forms of assessment.
- The benefits of an 'exchange' approach to assessment (Smale et al., 1993).
- The five core stages of assessment – preparation, data collection, weighing the data, analysing the data, utilising the analysis – as identified by Milner and O'Byrne (2002).

ASSESSMENT IN COMMUNITY CARE

One of the key objectives of *Caring for People* was 'to make proper assessment of need and good case management the cornerstone of high quality care' (DoH, 1989: 5). Indeed, the related concepts of assessment and care management – although separated for the purposes of this volume – were inextricably linked in much of the documentation that developed to assist the implementation of community care (see, for example, DoH/SSI, 1991a). The officially sanctioned 'seven stages' of care management included two that related specifically to assessment (DoH/SSI, 1991a). However, the priority that was accorded to assessment within the care management cycle can be seen in the official guidance, where 22 pages were devoted to the two stages of assessment, as opposed to 28 pages for the other five stages (Payne, 1995).

This can readily be explained by referring back to the 'deep normative core' (Lewis and Glennerster, 1996) of community care – the need to control costs.

One of the key purposes of assessment has been the definition of whether or not an individual is 'eligible' to receive care services. Questions of individual need have therefore become bound up with matters of resource allocation and prioritisation (Godfrey and Callaghan, 2000), leaving practitioners having to negotiate between what appear to be incompatible requirements (Parry-Jones and Soulsby, 2001). This was further complicated by the apparently contradictory aspects of the guidance on assessment and care management (DoH/SSI, 1991a), which gave primacy to the interests of service users at one point while elsewhere specifying that assessments were the responsibility of the practitioner (Caldock, 1996). Another element of contradiction can be observed in the insistence that assessments should be needs-led, as opposed to service-led (DoH/SSI, 1991a). While this was an important rhetorical commitment, it was substantially undercut by the parallel insistence that assessors should take account of the availability of services in the process of making their assessment, which is reflected in the confusion about these issues in the practice guidance (DoH/SSI, 1991a; see Middleton, 1997). As a result of this, it has been claimed that the definition of need is entirely dependent on the availability of resources (Tanner, 2003).

The concept of 'unmet need' has also been a key feature of community care (Cordingley et al., 2001; Godfrey and Callaghan, 2000); this too has been subject to considerable controversy. In its original conception, practitioners were supposed to record unmet needs: information would then be held by local authorities and used as part of their planning process. If patterns of unmet need could be established, this would theoretically lead to the commissioning of services to ensure that unmet needs could be satisfied in the future (DoH/SSI, 1991a). However, the reality has been much more problematic. Following concerns about the potential legal ramifications of an authority not being able to meet an assessed need, guidance was issued to the effect that unmet 'preferences' should be recorded, rather than unmet 'needs'. Clearly, this negated the ability of any authority to use aggregated unmet needs as the basis for future planning, thereby undermining a key element of community care policy (McDonald, 1999).

In addition to the problem of balancing apparently incompatible requirements, social workers have been hampered in their assessment tasks by both conceptual and practical barriers (Caldock, 1996; Parry-Jones and Soulsby, 2001). The fact that wide variations in the content of assessment schedules and the conduct of assessments have been characteristic of community care (Cordingley et al., 2001) is indicative of the fact that assessment has become a hugely contested area of practice. For social workers, one particular problem is the fact that assessments tend to focus much more on functional elements than on social, spiritual and emotional needs or strengths of an individual service user (Caldock, 1996; Phillips and Waterson, 2002). In addition, the primacy of needs-led assessment has been superseded by the pressing issue of risk assessment and management. Because this has had the effect of ensuring that services are targeted at those people deemed to be most at risk, it has also meant that a range of needs have not been met because they do not carry a high level of risk (Clark et al., 1998). There is little attempt at preventive work, as people who present with relatively low levels of need simply are deemed ineligible for services – at least until their needs have become much more pressing. Indeed, were preventive work to be more actively developed, there would be a greater obvious need for social work input:

> . . . serious preventive work must feature a focus on strengths, treat the service user as an expert in their own problem-solving, foster relationship-building, and allow time for the older person's narratives to be heard. (Tanner, 2003: 508–9)

Although this sort of process would take time – a precious commodity given the pressures on organisations and practitioners – it does appear central to the type of social work role envisaged in the Green Paper on Adult Social Care (DoH, 2005).

In the early stages of community care it was decided that there would be no national prescription on assessment within which local authorities had to work. Instead, each individual social services department had to produce its own eligibility criteria and assessment documentation. As a result of this there has been considerable variation both in the eligibility criteria used by various authorities and the structure and content of assessment documentation (Cordingley et al., 2001). The development of *Fair Access to Care Services* (DoH, 2002e) could be viewed as an attempt to bring about a more equitable approach to eligibility criteria – across England at least. This policy had been trailed in *Modernising Social Services*, where it was specified that it should 'introduce greater consistency' in the system for deciding who qualifies for social care services (DoH, 1998a: 26). To achieve this end, a national framework was introduced that should be used by councils in establishing their own eligibility criteria (DoH, 2002e). However, the policy embodies several key limitations. For example, the government stopped short of establishing national criteria; the general framework within which local authorities had to operate did not deprive authorities of their responsibility to take resources into account when making eligibility decisions (DoH, 2002e). As a result, the guidance specified that:

> . . . it is not the intention of the Department of Health that individuals with similar needs receive similar services up and down the country. . . . What is important is for people with similar needs to be assured of similar care outcomes, if they are eligible for help, irrespective of the services that are provided to meet eligible needs. (DoH, 2002e: 3)

The Department of Health issued policy guidance about how to describe the risks from which eligible needs would be identified and met, paragraph 16 being particularly important (DoH, 2002f). It was subsequently confirmed (DoH, 2003b) that this paragraph would have mandatory force, and that its wording had to be used by all councils. The flexibility for each social services department was limited to two areas:

- Each local authority had to decide where to draw the line about which needs it would meet, which would be subject to available resources.
- A local authority could include 'additional risk factors as bullet points within a band' (DoH, 2003b: 2), provided that these points clearly reflected the spirit of the guidance and that they referred to the key elements of independence within the rest of the guidance.

The eligibility framework contains four bands – 'critical', 'substantial', 'moderate' and 'low' – and a local authority's eligibility criteria should ensure that needs defined as 'critical' are met before those which are defined as 'substantial', and so on. If there are insufficient resources, the eligibility criteria could become comparatively restrictive. Given that resources are a key determinant of the services that people receive, it is therefore hard to see how people with similar needs can be *assured* of similar care outcomes. While the Department of Health is monitoring this aspect of implementation, with a view to ensuring a broad measure of equity across the country, the final decision rests with local authorities and represents, as throughout the life of community care, a balance between needs and resources. Therefore, the systems that have been developed may be *fairer*, but are not capable of achieving *absolute fairness*. Implementing eligibility criteria which are based on a national framework of needs and associated risks to independence may bring about a greater degree of consistency of approach to eligibility, but cannot achieve equity of outcome for all service users. In addition, as Tanner (2003) has pointed out, without additional funding to meet the needs of older people, the practice of social services departments will remain focused on people with the highest levels of need to the exclusion of those lower down the community care tariff. A similar criticism could also be directed towards the Green Paper on adult social care, which also does not attract additional resources, despite proposing a considerably enhanced role for social services organisations (DoH, 2005).

While the Fair Access to Care Services initiative may therefore not change the essential balance between needs and resources that characterises social work assessments in community care (Parry-Jones and Soulsby, 2001), two aspects of policy are having an immediate impact on what social workers are able to accomplish in practice. The first of these is the policy relating to hospital discharge, following the implementation of the Community Care (Delayed Discharges etc.) Act 2003. The second is the implementation of the single assessment process for older people, a key change that derives from the focus on improved 'person-centred care' in the *National Service Framework for Older People* (DoH, 2001a). The following two sections address these issues in turn.

CTION SUMMARY

This section has examined assessment in the context of community care, and has discussed the following issues:

- The priority given to assessment in the care management cycle.
- The contradiction between the needs-led rhetoric and the service-led reality of community care.
- The dilemma of responding to 'unmet needs'.
- The tendency of assessment to focus on functional tasks, downplaying other vital elements of an individual's existence.
- The lack of national prescriptions about how assessments should be carried out.
- The attempt to create greater consistency in assessments and outcomes through the *Fair Access to Care Services* initiative (DoH, 2002e).

ASSESSMENT AND DELAYED DISCHARGE

Although hospital discharge has long been considered to be a major problem in health and social policy (Glasby, 2003), its emergence into prominence in the early years of the twenty-first century does require some explanation. The starting point for this is the problem that confronts the NHS regarding the use of hospital beds:

- The health needs of the population are increasing at a rate that is creating problems of capacity within the NHS, particularly regarding hospital care.
- One way in which the use of hospital resources can be maximised is in a reduction of the length of time people spend occupying hospital beds.
- It is argued that delayed discharges are not in the interests of hospital patients, the majority of whom wish to leave as quickly as possible.
- It is also contended – erroneously, as the following paragraphs will demonstrate – that poor practice within social services departments is the primary cause of delay.

The purpose of the policy decided upon by government is quite simple: if it works well, discharge processes will be speeded up, leading to a reduction in the average length of stay for each individual in hospital. In turn, this will bring about a more efficient use of scarce hospital resources, enabling more people to have treatment. The Community Care (Delayed Discharges etc.) Act 2003 requires social services departments to facilitate rapid discharges from hospital of all people who need social care assistance following their discharge. If any discharge is delayed for reasons that are deemed to be within the control of social services, the hospital must be reimbursed to the extent of £100 per day (or £120 in Greater London). As the guidance specifies, there are a range of delays which are, and are not, covered by the Act (see DoH, 2003a: 8–13). The policy provides tight timescales first for the completion of an assessment, and then for the establishment of a package of care that can support the individual on discharge (DoH, 2003a).

As its implementation has demonstrated, however, there are a number of difficulties with the policy (Lymbery and Millward, 2004). As noted above, it rests on the highly dubious contention that poor practice within social services departments is the primary cause of delays. In reality, this is far from the case. For example, Glasby (2003) has analysed the various causes of delayed discharge, producing a list of eight potential causes that reflect its complex and multifaceted nature:

1   Structural barriers, including separate funding systems, lines of accountability, organisational priorities, etc.
2   Incompatible financial, organisational and professional systems.
3   Failure of health and social care practitioners to work together effectively.
4   Hospital-caused delays in the arrangement of transport and medication.
5   Failure to ensure that patients, carers and SSDs have been given adequate notice of discharge.
6   Failure to involve patients and carers appropriately in discharge and care planning.
7   Patient and carer dissatisfaction about the nature and extent of care services to be provided on discharge.
8   Lack of attention to the needs of carers.

In addition, there are three other potential causes of delay that Glasby does not address. These are:

9   Failure by social care staff to carry out assessments and care planning sufficiently quickly, often as a result of staff shortages.
10 Delays in the admission processes to residential or nursing homes (Phillips and Waterson, 2002).
11 Patient and/or carer resistance to the care services proposed (Cordingley et al., 2001).

An examination of the above list clearly identifies that these factors are not all within the direct control of social services departments. The first three points all turn on aspects of collaboration – the first two at the 'structural/organisational' level, the third at the 'professional/cultural' level (see Chapter 4). The fourth and the fifth are within the direct control of hospitals. The sixth, seventh and eighth all relate to the same theme – the failure to establish working relationships with patients and carers. The ninth and the tenth refer to the capability of social services staff to carry out their assessment and care planning responsibilities promptly, although neither are necessarily within practitioners' control. The eleventh is closely related to the seventh; however, whereas 'dissatisfaction' with the services provided implies that the services are inadequate, 'resistance' implies that although they are adequate, the patient or carer is resistant to their provision. Social services departments are only exclusively responsible for points 6–9; while they have some involvement in several of the others, they could not be held as solely accountable for them. Therefore, policy responses that focus primarily on social services departments are in danger of providing partial solutions, a point recognised by many within the health and social care world (Valios, 2004). It is interesting that the House of Commons Health Committee (2002), which had raised many of the concerns that led to the formation of the policy, was opposed to its introduction. Indeed, this committee took the view that there could be no resolution to the problem of delayed discharge without the creation of an integrated health and social care service (see also Glasby and Littlechild, 2004).

However, it has also been suggested that the introduction of the Community Care (Delayed Discharges etc.) Act 2003 has provided the catalyst for the development of ideas to help reduce the effects of delayed discharge (Lymbery and Millward, 2004). Indeed, since the introduction of the policy, 'the downward trend in the number of hospital discharge delays has been accelerated' (CSCI, 2004b: 4). While it may well be an over-simplified response to a complex problem (Glasby, in Valios, 2004), it has had some success in generating new thinking on the problem. Certainly, it is clear from the attention that the issue has generated in recent years that it is at the centre of thinking in health and social care. While discharge arrangements had been improved in advance of the introduction of the policy (Valios, 2004), it can also be argued that the policy itself has further concentrated attention on the problem (Lymbery and Millward, 2004). As the Commission for Social Care Inspection have concluded, the introduction of the policy has in fact seen an improvement of partnership working, despite some of the more gloomy predictions (CSCI, 2004b).

Of course, there are professional implications for social services staff – particularly social workers – through the implementation of the policy, particularly in the impact on practice of the tight timescales that dictate the processes of reimbursement. For example, following notification that an individual appears to require social care services on discharge, there are only three working days available to carry out such work (as presently defined these include Saturdays). Once the social services department has been notified that an individual is ready for discharge, there is one working day available to arrange it. Given that the priority for the organisation will be to ensure speed of discharge, those aspects of practice that will be more time-consuming – relationship building, dealing with the emotional and psychological impact of change – are even less likely to be carried out than would normally be the case. Even before the implementation of this policy, it had been suggested that the focus on discharge was at the expense of the involvement of social workers in treatment and rehabilitation (Loxley, 1997). There is a danger that this will further confirm the 'administrative' dominance of assessment practice, already highlighted in the previous section. Certainly, social workers' practice within hospital settings will emphasise their roles as 'disposal experts' and 'bed clearers' to which Rachman (1997) referred. Social workers still harbour a desire to be involved in activities that aid recovery or contribute to continuing care (Manthorpe and Bradley, 2000), which will arguably be less possible in future arrangements. However, the implementation of the single assessment process may provide an alternative, more positive direction for social work practice. It is to this development that the chapter now turns.

SECTION SUMMARY

This section has explored the impact of policy on delayed discharges, and has examined the following:

- The rationale for the policy and the detail of its implementation.
- The inadequate understandings of the causes of delayed discharge that have underpinned the policy,
- The perspective that the policy appears to have confirmed some of the improvements to hospital discharge that had already been underway.
- The problematic implications of the policy for social work practice.

THE SINGLE ASSESSMENT PROCESS AND SOCIAL WORK

The previous sections have set the context within which the single assessment process should be analysed. This section outlines the policy, charting its development from its introduction in the *National Service Framework for Older People* (DoH, 2001a), which introduced the issue of single assessments as follows:

All older people should receive good assessment which is matched to their individual circumstances. Some older people will benefit from a fuller assessment across a number of areas or domains . . . and some may need more detailed assessment of one, or a few, specialist areas. The single assessment process should be designed to identify all of their needs. For the older person, it will also mean far less duplication and worry – the fuller assessment can be carried out by one front-line professional and where other professionals need to be involved to provide specialist assessment this will be arranged for the older person, to provide a seamless service. (DoH, 2001a: 31)

Following the publication of the NSF, detailed general guidance for the implementation of the single assessment process was issued (DoH, 2002a, 2002b), with complementary guidance available for specific groups including social work practitioners (DoH, 2002c).

Four broad types of assessment were mentioned in the NSF – contact, overview, specialist and comprehensive. A specialist assessment will be indicated where there are specific sorts of issue – for example, cognitive impairment or mobility problems. Comprehensive assessments are indicated where the needs and circumstances of older people are problematic, or where the level of support/treatment is likely to be intensive or prolonged. Such assessments will consist of exploration of a set of 'standardised domains', specified first in the NSF itself (DoH, 2001a) and updated in subsequent guidance (DoH, 2002b); in the case of a comprehensive assessment all the domains should be surveyed and specialist assessment should be carried out in most of them. The 'fuller assessment' can be carried out by a range of different front-line staff, including social workers, community nurses, physiotherapists and occupational therapists. The guidance specifies the need for a comprehensive, multi-disciplinary assessment where admission to long-term care is a possibility (DoH, 2002a).

The introduction of the single assessment process has necessitated a fundamental review of assessment policies and practices – in itself, this creates an opportunity to clarify the precise role that social workers can play in the assessment process (see Lymbery, 2003). However, as indicated in previous chapters, much work will be required to ensure that different organisations and professionals are able to contribute fully to this process. For example, some of the fundamental premises of the policy are questionable. It appears to be governed by a sense that assessment is an uncontested area of practice. By contrast, in their review of the experience of multi-disciplinary community care assessments, Cornes and Clough (2004) depict a system where disputes over territories and boundaries are rife (in line with the theoretical material reviewed in Chapter 4). They argue that a successful single assessment process needs to recognise the actual state of practice rather than an idealised and inaccurate vision of harmony (Cornes and Clough, 2004). This is far from being acknowledged in the policy itself, or in the guidance about how it should be implemented.

Similarly, Caldock (1996) expressed doubt whether all professional groups would be equally committed to the multi-disciplinary assessment process. He was particularly concerned about the functional domination of such assessments, with too little attention paid to the strengths, wishes and capabilities of the service user: he argued that the social and psychological elements of assessment were particularly underplayed. More recently, McNally et al. (2003) have pointed out that assessment processes for health and social care tend to run more in parallel than in tandem, with relatively infrequent points at which there is multi-agency review (see also Cornes and Clough, 2004). It is also suggested that the fundamental changes that the single assessment process requires are unlikely to be delivered given the lack of additional resources for the implementation of the policy (Cornes and Clough, 2004; McNally et al., 2003).

Glasby (2004) has posed a number of questions regarding the implementation of the single assessment process, arguing that they need to be resolved if there is to be a successful outcome. These include:

- Will the various organisations involved be able to cooperate as the policy envisages?
- Will the social care elements of assessments be overshadowed by the medical?
- Will service users know who is legally responsible for each aspect of their service?
- Will the assessments, no matter how well coordinated, lead to the provision of services that are considered to be appropriate by service users?
- Will the various organisations be able to integrate separate information systems?
- Given the decision not to establish a national template, will there be duplication of effort across localities?

Several themes that have been addressed in this book underpin the above list of questions. For example, it is evident that if there are weaknesses in collaborative practice the aspirations of the single assessment process could be nullified. Similarly, in line with the issues explored in Chapters 4 and 5, there are concerns that the power of medicine might ensure that social care needs are overshadowed in the assessment process. As discussed earlier in this section, the availability of resources will remain a major constraint to assessment practice – there can be no guarantee that appropriate resources will be available, particularly since there has been no injection of additional funds from government to facilitate the development of the single assessment process.

Glasby (2004) is particularly concerned that individual agencies may be unwilling to use validated assessment tools, and will not have the resources or expertise to develop their own. While there can be little doubt about the potential value of scales and tools within assessment practice, over-reliance on such instruments could be dangerous unless accompanied by full appreciation of the nature of assessment. Middleton (1997) has conceptualised assessment as a holistic process, involving a number of different elements:

> Assessment involved gathering and interpreting information in order to *understand* a person and their circumstances, the desirability and feasibility of change and the services and resources which are necessary to it. It involves making *judgements* based on information. (Middleton, 1997: 5; emphasis added)

Middleton rejects the view that the quality of assessment can be determined by the deployment of assessment scales, commenting that this represents a 'growing and . . . dangerous belief' (Middleton, 1997: 8). Undeniably, assessment scales and tools can be *helpful* in the process of collecting, weighing and analysing data, but they cannot supplant the act of judgement on which an assessment depends. In addition, they cannot ensure the full involvement of a service user in the assessment process; indeed, unreflective use of assessment scales can relegate the individual's detailed knowledge of her/his own life and experiences to secondary rather than primary importance.

Despite concern about the practical implementation of the single assessment process, there remains scope for optimism about its ability to improve assessment practice for older people. There are structural and organisational issues to resolve, as Glasby (2004) has observed. In particular, the location of the key professionals in close proximity to each other will enable the close dialogue on which the process will depend. This argues for the creation of specialist teams serving the needs of older people; in community settings, these would be more effective if based within primary health care settings rather than in traditional social services offices (Lymbery and Millward, 2000, 2001). Of course, such a shift would have major implications for the organisation and management of services, as well as for the practitioners involved. In addition, as noted in Chapter 3, structural change alone will not ensure that assessment practice improves, but it can help to facilitate better communication and working relationships between individuals and professional groups.

SECTION SUMMARY

This section has addressed the development of the single assessment process, identifying the following key issues:

- Its origins in the *National Service Framework for Older People* (DoH, 2001a).
- The detail of what the policy envisages should occur in practice.
- The apparently uncontested vision of assessment on which the policy is based.
- A range of issues that remain to be resolved through the implementation process (see Glasby, 2004).

PRACTICE SCENARIO – ASSESSMENT

The following practice scenario is sub-divided into several distinct stages, mirroring the gradual accumulation of information in assessment practice. It is through this process that a more complete picture of the service user emerges, and this information is the basis for subsequent judgements about the course of action to be followed.

Practice Scenario 7.1

Lech Katlewski was born in 1920. He first came to Britain in 1939, where he followed a number of Polish refugees in joining the RAF. After meeting a local girl, Dorothy, they married in 1945 at the end of the war and he remained in this country. As a skilled mechanic in the RAF, Lech drew on these skills in civilian life, first working in a garage then setting up on his own. He and Dorothy had two children, both boys, Walter (born 1947) and Adam (born 1950). Both boys were very successful at school, and have gone on to have successful careers. Walter is an accountant in a London-based firm; Adam – a gifted linguist – works at the European Union in Brussels. Walter is married with five children, two of whom still live at home. Adam is divorced and has no contact with his former wife; he now lives with a Polish woman he met while working in Brussels. Dorothy died in 1980, after a long and painful struggle with cancer. Lech continued to work in the garage for a few more years, but the quality of his work suffered and the supply of customers started to dry up. He sold the business in 1986.

As a social worker, you receive a referral about Lech from a local GP, who has also referred him to the district nursing service. Apparently, Lech's general physical health is poor. He has angina, which is generally well controlled by medication. However, he also has moderately severe osteoarthritis in his knees and hips, and as a result is reported rarely to venture upstairs. Although his house is reported as having a downstairs toilet, there is no downstairs bathroom. He has been referred to the district nursing service specifically because he has a leg ulcer that requires the dressing to be changed on a daily basis. He has been referred to the social services department because the GP feels that he can no longer manage on his own.

As is reasonably typical of referral information, the above summary contains little detail about Lech and his home circumstances. While some information about his health is communicated, in and of itself this information would not seem to be unusual for a man of his years. There is nothing said about his personality, his interests, the condition of his home, his social life, what help he receives, etc. As a result, the tentative suggestion that he can no longer manage on his own is not supported by the sorts of evidence that a social worker would need. However, the GP has been involved in Lech's health care for the past 15 years; while you have little personal knowledge of him, his initial judgement will be based on that extensive knowledge and should not therefore be immediately discounted. The district nurse has been seeing Lech to treat his leg ulcer for the past three weeks, and has up-to-date information about his self-care: you have had considerable contact with her in the past and you are therefore confident that you can acquire accurate supplementary information in advance of visiting Lech in his home.

Practice Scenario 7.2

After discovering that Lech is happy to communicate with you through an exchange of letters, you write to arrange a home visit. As preparation for that visit you undertake three tasks. First, you check whether or not Lech has had any prior contact with the social services department. You find that, despite his age, he is not previously known to the department. Secondly, you have a conversation with the GP to ascertain why he feels that Lech can no longer manage on his own. The GP does not have any hard information to communicate, but is concerned that Lech – previously a fastidiously tidy man – is looking increasingly unkempt, and that his house is both dirty and rundown, with a number of basic maintenance tasks having apparently been neglected. Finally, you talk to the district nurse, who confirms the GP's perceptions. She also observes that Lech is extremely uncommunicative; she does not feel that he is hostile, but simply that he talks very little to her. She is also concerned that his self-care is poor.

At this stage, all the information that you have informally gathered confirms the need for a community care assessment. There are general concerns about Lech's health, alongside his ability to care for himself and his house, but the extent of these are as yet unclear. Although it is interesting that the district nurse views him as uncommunicative, it is uncertain whether this is significant: he may always have been taciturn, and she has only known him for three weeks. It may, however, prove difficult to win his confidence. There is no additional information about his family or social situation. Clearly, therefore, much more detail will be needed concerning a number of aspects of Lech's life. In such circumstances, a social worker needs to be highly observant during a home visit, while remaining sensitive to any cues that service users may give that could lead to more insight into their circumstances.

Practice Scenario 7.3

When you undertake the planned initial visit, you realise that Lech lives in a 1950s semi-detached house, in a reasonably affluent part of the town. From the location of the house, you believe that he is an owner-occupier. Your first impressions of the house reflect that of the GP, in that the garden is completely overgrown, the external decoration of the house is in need of renewal, the roof appears in need of attention, and the guttering at the front of the house has also broken. Lech takes a long time to answer the door, and clearly has mobility problems, as indicated by the GP. He is polite in his greeting to you, but – as indicated by the district nurse – does not appear to be communicative. He avoids eye contact and waits for you to initiate conversation; he does, however, engage readily enough, and his spoken English is very good. The inside of the house confirms the impression given by the outside; all the surfaces are thick with dust, indicating that cleaning has not recently taken place. It is unmodernised, without central heating and with window frames that appear to be unsound. The only source of heating in the house is a two-bar electric fire in the living room. There are grates for open fires, but these are not used. Lech confirms that he owns the house, where he and Dorothy lived from 1954 onwards. He acknowledges that he does not get around as well as he used to, and that he is therefore 'not bothered' about keeping the house clean. He also acknowledges that he is no longer able to use the upstairs rooms, and sleeps in his chair in the living room. When asked how he manages to bathe, he says that he uses the kitchen sink for washing, and that he goes to his sister-in law's bungalow every once in a while for a bath. Grace is Dorothy's younger sister; she was widowed a couple of years previously and lives alone in a small modern bungalow. She apparently does 'bits of shopping' for him, as he can no longer leave the house on his own. He claims to be eating well, although the fridge is empty and the kitchen appears little used.

At this first meeting, a limited range of additional information has been forthcoming. You have confirmed that Lech's mobility problems are more of a concern than had been realised, as he can no longer leave the house independently and does not use his upstairs rooms. This means that his sleeping, washing and bathing arrangements are less than ideal. You are still uncertain about the implications of his lack of mobility for day-to-day living. Although Lech's immediate family lives away, his sister-in-law provides some support for him including help with shopping and the opportunity to bathe occasionally. Although he professes to be eating well, there is sufficient doubt about this to make you concerned – particularly given the fact that little shopping is collected, along with a kitchen that does not seem to have been recently used. You recognise that Lech does not volunteer information readily, but are unsure about whether this is typical of his character, or indicative of a deeper problem. At a material level, the house is in need of considerable maintenance, both internally and externally. As a home owner, this could create financial difficulties for Lech, but such work will be essential to ensure his safety in the home. Certainly, his continued housing requirements will be a major feature of the assessment, but too little is yet known about Lech's wishes in this area.

In general terms, it is important to undertake the beginning stages of assessment by concentrating on establishing a rapport with the older person, without trying to resolve all of the possible issues at first contact. This means that the work must proceed at the pace of the older person, rather than the practitioner. This is vital where there appears to be some unwillingness to engage openly, as is the case with Lech. Failure to do this can fatally undercut the intention to use an 'exchange' approach to assessment, which depends on a basic readiness of the older person to share aspects of her/his life and experience. It could prove difficult to establish a productive working relationship with a service user unless adequate time and planning are devoted to the process, leading the assessment to become much more 'procedural' and 'questioning'. While such a change could result in a positive outcome for Lech, in that the outcome of assessment would still ensure that resources can be put in place to assist him in various aspects of daily living, it is much less likely to accord to his own wishes and desires.

Because there is much more that needs to be known about in advance of a future meeting, the social worker needs to remain clear about the tasks that should be accomplished:

- As regards the condition of the house, extensive modernisation may be a possibility, if Lech is able to pay or if some degree of financial support is available to him. It is therefore worth exploring the possibility of a grant towards such work from the local housing authority. As an older person living alone, Lech may be entitled to a mandatory grant to modernise the property. In addition, adaptations could be made – stairlift, bath aids, etc. – to ensure that he is able to use the full extent of the house. Alternatively, he may actually be happier to move to accommodation that is smaller and more convenient. It will be important to be clear about where Lech actually wishes to live and what options could be open to him. If he wishes to stay at home, it will be particularly important to involve an occupational therapist in the assessment to examine how best he can maintain himself in the house.
- Lech's arthritis has created a number of problems with various activities of daily living, certainly affecting his self-care, and probably also hindering his ability to prepare food. There are validated scales that can be used to assess his functioning in terms of the performance of the activities of daily living: this is one area where such assessment tools can usefully contribute to the overall assessment profile. It is important to work out what his physical capabilities are, and the extent to which they could be improved. The specialist involvement of a physiotherapist will be useful in this aspect of the assessment.

- Although Lech has no direct family living in the locality, his sister-in-law has provided some measure of caring support. As such, her opinions should be sought, in line with best practice and the legal requirement of the Community Care Assessment Directions 2004 (DoH, 2004a). If Lech is to be maintained in the community, Grace's role could be vital, if she is willing and able to continue to offer support. She is also somebody who has known Lech for many years, and therefore has a historical perspective that may be helpful. In addition, although his sons live at some distance, it will be important to find out what you can from them about their involvement with their father, and if this will change in the near future.

- Deeper knowledge of Lech's personality is potentially important, because his general demeanour, including his failure to communicate openly, has given you some cause to wonder if he could be depressed. If this hypothesis is correct, it may well compromise his ability to benefit from the range of improvements and services that could be arranged for him. Exploring Lech's psychological makeup is therefore far from irrelevant, as his state of mind will have a bearing on the viability of future services.

- Another aspect of Lech's life on which further information is needed concerns his range of social contacts. He has acknowledged that he rarely leaves the house due to his mobility problems, but little is known about whether he maintains an active social life through visitors to the home. In addition, Lech's own desires are not known – does he want to have a wider range of social contacts than is now available to him, or is he satisfied with the current situation? While a sense of this can be gathered from Grace, most detail will need to come from Lech directly.

One of the important ethical considerations at this point is to discuss with Lech the range of additional information that will be needed to complete the assessment, and to agree about the people whose input to the process will be sought. He has a right to know about the sorts of questions that will be asked and the people who will be involved in the assessment.

Practice Scenario 7.4

As preparation for your next meeting with Lech, you have undertaken a range of tasks. Regarding the house, you have confirmed that Lech would be entitled to a full improvement grant should he decide to remain there. This would include double-glazing, central heating and a new roof. You have also explored one or two other housing options for Lech, should he be interested in following any of these up. For example, there is a retirement 'village' not far from his

(Continued)

(Continued)

current house, comprising a range of supported housing options – bungalows, flats and maisonettes. Should he wish to move into this privately run facility, he would be able to generate sufficient cash from the sale of his house. There are no current vacancies, and a lengthy waiting list, for the two council-run warden-aided complexes in the locality. You have alerted the occupational therapy service that they may need to become involved in the assessment process. You have also informed the physiotherapy service that its involvement in Lech's assessment will also be needed to assess the possibility of him recovering some mobility.

As far as caring and social isolation are concerned, you have also discussed matters with Grace, offering her the opportunity to have her own needs assessed (an opportunity that she declined). She is considerably younger than him, and says that she is in robust physical health. She has always had what she describes as a 'close' relationship with Dorothy and Lech, but she describes him as having become increasingly uncommunicative in recent years. She says that she has offered more help than he is willing to take up – cleaning, shopping, cooking, etc. He claims that he is doing fine, but Grace thinks that he exaggerates his capacities. As justification for this, she says that he would never have tolerated the lack of cleanliness and order in the house in former years. In addition, until a few years ago, Lech was a keen gardener with a tidy, well-maintained plot to the front and rear of the house. Grace says that she has offered to find an odd-job man to keep the garden under control, but that Lech has never been interested in taking this offer forward. Even though it is 25 years since Dorothy died, Grace feels that he has 'never been the same man' since. While he used to enjoy an active social life – largely focused on the large Polish community centre in the town – this had started to drop off even before his mobility became so severely affected. Grace describes the only other social contact that Lech has as being a weekly visit from the Catholic priest. Other than that, he is said to watch television all day, but has no other hobbies to occupy his time.

The information from Grace is particularly important, as it provides extra evidence to support the tentative hypothesis that Lech may be experiencing depression. What Grace says about his past character and life appears to contradict the impression that is currently conveyed – the contrast between his previously active social life and his current lack of social contact is marked, indicating that Lech is not by nature an isolated individual. Grace's perceptions about there being a gap between what Lech claims to be capable of doing and the reality of his life reinforces the impression given by other informants, and is an important issue for further consideration. In general terms, one of the clearest contrasts between, for example, occupational therapists and social workers is that the former are less likely to take the claims of a service user about their performance of daily tasks at face value, preferring to ask to be 'shown' how a particular task is carried out. This is important, as accurate information about physical capacity is a vital element of a good assessment.

At this stage, therefore, the following issues are particularly important:

- *Housing*: The current state of Lech's house is unsatisfactory, and there are indications that it may be too much for him to manage. However, if he could be brought to accept the various forms of assistance, the house could be significantly improved, and become much easier for him to manage. In addition, given that he has lived in the same house for 50 years, it is reasonable to assume that he has a deep emotional attachment to it that will affect the judgement he makes. Having explored some other potential housing options, you will be able to discuss with Lech what most suits his needs and wishes.

- *Health*: From the discussion you have had with both the GP and the district Nurse, Lech has specific health needs that are currently reasonably well managed. No major issues appear to stem from this.

- *Depression*: Although Lech's psychological condition gives cause for concern, specialist involvement will be needed to make an accurate diagnosis and a referral for such an assessment appears indicated. Future support will depend on the nature of the diagnosis; possible options include the continued involvement of a community psychiatric nurse to monitor his condition, or the provision of counselling support. Resolving this issue successfully may be the key to Lech's future prospects, as it affects most aspects of his life.

- *Activities of daily living*: Lech's ability to carry out these activities – self-care, cooking, cleaning, etc. – is a major determinant of whether Lech is actually able to remain in his current house. His osteoarthritis has a significant ongoing impact on his ability to cope with various activities of daily living, but work could be accomplished with the assistance of occupational therapists and physiotherapists that would simultaneously improve his range of movement and his ability to manage within his home environment.

- *Carer's issues*: Grace had indicated that she carries out a range of tasks that would characterise the role of a carer, but has declined your offer of a carer's assessment (to which she would be entitled). She says that she will be happy to continue the sort of support that she has been providing, and that she would like to assist Lech in having more of a social life.

- *Social isolation*: In many ways, this problem is more difficult to resolve. Lech's limited mobility will affect him wherever he lives, but he is entitled to financial support (mobility allowance) that will help to pay for transport. However, a social life cannot simply be guaranteed by increasing Lech's ability to leave the house and attend social gatherings. Much will depend on what he is prepared to do: in this respect, the Polish Community Centre may be the best starting point, as this was the basis of much of his past social life. There is a particularly large population of older Polish men who use the centre, and specific activities are provided for this group. In addition, since the people who use the centre share similar cultural backgrounds, there may be other benefits to his attendance. For example, the Catholic priest pays regular visits to the centre; there are also regular social events drawing on their shared Polish experiences. However, as noted above, Lech's willingness to engage in more social interaction has to improve to take a benefit from what may be on offer at the centre.

The final assessment judgements and recommendations will come from balancing the various options for changing Lech's circumstances with what Lech actually wants. As the above range of options indicate, reaching a successful resolution is a complex matter, made particularly difficult by his psychological condition. There are a range of different occupations whose work will contribute significantly to the final assessment judgements and their involvement will need to be carefully coordinated. As discussed earlier in this chapter, while the adoption of various assessment tools and scales can help with the gathering of information on which the assessment outcome is based, this outcome will be the result of a process of discussion, negotiation and judgement. There is no single 'right' answer: there are too many unknown variables to be able to specify that one course of action would be the 'best'. It is particularly important for the social worker to ensure that the processes of the assessment are carried out well. This means ensuring as far as possible that Lech's wishes are paramount, that the proposed outcomes genuinely address his needs, that the wishes of Grace are taken into account, and that there is continuing dialogue with the full range of professionals involved in the assessment.

CONCLUSION

This chapter has examined the assessment of older people, drawing on material from the general literature on assessment (Middleton, 1997; Milner and O'Byrne, 2002) alongside material that is more specific to the roles and tasks of social workers in community care. It is clear that the future of assessment practice in community care for older people will be dominated by the impact of the policy on delayed discharge and (particularly) the development of the single assessment process. The continued uncertainty about the structural and organisational arrangements that will govern practice creates tensions in the implementation of the single assessment process and has led some commentators to conclude that the policy may be over-ambitious (McNally et al., 2003). This is critical as the experience of practitioners clearly identifies the impact of resource constraints on their practice (Gorman and Postle, 2003), which may particularly affect the depth of enquiry.

Nevertheless, a key goal for social workers in the assessment process should be to ensure that older people become more actively involved in defining what their own needs are and the best ways to ensure that they are met (Godfrey and Callaghan, 2000). This was illustrated through the practice scenario, outlining the need to work patiently to uncover the most appropriate way of responding to Lech's needs. As indicated in Chapter 2, this entails working in accordance with all the different aspects of social work's history. At the individualist-therapeutic level, the key element here is to engage with those issues that will affect his response to whatever services are arranged for him. If Lech's depression is not picked up at the point of assessment, the services organised on his behalf in the resulting care plan will be markedly less effective. Of course, these administratively oriented aspects of assessment are highly significant. Lech does have care needs to which existing services can respond effectively, and the assessor's role in linking Lech to resource providers is of great importance. Finally, the collectivist aspect of assessment can be seen in the developmental skills required to mobilise resources to combat Lech's social isolation. The assessment will only be comprehensive if all three aspects of social work are deployed. As noted above, there is an in-built tendency for social work with older people to focus only on the administrative aspects of practice; as this scenario demonstrates, this is to the detriment of an older person such as Lech.

At the organisational level, the responsibilities of a social worker involved with Lech's assessment will require effective inter-professional and multi-disciplinary working. This can be enhanced by the location of the social worker – certainly, research evidence would suggest that a primary health care setting could improve the quality of liaison work between social workers and both GPs and nurses (Lymbery and Millward, 2000), whereas the location of social workers in separate teams may serve to obstruct this development. The single assessment process is much more likely to lead to positive outcomes if changes are made to the organisational locations of key occupational groups. However, the financially driven nature of policy on delayed discharges could obstruct these benefits unless agencies act to develop cooperative approaches to the problem of hospital discharge. Indeed, unless cooperation is secured in this area of policy and practice it is highly unlikely that the single assessment process will succeed in its aim of improving assessment practice.

CHAPTER SUMMARY

The chapter has focused on the assessment of older people, and has addressed the following issues:

- The act of assessment is central to all social work.
- The importance of drawing on the ingredients of a successful assessment process (Hughes, 1995) and a framework whereby the process of assessment can be better understood (Milner and O'Byrne, 2002).

(Continued)

(Continued)

- The significance of resource constraints within community care, which have ensured that practice is dominated by the need for a high volume of mainly low-intensity assessment work, leading to unimaginative responses to need.
- The establishment of a national policy on delayed discharge from hospital care and the financial penalties that accrue to social services departments has led to a particular emphasis on the role of social workers in enabling the more cost-effective use of hospital resources, which has served to limit their wider involvement in treatment or rehabilitation even further.
- The establishment of the single assessment process has created the potential for more imaginative working between health and social care staff, but the effectiveness of the policy may be limited by the fact that no additional resources have been devoted to its implementation (McNally et al., 2003).
- The potential benefits of the policy were illustrated through a practice scenario, which indicated how effective cooperation can be enhanced by the thorough and painstaking approach of the social worker who is responsible (in this case) for coordinating the full assessment process.

Care Management and Social Work: a Marriage Made in Heaven?

...the rhetoric of community care has become the reality of care management.
(Gorman and Postle, 2003: 7)

When the Department of Health issued guidance on the development of care management in 1991 it was defined as a cyclical process, encompassing assessment, planning, intervention, monitoring and review (DoH/SSI, 1991a, 1991b). As the previous chapter has identified, assessment has been the element of the cycle that has been accorded most priority. One of the consequences of this has been the relative lack of development of other aspects of care management – particularly monitoring and review. This chapter examines the impact of this, focusing on the increased likelihood that the services older people receive are less likely to respond quickly to changes in the levels of need that they experience. It identifies the extent to which this limitation reflects an ageist ethos, arguing that the outcomes for older people are consequently less likely to reflect either their needs or wishes. However, care management has become the dominant form of practice across all adult services, with a particular bearing on work with older people. In this context, the chapter also identifies the extent to which financially driven priorities, particularly when combined with routinised assessment processes, have created a sterile and unsatisfying form of practice.

The chapter commences by examining the centrality of care management to community care, discussing the impact of the model of practice that has been developed since 1993. It examines how similar principles are becoming entrenched into community health services, with the focus on care management processes as a means of managing 'chronic disease'. It then engages with an argument that is central to the future of social work with older people: to what extent can care management be seen as consistent with the core principles of social work? In arguing that it has been characterised by bureaucratised 'administrative' forms of practice, the chapter suggests that re-engagement with both the 'individualist-therapeutic' and 'collectivist' traditions of social work could potentially enable the establishment of an approach to care management practice that would be more in the interests of older people. Through such developments, the importance of social work to the needs of older people can become more strongly emphasised. While recognising that this runs counter to much contemporary practice, the chapter outlines ways in which the social work role can be enhanced, focusing on the elements that clearly distinguish it from other occupations. The issues and themes developed in this chapter are illustrated through a practice scenario, which indicates how the continued involvement of a social worker can provide an additional quality of support for many older service users.

CARE MANAGEMENT IN COMMUNITY CARE

Since care management was one of the most significant creations of new community care policy, it is vital to generate a clear understanding about what is meant by the term. In particular, it is important to trace its roots: the origins of care management provide a useful perspective on its subsequent development in British policy. As Payne (1995) has demonstrated, the British variant of care management that has come to dominate community care for older people has some clearly defined antecedents. These can be briefly defined as follows:

- It was first developed in the context of social services in the USA, where service provision is characterised by its uncoordinated nature and its uneven geographical distribution (Payne, 1995). Care management – or 'case management' as it was known in its American context – was seen as a way to ensure increased coordination of services. Initially, it was directed towards the needs of people with long-term mental ill-health, and particularly focused on their discharge from long-stay hospital care into the community. However, the concept was soon applied to other groups of service users (Payne, 1995).
- Care management principles were first applied in Britain by projects fostered and developed by the Personal Social Services Research Unit based at the University of Kent (see, for example, Challis and Davies, 1986; Challis et al., 1995). These were well-funded demonstration projects, focusing particularly on defined populations, with decentralised responsibility for budgetary management, the ability to commission services from existing or new providers, and staffed by qualified social workers who carried low caseloads (Bauld et al., 2000).
- The translation of these experiences into frameworks that could be applied within community care was gradual, with models of case/care management evident in the Griffiths Report (1988) and in *Caring for People* (DoH, 1989).

The approach to be adopted was more fully articulated in the *Policy Guidance* (DoH, 1990). As Payne (1995) has argued, these documents define care management as the process of assessment followed by the design, implementation and monitoring of the resultant care plan. Although there is mention of the need to maintain strong interpersonal relationships, this element of the guidance is secondary to the preoccupation with care management as a primarily 'administrative task'.

- The most detailed information on the implementation of care management within community care is contained in the guidance published on care management and assessment – one of which was for practitioners (DoH/SSI, 1991a), the other for managers (DoH/SSI, 1991b). These documents defined care management as containing seven stages, with stages 3–7 representing a circular process. Its cyclical nature is important, as monitoring and review are necessary in order to ensure that services continue to be appropriate for the service user, given likely changes in the nature and level of need. As I will explain later in this section, the lack of development given to monitoring and review has proved to be a major obstacle to the operation of care management. As the guidance makes explicit, judgements about need and eligibility, which are both central to the operation of the care management cycle, rest with the local authority. Another key aspect of the guidance, and a significant departure from previous experience, is that it specified that this process of care management would apply to all people seeking assistance from social services; the previous pilot projects had operated on the basis that although a service user should be fully engaged in the process, it is owned and put into effect by the local authority.

From its origins in the United States, through the early projects in Britain, to its centrality in community care policy, specific aspects of care management have been favoured, while others have been downplayed or ignored. Its weaknesses and limitations in contemporary practice can all be traced to these decisions, the implications of which have been critical for its development.

One major problem has stemmed from the differences between the limited scope of the pilot projects and the breadth of the vision of care management in community care. Whereas the original projects in Britain were targeted on tightly defined groups of service users, care management has been applied widely to all service users. As Bauld et al. (2000) observed, this failed to recognise that the benefits of the pilot projects were closely bound up in the fact that they focused on specific service user groups. Therefore, it was simply unknown whether the broader approach would be successful, because none of the pilot projects on which the policy relied had tested it out in this way. A key consequence of this has been the distinction between care management as a process and care management as a specific role – a distinction that is particularly significant for social work. In the origins of case management in the United States, particular emphasis had been placed on the role and skills of the social worker, not just in coordinating packages of care but in building and sustaining high quality interpersonal relationships with service users. This element of the care management role has been actively discouraged in the British context (Gorman and Postle, 2003; Sturges, 1996), leading to concerns about the de-professionalisation of this area of social work (Hugman, 1998a). Certainly if care management is to be defined as a purely administrative process there is little reason to insist on a qualification requirement for its practitioners.

In addition, in another illustration of the highly skilled nature of the practitioner role as originally devised, the pilot projects featured a high level of worker accountability; practitioners had devolved responsibility for decision-making and individual budgets on which to draw. It was expected that they would act to create services if needs were inadequately met by what currently existed. They also had to make complex judgements concerning the allocation of resources for each individual in the context of this overall responsibility. When community care was implemented, the bureaucratic demands of organisations required that financial accountability be held above the level of individual practitioners, and devolved budgets became a rarity. There has also been little evidence of innovation and flexibility in the way in which people's needs are addressed. Rather, care management has been dominated by stereotyped and unimaginative responses to need (Postle, 2002). One of the contributory reasons for this has been the relatively slow development of services that could act as alternatives to the standard provision of residential or domiciliary care. This trend has also been accentuated by the volume of work that care managers have to process. Because the care management approach was applied to all people in need of social care services, the low caseloads that had been a feature of the original pilots were replaced by their opposite – particularly in respect of practitioners working with older people (Sturges, 1996) – with obvious consequences for the quality of practice.

Despite the fact that the care management cycle placed monitoring and review as key elements of the process, these have become neglected within the British context. This has led to a critical break in the cycle; without these essential elements, the effectiveness of care management as a process is called into question (Bauld et al., 2000). Without regular monitoring and review, it is impossible to ensure that a care package continues to meet an individual's needs effectively. Where monitoring does take place on a case-by-case basis it is more likely to be undertaken by the provider of care services. While providers are likely to inform care managers on occasions where there has been an increase in need, there is a financial disincentive to do so when an individual's circumstances improve. The separation of these essential roles from the bulk of care management activity, added to the ideological preference for a separation between the roles of 'purchaser' and 'provider' (DoH, 1990) has led some commentators to see care management as characterised by fragmentation (Lymbery, 2004a; Sturges, 1996) rather than integration.

As Payne (2000) has observed, some of the practical problems are related to the model of care management that was adopted – that of 'social care entrepreneurship', where a range of care services from different sources are coordinated by a worker on behalf of the service user (Payne, 1995). The effectiveness of this approach has been constrained by the resource-driven nature of community care, which has had an impact in three related ways:

- Care management for older people has become a highly bureaucratised, routinised process, where the emphasis has been to 'resolve' needs as quickly and as cost-effectively as possible (Lymbery, 1998a; Payne, 2000; Postle, 2002; Sturges, 1996).
- The unremittingly high levels of referral have ensured that caseloads are sufficiently high to ensure that innovative and creative practice is rare (Carey, 2003; Postle, 2002).
- The pressure of incoming assessment work has served to marginalise the functions of monitoring and review, leaving these vital aspects of the care management cycle undeveloped (Bauld et al., 2000).

In both the other possible models for care management – 'service brokerage' (most common in services for people with disabilities) and 'multi-professional' (which predominates in mental health work) – there are clearly defined professional roles, which build on the skills and strengths of social workers (Payne, 2000). Indeed, the concept of service brokerage appears to underpin the government's vision of the future of social care for adults (DoH, 2005), while the centrality of multi-professional working is clear in the single assessment process (DoH, 2002a). However, neither model is suited to the high volume of work that has been characteristic of community care for older people.

The lack of monitoring and review underpinned a key element of the *Fair Access to Care Services* policy (DoH, 2002e): one of its key purposes was to ensure that there are regular reviews of care plans leading to a reassessment of individuals' needs (DoH, 2002e). The Policy Guidance sets out more detail concerning how this should be implemented, laying down timescales for first and subsequent reviews (DoH, 2002f). Although this requirement was linked to the general policy guidance for community care issued a decade earlier (DoH, 2003b), the fact that *Fair Access to Care Services* had to include an injunction to improve the frequency and quality of review processes testifies to the fact that these had been neglected. However, the responses of social services departments have not necessarily boosted the care management function, as the task of reviewing care – particularly for people in long-stay institutional settings – has often been delegated to specialist teams, unconnected to the original assessment decisions. The lack of continuity in this process is stark, even though it meets the requirement that reviews should be carried out 'by competent professionals who are independent of the services they are reviewing' (DoH, 2003b: 20). Older people who have been admitted to any form of long-stay institutional care often have the most intensive care needs, and yet have typically been provided with less care management support than others: this is an anomalous outcome of community care policy.

Another variant of care/case management is being developed in health care. In an interesting reflection of care management for older people in social care, a parallel concept is being promoted to resolve the problems of people with chronic incurable diseases. It is recognised that these issues represent a particular problem for health care systems globally, as 'the care of people with chronic care conditions also consumes a large proportion of health and social care resources' (DoH, 2004b: 3). It is suggested that:

> The complexity and challenge of managing chronic care increases as people develop multiple conditions as they age. However, while individual people may have complex conditions the systems for managing chronic care can be simple. Different interventions can be used for patients with different degrees of complexity. (DoH, 2004b: 4)

It has long been recognised that the system of health care places more emphasis on 'cure' over 'care', so it is encouraging that there is official recognition of the desirability of improving the systems of care for people with chronic conditions. It is interesting that the illustrative examples of the system to be adopted (see DoH, 2004c) include a range of people including one child, two adults and one older person. It seems probable that, in reality, the population to whom this policy will apply will be predominantly older people, as they are more likely to have the mix of conditions specified (DoH, 2004b).

It is intended to identify three levels at which chronic disease management could take place. At the lowest level – estimated as being 70%–80% of the population who require 'chronic disease management' – the emphasis will be on supporting people with their own care, assisting them to manage their own conditions. At the second level, defined as being for 'high risk patients', a version of 'care management' through multi-disciplinary teams is promoted. At the third level, for 'highly complex patients' (*sic!*) it is proposed to develop systems of 'case management' with a key worker (who will often be a nurse) actively managing and coordinating the care for this group of people. It is also interesting that this policy is re-creating a distinction between 'care' and 'case' management that runs counter to the policy that has underpinned care management in community care (DoH/SSI, 1991a).

There are obvious links between these proposals and the systems of care management that currently operate. For example, many people in receipt of intensive packages of social care have chronic conditions that would place them under the terms of this policy. However, while there is some recognition that it will have an impact on social care, the policy is devised from a predominantly health service perspective: the consistent use of the term 'patients' is an obvious indicator of this. The precise nature of its effect on social care is unclear, except that it favours the extension of systems of direct payment for older people as a means to enable them to manage their own conditions (DoH, 2004c). This theme has been extended in the Green Paper on the future of adult social care (DoH, 2005). It also places an even greater emphasis on effective collaborative working (discussed in Chapter 4), and is particularly dependent upon the development of an effective single assessment process (discussed in Chapter 7).

Perhaps the most significant parallel with care management under community care comes in the fact that both were imported from the USA, with scant recognition of the major service differences that exist in the two countries. Primary care is relatively undeveloped in the USA, and questions have therefore been asked about whether it is possible or desirable to transfer 'managed care' systems from the USA to Britain, given that a much more developed primary care infrastructure exists in this country (Peckham and Exworthy, 2003). Moreover, three of the four examples of the potential benefits of such systems derive directly from the USA, with no recognition of the extent to which such benefits would necessarily accrue in a different environment (DoH, 2004b). As this section has previously discussed, precisely the same lack of comparative understanding hampered the introduction of care management in community care.

SECTION SUMMARY

This section has explored the development of care management policy in the context of community care, and has addressed the following issues:

- Its development as a policy from its origins in the United States to its centrality in community care.
- The fact that it has become a highly 'administrative' form of practice in community care, with the interpersonal elements of the role downplayed.
- The limited emphasis within care management on the vital aspects of monitoring and review.
- The links between care management and 'chronic disease management'.

CARE MANAGEMENT AND SOCIAL WORK

A recurring theme in the literature on care management has been the question of the extent to which it represents a break with social work, or is better seen as a continuation of social work into a different direction. This debate is not assisted by the fact that the concept of 'social work', on which such discussions depend, is not clearly defined. Therefore, while some contemporary commentators have argued that there is little relationship between the practice of care management and the core nature of social work (Carey, 2003), pointing to the way in which care management focuses on essentially administrative tasks, this ignores the fact that there has always been a strong administrative focus within social work with older people. Perhaps in recognition of this, others have been more cautious in their analysis. For example, while accepting that there has been an element of deskilling of practitioners in care management work, Gorman (2003) has concluded that the range of skills that they require are much more varied than the procedural and bureaucratic elements that have dominated other accounts. In an earlier study, Hardiker and Barker (1999) reached a similar conclusion, arguing that while the balance between different aspects of the role may have altered, there remains something distinctive that social workers can contribute to it. As Lloyd (2002) has argued, there should be little surprise about the nature of this debate. She has suggested that the history and development of social welfare, the organisational structure of social services departments and the tradition of social work have interacted to create contention about the nature of care management activity. For example, as defined in Chapter 3, community care represented an attempt to get to grips with areas of policy difficulty while controlling the amount of expenditure on them. It was therefore inevitable that departments would introduce an administratively oriented approach to the problem of resolving burgeoning levels of need with inadequate resources (Lloyd, 2002).

In the early care management projects – both in Britain and in the United States – the social worker had a core role in the process, with counselling, therapeutic and interpersonal expertise considered as vital to successful outcomes (Payne, 1995; Sheppard, 1995). In the British context, Challis et al. (1995) contended that the range of skills required by a care manager would be greater than those which would normally be deployed by a social worker. Certainly, as Gorman (2003) has observed, while 'traditional' relationship skills were still defined as central to the successful performance of the care management role, in practice these skills needed to be complemented by abilities that were less securely associated with social work's history – coordination, liaison, management and budgeting (although these have often been part of social work's administrative heritage). It is the place of the more traditional skills that has been subject to particular debate. For example, Gorman and Postle (2003) have argued that while such skills are still used, they are in danger of being squeezed out by the pressing bureaucratic demands of the role. Carey (2003) has taken this argument a step further, claiming that the performance of administrative tasks has taken over from the face-to-face practice that had previously characterised social work, leaving practitioners demoralised and stressed.

While there is little argument that the introduction of care management has affected the focus and content of practice, there remains debate about the extent of this change, as the previous paragraphs have demonstrated. Certainly, the testimony of practitioners (Carey, 2003; Gorman and Postle, 2003; Postle, 2002) appears to emphasise the unsatisfying nature of the care manager's role – a perspective that relates to more general research into the contemporary nature of social work practice (Jones, 2001). However, other commentators insist that there is potential to make something more positive from the care management role (Lloyd, 2002; McDonald, 1999), even if this would entail altering the direction of current practice to accommodate a wider vision of its scope. In this book I align myself with the latter group, despite the force of the sometimes despairing visions of care management practice. As I have argued elsewhere (Lymbery, 2004a), it is possible to develop forms of care management practice that are consistent with the principles and heritage of social work.

However, the introduction of care management certainly created a number of challenges to the role and status of social work (Lloyd, 2002). These have come from many different yet related directions:

- The failure to define a preferred qualification for the care management role has meant that it has been open to people from other professional backgrounds as well as social work.
- The way in which the role has developed has privileged the administrative and bureaucratic functions, has led to claims that it represents a threat to the professional status of the social worker/care manager (Lymbery, 1998a).
- At the same time, this procedurally oriented approach has potentially opened up the care manager role to those people without formal professional qualifications: after all, if the essence of the job entails the efficient administration of set policies and procedures, a professional qualification could be held to be unnecessary.

The ongoing confusion between care management as a targeted service for tightly defined groups of service users as opposed to a process through which the needs of all adults are addressed (McDonald, 1999) adds further complexity to this debate. The first variant was the one which dominated the early projects both in the United States and Britain, where the knowledge, skills and values of social workers occupied a central role in its performance. The second variant has come to prominence under community care policy; there is a less obvious role for social work within it, as numerous writers have recognised. Indeed, the development of parallel systems of case/care management in the process of 'chronic disease management' (DoH, 2004b) could represent a third variant. If a social work role is deemed as necessary within any of these approaches, there must be clarity about what it is that a social worker will offer that provides 'added value' to the care management task (Lloyd, 2002). This is not entirely straightforward, particularly if one accepts the constraints that have been placed on the care manager role by the factors listed above.

As I argued in Chapter 2, the history of social work can be seen as comprising elements of three strands – the 'administrative', 'individualist/therapeutic' and 'collectivist' traditions. I suggested that social workers should embrace all three of these elements, seeking to integrate their practice by drawing on each of these traditions as appropriate. One of the particular problems in the development of the care management role is that it has emphasised one aspect of social work – the 'administrative' – and hence downplayed the importance of both the 'individualist/therapeutic' and 'collectivist' elements. In making the argument for a broader interpretation of the social work role I am seeking to extend the arguments of others who have recognised the limitations in much contemporary practice. For example, Payne (1995) is surely correct in pointing out that the collectivist approach to social work could have an important part to play in the growth of new responses to need, drawing on community development approaches. Also, the relational focus of social work has also been undervalued, as organisational policies appear resolutely to simplify the complexity of the needs of older people, in order to fit them into the pre-packaged services that remain the staple of practice (McDonald, 1999). The essence of the social work contribution to care management would therefore rest in the combination of the three core elements of the social work role.

SECTION SUMMARY

This section has explored the links and connections between care management and social work, identifying the following issues:

- The extent to which care management practice is consistent with social work.
- The key social work role in the early forms of case management in the United States.
- The demoralising impact of many of the changes in care management upon its practitioners.
- The need to revive the concept of care management by reference to the 'missing' elements of the social work tradition, notably the 'individualist-therapeutic' and the 'collectivist' strands.

THE FUTURE OF CARE MANAGEMENT

As the quotation at the beginning of this chapter implies, the overall health of community care can be measured by the condition of care management. From the evidence presented so far, a gloomy prognosis would seem guaranteed. Some detractors have claimed that while it has managed to achieve the fulfilment of the financially driven priorities of community care, it has become a form of practice that is sterile and unimaginative for practitioners, and profoundly unsatisfactory for service users (Carey, 2003). Other commentators have accepted that there have been many problems in its implementation, but also that it is possible to devise successful care management practice (Lloyd, 2002; Lymbery, 2004a).

At the conclusion of the previous section, it was suggested that such a development would require the re-integration of the different aspects of the social work role. There are obvious difficulties associated with this task, however. The pressure of work that confronts social workers will not quickly reduce, nor is it likely that large numbers of additional qualified social workers will be recruited. In the light of this, how can additional time be found for work which focuses on the interpersonal, and for the developmental activities that will be required to generate new service responses? Greater levels of activity drawing on both of these approaches would potentially reduce the scope for social workers to carry out the assessment tasks that have become their core function. A ready way to help resolve this would be to allocate a greater proportion of social services resources to older people – particularly in terms of the ratio of qualified staff deemed appropriate for the work. However, calls for extra resources for this particular service user group are unlikely to be successful, particularly given the competing pressures on child care amongst other areas of social services expenditure. After all, it has been felt that the single assessment process can be implemented without the allocation of significant extra resources, despite the manifest absurdity of such a proposition (McNally et al., 2003). Similarly, it is suggested that the radical re-orientation of the Green Paper on the future of social care is to be achieved without additional resources (DoH, 2005). Another possible approach to the problem would be to reduce the proportion of older people who receive the services of a qualified social worker, reserving the social worker's input for more complex cases – possibly involving allegations of abuse, or dealing with complex family dynamics. This would appear to be a pragmatic way of resolving the problem, and as such could be managerially attractive. However, it would feed into some of the worst stereotypes about the needs of older people (addressed in Chapter 1) and further downgrade the status of work with older people (discussed in Chapter 6). As a result, this is not an approach that I would recommend, although it is already quite common in the social services world.

A more fundamental shift could be brought about by changing the entire way in which services are organised, expanding the scope of a social worker's responsibilities. The key to such a transformation is the relationship between the qualified social worker and the unqualified practitioners – with job titles such as community care officers, social work assistants, etc. – who also work with older people. Traditionally, social workers have not had management responsibility for such practitioners, whose work has been overseen by the same first line manager who supervises the practice of the qualified social worker. This is a different arrangement than exists in many primary health settings. For example, district nurses are responsible for all work carried out in their areas, and therefore also accountable for the work carried out by lesser qualified practitioners. While all qualified nurses take personal responsibility for their practice, this gives the district nurse an oversight into the work carried out under her/his authority. If such a model were to be transferred to social care, the qualified social worker would become accountable for the practice of others, would be directly familiar with the issues encountered by other staff and would have the capacity to decide that her/his own input is needed at a particular juncture in the work. In care management practice, where there should be adjustments to varying levels of need at different times, a team approach makes eminent sense, with a social worker being in a position to coordinate the contributions of others. In particular, it potentially links the review process more closely to the source of the original assessment, which should be helpful in improving levels of continuity. It should also increase the likelihood that an older person's needs are reviewed by somebody with a prior experience of that person and that the older person would be familiar with the person undertaking the review. In reality, as the foregoing has made clear, social workers are too little involved in reviewing activities, but this shift in organisational arrangements should ensure an improvement in this respect.

The development of such a role would require a transformation of the occupational structure of social work. For example, social workers would need to develop an understanding of some essential managerial issues, such as the motivation of staff. They would need to have well developed skills in being able to balance their managerial and practitioner functions. It would clearly also affect the structure and organisation of social services departments. Social workers occupying such positions could legitimately expect to be rewarded with higher salaries, in recognition of the enhanced nature of their role. A similar precedent has already been developed in some authorities in respect of a 'senior practitioner' role in child care, which has a broadly similar range of responsibilities to that outlined here. The physical location of such workers is also highly important. As noted in Chapter 4, the success of such practitioners in relation to their essential collaborative activities will be enhanced if they are located so that they can have ready access to colleagues in health-related roles. If the role of social workers is amended, then so too will be the role of the current first line manager, some of whose responsibilities will transfer to the practitioners.

While a book of this nature cannot flesh out the detail of how such arrangements could work, it is suggested that this might help to provide a better, more rounded and consistent service to older people, as well as a more satisfying role for social workers. That it would take considerable effort to put such an idea into practice is also apparent; however, the poor state of much contemporary care management practice would indicate that a radical change to how it is conceived and organised may be long overdue. The following practice scenario is written on the basis that such an arrangement is in place, while also building on the advantages of co-location, noted in an earlier chapter.

SECTION SUMMARY

This section has explored the possible future of care management. It has addressed the following issues:

- Some of the options for reorganisation of the care management role.
- A suggestion that the care management role could best be enhanced by a fundamental reorganisation of the way in which social services departments are structured in relation to services for older people.

PRACTICE SCENARIO – CARE MANAGEMENT

The purpose of the following practice scenario is to follow the care management cycle, with a particular focus on the constant need to review and reassess when circumstances change. It is designed to demonstrate the benefits of continuity in the care management process, while also indicating the advantages for a social worker with older people to be located in a primary health care setting.

Practice Scenario 8.1

Gladys Evans is a 78-year-old woman, who has been recently widowed. Of Welsh origin, she lives in a council house in a run-down part of a city. She is a frequent visitor to the local health centre, often calling for what appears to be emotional support rather than any physical ailment. You are a social worker based in this health centre, with supervisory responsibility for an unqualified community care officer, who is a very experienced and mature worker. The General Practitioner involved has referred her to you because she believes that she may have unmet social care needs. In addition, as she acknowledges, Gladys takes up a lot of her time to no particular benefit. The only indication of these needs is that Gladys is described as being depressed.

In a spirit of cooperation you accept the referral, aware that Gladys may not meet the social services eligibility criteria. However, you recognise that her over-use of the GP for support is not the most productive arrangement, and suspect that you may be able to provide more effective assistance. Because of the likely level of need, you ask the community care officer, Meg, to undertake the initial assessment.

Practice Scenario 8.2

Meg first sees Gladys at the Health Centre, and is introduced to her by the GP. In the course of the conversation Gladys talks a lot about her recently deceased husband, Emrys. According to Gladys she was fine until he died, which was about 18 months before the meeting. She even says that she had 'never had a day's illness in her life' until his death, and acknowledges that she now often feels below par. Because of the repeated minor ailments, Gladys says that she gets out much less than she used to. Apparently, while Emrys was alive they were out and about a lot, being active members of a local bowls club. She says that if she could only feel physically better she could get her life back on track, but that she simply doesn't feel like doing much at the moment. At the end of the conversation Gladys says that she feels better. Back in the office, Meg checks with you her understanding of what had taken place, expressing the view that Gladys seemed physically OK, but that she also seemed to be 'low' in spirit. You contact the GP, who reiterates that she does not feel that there is ever much physically wrong with Gladys, viewing the symptoms as largely psychosomatic. Given that neither you nor Meg has seen Gladys in her own home, you suggest that Meg pays her a visit to carry out a simple assessment; you indicate to Meg that Gladys might like to consider counselling support, as Emrys's death appears to have generated strong feelings of loss and sadness. You suggest that Meg should take along some leaflets that outline the bereavement counselling service of CRUSE.

On her return from visiting Gladys, Meg confirms that her house is well cared for, and that she does not appear to have any immediate care needs. Gladys acknowledged that she didn't go out much at the moment, stating that she 'didn't feel up to it' most of the time. Meg discussed with Gladys her feelings about being alone, which she accepted had come as a shock to her. Meg reports that Gladys simply said that Emrys was 'her life' and that she doesn't know what to do now that he has gone. Apparently his death was sudden and she had been quite unprepared for it. When Meg asked what support she had received after his death she says that her children – three daughters, who all live locally – have been 'wonderful'. However, Gladys also stated that they no longer want her to talk about Emrys so much, feeling that continually dwelling on him is stopping her from moving on. Meg discussed the possibility of Gladys receiving professional counselling help, and gave her the details of the CRUSE bereavement counselling service. Gladys indicates that she was unaware that such a service existed and that she would 'give it a go'. Meg indicates that she had agreed with Gladys that she would not follow up, but gave her information about how to contact her in future. The assessment documentation was completed and the 'case' was closed. Three months after the meeting Gladys called in to see Meg, looking visibly better. She indicated that she was attending counselling sessions and that they were helping her a great deal. Out of curiosity, you contact the GP and find that Gladys has only been to see her once in the past three months, as opposed to the numerous visits that had taken place before.

Practice Scenario 8.3

A couple of years go by without any contact from Gladys, until she suffers a severe bout of bronchitis in the winter months, which leaves her unable to undertake any physical activity. Again, the GP makes the referral, saying that she was concerned about Gladys' self-care with the infection proving slow to shift. Given that Meg had previously had contact with Gladys, you decide that she should undertake the initial visit to make a preliminary judgement about Gladys' needs and the most appropriate way of meeting them. Given the state of Gladys' health you suggest to Meg that this visit should take some priority; in the meantime, you undertake to make some telephone calls to see if she is currently in receipt of other forms of service. You discover that Gladys has had no ongoing contact with any form of health or social care since the previous contact with Meg. Once again, Meg's responsibilities are to start the assessment process.

On visiting Gladys, Meg discovers that she is confined to bed, and also that one of her daughters, Beth, is in attendance. Gladys does not talk much, but the house appears clean and well cared for. Meg asks Gladys if it would be all right for her to have a chat to Beth to find out what arrangements for support were in place for Gladys. Apparently all three daughters are arranging to spend as much time with Gladys as they can, and have developed an informal rota. Beth is the eldest daughter; she lives alone, following the breakdown of a long-term relationship, and has no other caring commitments. She works full-time in a local supermarket, a job which involves a shifting pattern of work hours, across all seven days in the week. Jenny is the second daughter; she is married with grown children and works part-time for the local council as a community care assistant. Helen is the youngest; she is divorced and is a single parent to two teenage boys, one of whom has learning disabilities. Although they have been able to provide considerable support to Gladys in a variety of ways – Beth does her shopping, Helen prepares and freezes most of her meals, while Jenny ensures that her personal care and hygiene are looked after – Beth says that they have particular problems at two points in the day, first thing in the morning and last thing at night. This is liable to become an increased problem as Gladys improves, as she is likely to need assistance in getting up and preparing for bed. Although the weekends are always covered in this respect, the weekdays have been more difficult due to difficulties with the daughters' shift patterns and family commitments. Beth says that all the family members are feeling 'stressed out' by this problem, as it compounds their anxiety about their mother's condition. As the prognosis from the GP is that the bronchitis should improve with time, any additional assistance that the family require should be of a short duration, and that Gladys should be able to return to being fully self-caring in a short time. With this in mind, you agree with Meg that time-limited domiciliary assistance will be offered to Gladys to assist with her self-care for weekdays only. Meg arranges to visit Gladys again, and has asked if one of the daughters can also be present at the meeting.

When this takes place, Gladys is slightly improved, although still appearing unwell. The offer of assistance is carefully explained, with particular focus on its purpose and likely duration. This is welcomed very readily by both Gladys and Jenny, who had been able to be present at the meeting. It is agreed that such care would be put in place for the following week, and reviewed after three weeks. Gladys and Jenny are quite agreeable to this arrangement. After the meeting, Meg arranges for the care to be supplied by a local provider of home care services in the private sector, stressing the nature of the service, the amount of time to be devoted to each visit – twice daily for 30 minutes a time – and the fact that it will be reviewed after the three-week period. She also negotiates a price for the service, based on the standard fees contractually agreed with home care providers. This will be paid from the budget for which you are responsible. If there are changes in Gladys' condition – either positive or negative – the home care provider is to contact Meg; otherwise the service will be reviewed after three weeks. The family are also asked to contact Meg if they notice any change. The provider is also requested to ensure that Gladys is assisted to perform any self-care tasks herself, if she is capable of so doing, in order not to lose her abilities in this respect.

There having been no reports of any problem or change in the three-week period, Meg convenes the pre-arranged review meeting. Gladys is much better, and was able to get herself in and out of bed with no direct assistance on the final week, with the care assistant simply overseeing her carrying out these tasks. The family – represented by Beth at this meeting – are relieved that their mother's health is improved and now feel much more confident in her safety at those times when one of them cannot be present. As a result, it is decided that the paid assistance will no longer be required. Meg agrees to check on Gladys' progress in a further two weeks, with the understanding that her involvement will cease if the improvement is sustained. This is also agreeable to the family, who are also encouraged to contact Meg if there are any problems. None arise, and – following the agreed visit from Meg – further support is held not to be necessary and Meg withdraws from the situation.

Practice Scenario 8.4

Once again, an extended period of time goes by without further contact with Gladys. This situation changes after approximately 18 months, when Beth comes to see Meg at the health centre. She is quite agitated, saying that her mother has suddenly become forgetful over the last few weeks. She is reported to have forgotten her grandchildren's names, and to have left pans to boil dry on the hob on 'two or three occasions'. Having had most prior contact with the family, you agree that Meg should make the first contact. When she arrives on the visit, Gladys doesn't recognise her – even when reminded, she has no recollection of any past contact with Meg. She is vague about many events of the recent past, and talks about her children as if they were at school. Although the physical condition of the house seems good, Meg is concerned about Gladys' state of mind. She also seems clumsy and her speech is somewhat indistinct.

On her return from the visit, Meg approaches you with her concerns. Her sudden memory loss and forgetfulness is very concerning to both of you. It is clear that Gladys' needs have once again changed markedly, and there is an urgent need to establish a thorough, in-depth assessment, involving specialist information from medical personnel. In your judgement, there is an urgent need to involve medical opinion at this stage – the apparently sudden onset of confusion and memory loss could be the result of a stroke; alternatively, it could derive from an undiagnosed infection. Until a diagnosis is made it will be impossible to plan to meet Gladys' needs. Her prognosis will undoubtedly affect the nature of any subsequent intervention.

Practice Scenario 8.5

Following medical investigation, it appears that Gladys has suffered a series of small strokes, which has caused the relatively uncommon multi-infarct dementia. Although the effects of these strokes on her memory and cognition are irreversible, they are not progressive – her condition will not worsen unless she experiences more strokes, in which case there could be a 'stepwise' deterioration (Briggs, 1993) in her condition. Following receipt of this information, you ask an occupational therapist to contribute to the assessment of Gladys' needs, looking specifically at the range of tasks that Gladys can accomplish on her own at home, as well as those with which she requires additional assistance. It seems that she can manage most tasks of daily living, although needing assistance with some aspects of cooking and cleaning. In terms of her personal care, she is occasionally incontinent of urine, which causes her considerable embarrassment. As a result of the intersection of all of these factors, you feel it is important to convene a family meeting to discuss the implications of Gladys' condition. This will enable you to hear the opinions of all parties, and be able to begin to plan an approach that responds to their concerns and is respectful of their wishes. Due to the potential complexities in Gladys' circumstances you decide that you should carry out this work personally.

At the family meeting, you discover that there has been no further appreciable deterioration in Gladys' condition. She appears to know where she is, and the identities of all of her children. However, her condition is described as being somewhat 'up and down'. Although her daughters are very worried about the overall decline in their mother's condition, the fact that it is not the progressive form of Alzheimer's disease is something of a relief to them. You are able to explain the likely progress of an individual with multi-infarct dementia, and the likelihood that more small strokes can effect a similar decline. Gladys is able to say that she wishes to remain at home for as long as possible; although anxious about their mother's safety, all three daughters indicate that they are prepared to support Gladys in her desire for as long as possible. If they rally round as before, they believe that all of her needs can be catered for without the need for additional paid care. In respect of her incontinence, you ask the district nurse with whom you share an office to pay a visit to provide some advice and guidance, aware that continence advice is one of her specialised areas of practice. As Jenny points out, if there is a decline in Gladys' condition, it will be increasingly difficult for the family to manage. In the light of this, and the likelihood of such deterioration happening at any time, you decide to maintain an active oversight and monitoring of the situation. You specially seek to reassure the family members that you will respond quickly to any change in circumstances.

Aware of the toll that dementia can take on families and carers, you also recognise how important it is for family members to discuss the feelings that each person has about what is happening to Gladys, and to explore the most appropriate means of support for them as carers. For example, there have been numerous developments in supporting people with dementia and their families: various forms of support group have been established (Dröes et al., 2004), with the Alzheimer café concept being a development that is particularly well established in the Netherlands (Miesen and Jones, 2004). The need for appropriate support in such circumstances is important, and it is therefore vital that you are familiar with the range of formal and informal support that may be available in the locality, and are able to discuss with family members what might be most effective for them. As well as being in the best interests of the family themselves, it also provides the best chance that they will be capable of maintaining the appropriate level of care and support for their mother.

Practice Scenario 8.6

Matters proceed relatively unchanged for a few months, with periodic messages from the family that things are 'as well as could be expected'. However, you then receive a visit from Beth to let you know that Gladys has deteriorated rapidly again, with markedly increased levels of confusion, memory loss and failures of cognition. The family are once again very concerned about the turn events have taken, as they are finding it difficult to provide the increasing levels of support that Gladys now requires. Beth is particularly upset by what has occurred, the impact of which has been exacerbated by a number of other events in the family. Beth herself is currently being treated with chemotherapy, following a diagnosis of breast cancer followed by a radical mastectomy. At the same time, Helen's youngest boy, Simon, has been experiencing particular problems at his school, involving allegations of bullying. As a result, the family network of care support is not as strong as it once was. Beth is very emotional and feels that admission to residential care is more or less inevitable, as Gladys can no longer look after herself, even with family support.

You recognise that this is something of a crisis for Gladys and her family, and that Beth's fears may be justified. Once again you need first to gather accurate assessment data concerning Gladys' health – although it could be assumed that this is a further progression in her dementia, the deterioration could have been caused by other physical conditions and may conceivably be reversible. If that were to be the case, it may be possible to construct a care package that continues to maintain Gladys at home, using a greater proportion of paid care to supplement the inability of the family to maintain their own support at the previous high level. To this end you refer Gladys for specialist medical assessment, while undertaking a home visit to observe how Gladys is managing in her own home with the decline in her memory and cognition. You organise the visit for a time when Jenny will be there, in order to receive some corroboration about the extent of Gladys' capabilities. While Gladys seems cheerful enough at the start of your visit, Jenny indicates that her moods have become much more changeable. Gladys does not recognise you or appear to understand the reason for your visit. She is difficult to engage in conversation, appearing to be concentrating on something else. Gradually, from a combination of her and Jenny you gather that her ability to look after herself is compromised. She is routinely incontinent of urine; Jenny says that the most difficult thing for her is that her mother no longer seems bothered about this, having previously seen it as upsetting and humiliating. When engaged in conversation about her social life, Gladys talks a lot about going out and about with Emrys – but refers to this in the present rather than the past tense. Jenny says that Gladys actually no longer exhibits any real interest in social activities. While both Gladys and the house remain well cared for physically, Jenny also indicates that it is very hard to maintain these standards, particularly since her mother is increasingly prone to wandering and distracted behaviour. She also says that she is now very worried about how Gladys is faring during the times when she is alone, during the night-time in particular.

When the medical judgement is given, this confirms the fact that there has been a further step in the progress of her dementia, which cannot be reversed. The medical view is that Gladys now requires 24-hour care. When combined with the evidence of the visit to Gladys, this information confirms the fact that this is a condition of some crisis. Given the full and active involvement of the family in the provision of care, you once again take the view that it is appropriate to convene a family meeting to discuss the best course of action. In calling such a meeting, you are seeking to balance the wishes and desires of all the family members, paying particular regard to Gladys. In addition, if there is both a desire and a possibility to maintain Gladys in her own home, you also have to balance the level of support required by Gladys with the capabilities of the family, supplemented by paid care support. Finally, you have to be aware of the financial cost of any care package, and be able to balance the requirements of Gladys and her family against other calls upon the budget. (One of the key implications of the organisational arrangement suggested earlier in this chapter is the reality that difficult decisions of this nature will have to be taken by social workers, who will need to be aware of the need for an equitable distribution of resources as well as seeking to achieve the best outcomes for service users.)

The family meeting takes place in a heightened emotional atmosphere, with Beth, Helen and Jenny united in the belief that they cannot continue to meet all of their mother's needs. They all say that they feel that she can no longer be left safely, and are very worried when they have to leave her on her own. Gladys seems unable to follow the conversation, and is unable to respond when asked about what she would like to occur. However, she does recognise her daughters' presence, responding to touch and various forms of non-verbal communication. In the light of the medical report, it seems clear that the current situation cannot be sustained. You therefore decide to pursue the alternative options that are open to the family in deciding a future course of action. First, you explore the possibility of Gladys remaining in her own home, supported by substantially increased paid care to supplement the family's efforts. While this would be the preferred option in many ways, not least because the familiarity of her surroundings may assist Gladys, it would inevitably be reliant on a continued high level of practical and personal support from the family. In the light of the changed circumstances of Beth and Jenny in particular they do not believe that it will be possible to maintain this support. None of them are realistically able to live with Gladys; only Beth could conceivably do this, but she also requires a lot of support at the moment due to the effects of the chemotherapy and is not able to consider taking more responsibility for her mother's care by moving to live with her. You discuss the notion of 24-hour paid care, but none of the family is attracted to this option. They all believe that Gladys would be better cared for in a residential home, where she could have access to some degree of social contact as well as trained care. As Gladys meets the eligibility criteria for long-term care, there is no financial obstacle to pursuing this course of action. You explain what the process of choosing a home would entail and identify the sorts of factors that the family might like to consider. Jenny agrees to take the lead in the process of finding a suitable home, having more experience in the care world and more time in which to visit them. You indicate that you will ask Meg to act as liaison with the family in this process to ensure that they have continued advice and guidance to enable them to make the best choice.

Practice Scenario 8.7

On returning to the office you leave a message for Meg asking her to contact you on her return. You indicate that the decision of the family is to seek residential care for Gladys. Although she does not require nursing care, she does need to be placed in an environment which is capable of responding appropriately to her needs, particularly those deriving from her dementia. You also ask Meg to ensure that the process of choosing a home runs smoothly, with the family being provided with information and guidance throughout. This is an activity that Meg has undertaken many times in the past, and she is very familiar with the range of homes available, as well as the particular strengths and limitations of them.

In the organisational framework proposed, decisions regarding which practitioner takes on a particular role such as assisting a service user and her/his family to choose a suitable residential home are highly significant. In this practice scenario, both the social worker and Meg as an unqualified practitioner have been substantially involved at different times, and both are familiar with the issues that have arisen. In this case, a relatively straightforward task is as well carried out by the experienced yet unqualified practitioner as by the qualified social worker. In another scenario a different decision could be taken: the important issue is to reach an informed judgement which should be based on clear reasoning and principles. In this scenario, Meg was very well placed to assist Gladys' family to decide which of the possible residential homes would be most suitable for their mother. Similarly, once a residential place has been secured, Meg would be an appropriate person to maintain contact with Gladys and her family through reviewing processes.

CONCLUSION

This chapter has examined the role of care management in social work with older people, exploring its history, development and potential. While there is considerable critical literature about care management within community care, the chapter has adopted a positive outlook. It has suggested that there are potential ways in which the practice of care management can have a beneficial impact on the lives of service users. It has recognised that this would require that the functions of monitoring and review – integral to the theory of care management, yet sadly neglected in its practice – are given a much more active profile within the policies and practices of agencies.

Underpinning the practice scenario is the belief that social work services are better delivered from settings which are closer to the service user and which enable better working relationships to develop with a range of other professional groups. As evidenced elsewhere (Lymbery and Millward, 2000), there are numerous advantages in locating social workers within primary health settings, which can help to promote the sorts of collaborative working on which effective care management will depend. In addition, the practice scenario is written to illustrate the potential benefits that could accrue from changed organisational arrangements within social services.

In addition, the chapter illustrates how different aspects of social work can be used effectively. For example, the importance of individual work with Gladys and her daughters was evident throughout, with the social worker being able to recognise where there were issues that required more than simply a service-led response. Without the ability to recognise that Gladys' regular attendance at the surgery was being caused by other factors than her health, it is unlikely that she would have been given the necessary support to address her feelings of loss. In addition, there were a number of occasions when a sensitive understanding of the needs of Gladys' daughters was a vital component in an effective response. However, there were also key moments when the speedy introduction of formal care services and resources – the 'administrative' aspects of social work – were a vital part of the care management response. There is also a clear example where a 'collectivist' approach to practice is indicated, when considering the family's support needs. If there are good support networks for carers of people with dementia, it will have been a relatively straightforward task to link the family to them. However, 'collectivist' action would clearly have been indicated if those support networks did not exist: there is a role for the social worker to facilitate their development, drawing on the skills of community development and social action noted in Chapter 2.

CHAPTER SUMMARY

The chapter has engaged with a number of critical issues in care management:

- Its origins in the USA, and its subsequent development in various projects in Britain, many of which were developed and evaluated by the Personal Social Services Research Unit. The chapter suggested that insufficient attention was given to the many issues that affect the transfer of policy from one type of environment to another – in particular, the difference between social welfare in the USA and Britain. The chapter has also observed how a similar process is being set in train in respect of 'chronic disease management'.
- The relationship between care management and social work, specifically pointing out the fact that while social workers were key agents in the early examples of care management, in post-community care versions the professional role of social work has been neglected.
- Building on the insights in the two above themes, the chapter has also sketched out a vision for the development of care management that reasserts the central place of social work as a professional discipline. This entails recognising the distinctive contribution that social workers can make to the continuing care of older people, and developing their supervisory work with social care staff who are themselves not professionally qualified.
- The theoretical and conceptual insights were then brought together through a practice scenario which indicated how a social worker, acting in concert with an unqualified worker as well as members from other professional groups can help to provide a more consistent and coherent management of an individual's care needs, working in conjunction with family members and informal carers.

Intermediate Care: Social Work – the Forgotten Profession?

Intermediate care has made great strides but needs to move on to the next phase in its development if it is to be fully accepted and realise its potential to transform the way in which services are delivered and the experiences of people who receive those services. (DoH, 2002g: 16)

One of the key developments in the delivery of services for older people is the growth of systems of intermediate care, which it is claimed will simultaneously enable more people to maintain their independence and reduce the numbers of people occupying hospital beds (DoH, 2000b, 2001a). While the financial motivation of the government is apparent, the benefits for older people also appear clear-cut. As a result, intermediate care policy could potentially resolve the dilemma that has beset health and social care policy since community care was implemented: how to make financial savings while also providing a service that is welcomed by older people? Although intermediate care services have been developed as a matter of some urgency, this task has been hampered by a lack of evidence concerning the forms of intermediate care that would best help individuals at particular points in their lives. Although the policy has been advanced in a confident manner, there is a crucial gap in its evidence base; this is distinctly ironic, given its introduction in a document that explicitly promoted evidence-based policy and practice (DoH, 2001a). In addition, the development of policy has not been aided by a definitional problem: what exactly *is* intermediate care, and how best should it be organised (Wilson, 2003)? Criticism has also been made of the extent to which the development of intermediate care could encourage the fragmentation of services and hence work against the parallel policy goal of integration (Petch, 2003).

This chapter seeks to explore the rhetoric of intermediate care, drawing on influential government documents that have introduced and refined the policy (DoH, 2000b, 2001a, 2001c, 2002g). It identifies how the policy came into being, moving on to review the different forms of intermediate care that have been developed. Although much practice has been built on the concept of rehabilitation (Robinson and Stevenson, 1999; Mountain, 2001), the relative absence of the discipline of social work from accounts of intermediate care would suggest that a partial view of rehabilitation has been developed, focusing particularly on functional processes that tend to exclude a more socially-based conception. This perspective is substantiated through an examination of the various forms of intermediate care that have been developed. The chapter then argues that social work has a potentially active role to play in the construction of viable systems of intermediate care, focusing particularly on its critical role in seeing an individual in a holistic context, encompassing family, friends and the community. It is suggested that the further development of a specific social work contribution could help to make intermediate care both more acceptable and more successful, in the ways envisaged by the Department of Health (DoH, 2002g). The themes that are outlined in this section are given substance in a practice scenario, indicating the scope of social work involvement in intermediate care.

INTERMEDIATE CARE: THE BIRTH OF A POLICY

As with other elements of community care, there have been strongly resource-driven aspects of intermediate care policy. For example, it was argued that large numbers of older people were being admitted into long-term residential care, nursing home care or hospitals, creating political and practical difficulties in a number of ways. This created pressures on the budgets of the health service (through the use of costly hospital beds) and social services (through unnecessary admissions into long-term residential and nursing home care). The expenditure on these forms of care effectively limited the development of the very schemes that could have helped to reduce the levels of admission, the 'vicious circle' identified in the Audit Commission's seminal document (1997). In addition, it was contrary to the stated policies of successive governments that a greater proportion of older people should be maintained in their own homes.

While there has been a measure of consensus about the nature of the problem to be addressed, there has been little agreement about the best way to respond to it. Indeed, the years immediately preceding the formal adoption of a national policy featured a bewildering array of local developments, as practitioners sought to develop a range of services that could improve the abilities of older people while avoiding or delaying the need for them to enter expensive hospital or institutional care (Wilson, 2003). In essence, these were *ad hoc* developments, created within the context of local services, using minimal resources from a range of different budgetary headings. Many of these early schemes were explicitly based on a concept of rehabilitation, following publication of the Audit Commission's *Coming of Age* (1997). It was felt that effective rehabilitation was the best means to enable older people to return home more rapidly and safely, while also reducing expenditure (Robinson and Turnock, 1998). While there is uncertainty about the precise definition of the term 'rehabilitation' (Mountain, 2001), Nocon and Baldwin (1998) have argued that it has a core of three elements:

- It aims to restore an individual to a previous state.
- It involves some element of purposeful therapeutic activity.
- It can be achieved through a diversity of approaches.

Plant (2002) has suggested that rehabilitation for older people ought to be a core element of all services, rather than a discrete specialist service. However, this is often not the case, perhaps in recognition of the fact that it requires attitudes and skills that are often not present in standard work with older people (Squires, 2002a). Indeed, in some cases workers within intermediate care have been able to recognise how their past practice failed to recognise the potential of older people to benefit from rehabilitative programmes (Hart et al., 2005).

Relatively little is known about the nature and effectiveness of the different approaches that could be used to reduce the need for institutionalisation (Sutherland Report, 1999). On assuming power in 1997, the 'new' Labour government consistently emphasised the theme of rehabilitation for older people in its official publications. For example, this was a central feature of the *Better Services for Vulnerable People* Executive Letter (DoH, 1997b), as well as being a major component of the White Paper *Modernising Social Services* (DoH, 1998a), where the related themes of prevention and rehabilitation were located within the overarching goal of 'Promoting Independence'; as the Green Paper on the future of adult social care indicates, this theme is of continuing significance (DoH, 2005). Because the concept of rehabilitation was central to policy at this time, much literature discussed the role of therapists in its implementation (see, for example, Shield, 1998); by contrast little specifically explored the contribution of social workers (Lymbery, 2003).

By the time of the publication of the *NHS Plan* (DoH, 2000b) there was a shift in focus, with the more general concept of 'intermediate care' being used instead of the specific notion of 'rehabilitation' (Vaughan and Lathlean, 1999). Of particular significance in the *NHS Plan* was the promise of extra resources to facilitate the development of intermediate care: an additional £900 m for various forms of such care was to be made available by 2003/04. Soon thereafter, the Department of Health issued a circular defining both the nature and scope of intermediate care services (DoH, 2001c), which specified that to be labelled 'intermediate care', services had to meet each of the following five criteria:

1   They must be targeted at those people who would otherwise face either unnecessarily prolonged hospital stays, or inappropriate admission to acute hospital in-patient care, or long-term residential or nursing home care, or continuing NHS in-patient care.
2   They must be provided on the basis of a comprehensive assessment, the outcome of which being a structured individual care plan that would involve active therapy, treatment or opportunity for recovery.
3   They would have a planned outcome of maximising independence, which would – in most circumstances – enable people to resume living at home.
4   They would be time-limited, normally lasting for no longer than six weeks, and frequently being for shorter periods of one to two weeks.
5   They must also involve cross-professional working, including a single assessment framework, single professional records and shared protocols between health and social care agencies. (DoH, 2001c: 6)

The circular also stressed the need for intermediate care to be placed within a continuum of other services, including health promotion, preventive services, community health and social care services, hospital care and support for carers (see also Plant, 2002). It insisted that there should be a clear distinction between intermediate care and other services that fulfil similar functions – other forms of transitional care that 'do not involve active therapy or other interventions to maximise independence' (DoH, 2001c: 6), longer term rehabilitation services or rehabilitation that is part of ordinary acute hospital care.

The circular also outlined the various models that could be developed in line with the criteria specified. These included the following types of service:

* *Rapid response*: services designed to avoid acute admissions by providing 24-hour access to short-term support in the service user's own home.
* *'Hospital at home'*: intensive medical support (in excess of what would normally be available in primary care) provided within the person's own home, as a means of avoiding hospital admission or facilitating early discharge from hospital.
* *Residential rehabilitation*: a short-term period of time in a residential setting, with therapeutic support to enable people to return home safely thereafter. Again, this could either be used to facilitate speedy and safe discharge from hospital or to prevent long-term hospital or other institutional care.
* *Supported discharge*: a short-term period of nursing and/or therapeutic support in a patient's home, to enable safe early discharge from hospital.
* *Day rehabilitation*: a short-term period of therapeutic support provided at a day hospital or day centre. (DoH, 2001c: 7–8)

Successful intermediate care would be dependent upon the establishment of excellent collaborative working between health and social services (see also Squires, 2002a), with the circular noting the potentially vital role of the independent sector.

It was apparent that the establishment of intermediate care services was to be a major priority in work with older people, an impression which was confirmed when intermediate care became one of the four themes of the *National Service Framework for Older People* (DoH, 2001a), as well as one of the eight standards against which progress would be measured. While repeating much of the detail that was introduced in the earlier circular (DoH, 2001c), the *National Service Framework* also clarified some aspects of the development of intermediate care, notably through its definition of the points on the care pathway on which such services should focus. These were defined as follows:

- responding to or averting a crisis
- active rehabilitation following an acute hospital stay
- where long-term care is being considered (DoH, 2001a: 44).

Recognising the strategic importance of intermediate care, the Department of Health issued another significant document to support the implementation process (DoH, 2002g). This recognised that intermediate care would necessarily entail many changes to patterns of service and to the relationships between service providers. In noting that there had been relatively little progress in the development of intermediate care in many places – caused by inconsistency, fragmentation, lack of coherence between services, and poor integration between organisations and services (DoH, 2002g) – the document insisted that further progress was needed to ensure that intermediate care produced genuine benefits for service users. In that spirit, one of its key purposes was to offer additional information through which services could be improved, particularly through the publication of a number of 'good practice examples' (DoH, 2002g: 17–24). These reflected the diverse nature of intermediate care, as many of the projects described had been developed before the policy had become formalised.

The *Moving Forward* document reiterated the four guiding principles that should underpin the entire *National Service Framework*, including intermediate care. These are defined as follows:

- *Person-centred care*: the need to ensure that older people are treated as individuals, on the basis of their needs, circumstances and priorities.
- *Whole system working*: the development of 'an inclusive approach that recognises the contribution of all partners in the local system' (DoH, 2002g: 7), which requires the effective integration of services, and is dependent upon the establishment of a single process for assessing needs and sharing information.

- *Timely access to specialist care*: the need to ensure that older people have appropriate access to specialist care, and that intermediate care is not used as a mechanism to deny older people such care (which had been one of the criticisms of Grimley Evans and Tallis, 2001).
- *Promoting health and active life*: the principle that intermediate care should contribute to this end. (DoH, 2002g: 7–8)

It also identified specific areas where further progress would be particularly needed; these included working with older people with mental health needs, and the link between intermediate care and housing.

More critical observations were contained in the House of Commons Health Committee Report (2002), which expressed concern about a number of issues, including continuing lack of clarity about what 'intermediate care' is (see also Wilson, 2003), the difficulty of achieving a strategically focused and integrated care system, the failure to identify people who would be appropriate for each scheme, the tendency to 're-badge' existing services as intermediate care rather than develop new services and the use of government guidance as prescriptive when it had not been intended as such – particularly in relation to the six-week timescales (see also Glasby and Littlechild, 2004). Underlying these criticisms is the continuing difficulty of establishing collaborative systems of working (to which this book has made repeated reference) even though it is acknowledged that effective intermediate care is only possible if excellent systems of collaboration are in place (Squires, 2002a). However, it should be acknowledged that health and social services organisations were required to develop intermediate care substantially in advance of any robust research evidence concerning its effectiveness. In the light of this, the following section examines the evidence base for intermediate care.

SECTION SUMMARY

This section has examined the genesis of policy around intermediate care, with particular reference to the following:

- The perception that successful intermediate care could save money from both health and social care budgets.
- The dominance of the concept of 'rehabilitation' in early government discussions about intermediate care.
- The different types of intermediate care that could be developed.
- The generally patchy and reactive pattern of intermediate care services across the country.
- A number of practical and conceptual problems with its development.

FORMS OF INTERMEDIATE CARE:
THE RESEARCH EVIDENCE

Service development in intermediate care has been uneven across the country (DoH, 2002g; Mountain, 2001; Wilson, 2003). Broadly speaking, there are three main different locations of intermediate care service, each containing numerous sub-divisions. These are as follows:

1   Hospital-based, including day and community hospitals.
2   In residential or nursing care homes.
3   In the community, including hospital-at-home schemes.

As noted above, developments have been localised, often building on projects instigated before the full implementation of intermediate care policies. As with the single assessment process, there has been no blueprint for intermediate care, although government guidance does stress the fact that there are a number of key factors that underpin the most successful projects (DoH, 2002g).

In addition, the quality of research evidence regarding the effectiveness of various forms of intervention is relatively weak (Parker et al., 2000). In reality, many schemes have been developed in advance of robust research evidence concerning their effectiveness. This was acknowledged in *Intermediate Care: Moving Forward* (DoH, 2002g), which contained an appendix reviewing the research evidence that was available at the point of production. In line with the *National Service Framework for Older People* (DoH, 2001a) this review gave particular credence to large scale randomised controlled trials, paying little attention to the plethora of other forms of research evidence that had been generated. While this is understandable given that much of the early research evidence focused on self-reported projects and schemes, which were unsurprisingly deemed to be highly successful (Wilson, 2003), it has limited the type of research data that has been collected. The evidence therefore appears to contain some glaring flaws:

- It has failed to engage with the national policy context within which the research takes place, including the political pressure on health and social care providers to develop *something* that they can label as intermediate care.
- In focusing on the outcomes of the intervention process, randomised controlled trials do not typically generate much understanding of the local context within which they take place. Therefore, even if a service is deemed to be effective, there is little chance of it being capable of replication.

- It fails to encompass the views of older people, which is a critical failure when the policy seeks to work from a basis of 'person-centred care'.
- It also does not take into account the perceptions of those staff who operate the service, therefore ignoring their insights and expertise. A particular absence in this respect is any consideration of the social work role in intermediate care.

A recently concluded research project sought to improve the quality of research evidence relating to residential forms of intermediate care, containing both a randomised controlled trial and an ethnographic study within the research design (Fleming et al., 2004; Hart et al., 2005). While this produced interesting but inconclusive evidence, its main contribution to learning may well be methodological – as a demonstration of the way in which different approaches to research may be deployed to achieve a much greater depth of understanding (Hart et al., in press). A particular problem with such an approach is to ensure parity of esteem and value to all aspects of the study – which is difficult, given the dominant position of quantitative methods (including randomised controlled trials) in the hierarchy of research evidence (DoH, 2001a). It is cited here as an example of an approach to research that could avoid the pitfalls of an entirely quantitative approach, cited above.

The randomised controlled trial (RCT) used a number of measures as the proxies for success. However, it found that the intermediate care programme had no measurable impact upon survival, rates of admission to long-term residential or nursing home care, or the proportion continuing to live at home. In addition, there was no significant impact of allocation to the scheme on an individual's ability to undertake activities of daily living. The scheme did succeed in diverting people from inpatient hospital settings, but this was at the expense of a longer stay in the intermediate care unit (Fleming et al., 2004). By contrast, the ethnographic study identified differences in the practical organisation of the intermediate care scheme in the six settings. It also identified a strong belief in the success of the project amongst staff working within it, alongside a more varied range of perspectives from users of the service. From the perceptions of rehabilitation staff a more positive view emerged regarding the potential of older people to benefit from rehabilitation. However, it also concluded that the concept of 'rehabilitation' was becoming replaced by older people's 'adaptation' to the norms and routines of the unit (Hart et al., 2005).

Putting the two forms of knowledge together enables a more nuanced view of the project than could be achieved from either part of the study alone. The randomised controlled trial was able to show that many of the anticipated benefits of the scheme did not materialise. The project succeeded more in terms of facilitating early discharge from hospital than in enabling improvements to the physical or psychological health of service users, its original intention. The ethnographic study identified the strong belief of many staff in the success of the project, even though this success appeared not to be justified by the data generated by the RCT. It also enabled a better understanding of the context within which the research took place, as well as allowing the voices to be heard of people who feature relatively little in the published literature – that of older people themselves and of care staff. The combination of methodological approaches therefore created a more useful set of data, although the practicalities of creating a project in which different research approaches are accorded equal validity was challenging (Hart et al., in press).

As yet, there is little understanding of the nature of the disciplinary roles to be undertaken within intermediate care teams: for the purposes of this book, the lack of clarity concerning social work is of particular concern. For example, while Nancarrow (2004) has examined role boundaries within intermediate care, her research sample only included one social worker, whose role did not feature significantly in the outcomes reported. In general terms, Nancarrow (2004) did report that there had been a blurring of boundaries between occupational therapists and physiotherapists, with nurses having a more clearly defined, medically oriented role. However, the specific contribution of the social worker to intermediate care teams remains relatively little explored in the literature (Lymbery, 2003). Indeed, there is concern that their potential contribution to intermediate care could become marginalised (Manthorpe, 2002). It is to this topic that the chapter now turns.

SECTION SUMMARY

This section has reviewed the research evidence around intermediate care, concluding that:

- There is a relative dearth of good quality research evidence that attests to the success of intermediate care.
- In official documents, there is an explicit preference for hard, quantitative data of the sort provided by randomised controlled trials.
- By contrast, most of the small-scale projects that have been evaluated have relied on more qualitative data.
- Effective evaluation needs to combine both forms of research approach, as was demonstrated using the example of a project that sought to combine a randomised controlled trial with an ethnographic study.

SOCIAL WORK AND INTERMEDIATE CARE: AN OCCUPATION MARKED BY ITS ABSENCE?

The early examples of intermediate care that feature in the literature do not focus on the social work role to any great extent, despite the fact that social workers are seen as a crucial occupational group in the *National Service Framework* (DoH, 2001a). Where disciplinary roles are identified they are usually of occupational therapists or physiotherapists (see, for example, Nancarrow, 2004; Shield, 1998), perhaps reflecting the fact that the concept of rehabilitation – generally seen as the province of therapists – has been dominant in the development of policy, as noted in an earlier section. Indeed, the term 'rehabilitation' is not widely used within social work circles (Manthorpe, 2002). However, there are aspects of intermediate care where the social worker has a potentially pivotal role to play. As Squires (2002b) has pointed out, social workers are more familiar at working within an anti-ageist and person-centred focus, even if a lack of resources has hampered their efforts in this area. It is the purpose of this section to sketch out the various roles that a social worker can productively fulfil within intermediate care teams, irrespective of location. Although there are various potential locations for intermediate care teams, the tasks that need to be undertaken are broadly similar. Therefore, the roles of social workers within intermediate care are transferable between settings.

The social worker's contribution to intermediate care can be located in a number of different areas of activity, all drawing on the core capabilities of social work, as outlined in previous chapters. Manthorpe (2002) has defined the range of skills and experience that social workers can bring to intermediate care:

- Independence of thought from hospital and general health systems.
- The ability to represent older people's points of view, and to advocate on their behalf.
- The capacity to manage tensions within social relationships.
- Managing complex packages of support, particularly those that involve the independent sector.
- Working with carers.
- Managing risk.

In essence, the social work role can therefore be found on the boundaries between an individual and her/his social world, in a space that is inhabited by no other professional. The first of the distinctive contributions of social work has been heralded in Chapter 7, and relates to the initial assessment of need. As this is the key to successful services, a good quality assessment must consist of much more than simply a mechanical process that measures a person's eligibility for services. Such a 'procedural' (Smale et al., 1993) approach would not uncover the range of issues that need to be addressed within intermediate care. Similarly, it must not only address an individual's functional capacity to benefit from intermediate care services. While other members of an intermediate care team – physiotherapists, occupational therapists, nurses and doctors – all have significant contributions to this process, a number of factors which fall within the domain of social work's expertise must also be addressed, as the following examples illustrate:

- It is vital to determine the attitude of the older person to rehabilitation and the prospect of regaining her/his independence, as this is a key determinant of success. Some older people are physically capable of rehabilitation, but do not have the desire or the confidence to engage in rehabilitative processes.
- The external circumstances of individuals must also be explored, as these will have a major effect on people's willingness to engage in the processes of intermediate care. This includes gathering a sense of the concerns of carers and other family members, and the impact of these on the individual, as well as wider issues such as finance and housing (Lymbery, 2003).
- From this, it is important to balance the needs and wishes of individuals, including their potential to benefit from a period of intermediate care and their attitude to it, with the concerns of wider family and other networks. A commitment to meeting the needs of the individual service user does not preclude full consideration of the issues that carers and family members might have.

If intermediate care is to be successful, the initial assessment must not be seen as predominantly functional in nature; other social and psychological factors are of equal importance (Dinagly and Baillie, 2002). If these issues are not addressed in the assessment process, factors that may be critical to the success or failure of the intervention could be ignored.

Similarly, there are defined roles and tasks during the process of intermediate care that call for the involvement of social workers; these relate to the processes of care management, discussed in Chapter 8. As before, the critical role of social work is in continuing to hold in balance the needs and wishes of individuals and their families. Many issues may occur during the process of intermediate care that require social work skills, deriving from each of the 'individualist-therapeutic', 'administrative' and 'collectivist' traditions. At the 'individualist-therapeutic' level, for example, the decline of an individual's capabilities may be related to psychological factors – possibly deriving from depression, anxiety, loss and bereavement, memory impairment, etc. (Dinagly and Baillie, 2002) – as well as to organic physical changes. A social worker would need to recognise what these factors might be, and ensure that any psychological issues are addressed through the intermediate care programme. Indeed, since many of these psychological factors are associated with social factors such as poor health and poverty (Dinagly and Baillie, 2002) a social worker may be particularly well placed to identify whether they are likely to be in existence. In addition, a person's attitude towards intermediate care will be affected by the concerns of her/his close family, who may have a desire to accentuate the need for 'safety' and hence be unwilling to allow for the element of 'risk' that is inherent within the process of rehabilitation. The motivation of an older person will be materially affected by these sorts of issue (Dinagly and Baillie, 2002), and it may be that the social worker is best placed within the intermediate care team to help the older person and her/his family to manage these tensions. Following discharge, there will be a continued role in ensuring that any family concerns are addressed so that they do not destabilise the independence of the older person. Finally, the social worker will need to ensure that the older person's morale and confidence remain high once s/he has returned to a more independent life, paying due attention to what that person perceives about her or his own situation.

Physical decline may also have been affected by a degree of social isolation, with the older person having less contact than before with family, friends, neighbours and the wider community. Here skills deriving from social work's 'collectivist' tradition can be useful, with a social worker drawing on – and promoting – community-based resources that might enable the older person to re-create a wider social involvement, which might in turn help to maintain any physical improvements that the intermediate care programme has generated. At the 'administrative' level, there are continuing tasks to be accomplished on and after the point of discharge from intermediate care programmes. It is likely that systems of formal and informal care arrangements will need to be put in place, and effectively monitored and reviewed, in order to maintain the person independently; this is a core task of care management, drawing on a social worker's specific skills and abilities (Manthorpe, 2002).

Ideally, as the above summary indicates, the work of the social worker in relation to intermediate care would not be the short-term task-focused work that has characterised much community care (Lymbery, 1998a; Postle, 2002). The issues to be resolved – helping an older person come to terms with changed circumstances, enabling an older person's family to adjust to these changes, supporting the older person and the family following discharge – require in-depth work. While it may be of relatively short duration, it would be of a level of intensity that is uncommon in contemporary practice. In addition, older people's needs will change and it is crucial that these changes are captured through effective processes of monitoring and review, elements that have not featured strongly in much care management practice (see Chapter 8).

SECTION SUMMARY

This section has explored the potential contribution of social workers to intermediate care, with particular reference to the following:

- The specific skills and values that are unique to social workers, drawing on Manthorpe (2002).
- The fact that a social worker is unique in working on the boundaries between an individual and her/his social world.
- The ability of a social worker to work with an older person's attitudes to intermediate care, their external circumstances, and in accordance with the wishes of her/himself and other family members is critical.
- The need to recognise that much of this work requires a longer-term involvement of practitioners than has hitherto been the case.
- The application of elements of social work's 'individualist-therapeutic', 'collectivist' and 'administrative' traditions to the circumstances of intermediate care.

PRACTICE SCENARIO – INTERMEDIATE CARE

Because intermediate care is – by definition – a time limited intervention, the possible social work roles are illustrated through a practice scenario that encompasses both residential and community intermediate care. In the first part of the scenario the service user – Delia Blackmore – is living within a residential setting, following a discharge from hospital. In the latter stages of the scenario, she is provided with intermediate care services within her own home. Although, as noted earlier in this chapter, the social work skills required to practise successfully in these sorts of settings can readily be transferred to other intermediate care environments, it is helpful to have concrete examples of diverse sorts of environment for illustrative purpose, as they highlight different issues for practice.

Practice Scenario 9.1

As a social worker, you first become aware of Delia's circumstances when she is accepted onto the residential intermediate care programme, following an extended stay in hospital. She was originally admitted after a fall had left her with a broken hip. While in hospital, she contracted a sequence of infections which prolonged her stay. One of them was sufficiently serious as to leave her on the verge of death. By the time of discharge, Delia had been in hospital for over six months. When people enter the residential intermediate care programme, your role is to ensure that their family and home circumstances will be capable of supporting independent living; the issues of functional rehabilitation are the primary responsibility of occupational therapists and physiotherapists. At the point of referral, very little is communicated to you about her family and home circumstances.

As with all social work intervention, irrespective of location and overarching purpose, the first task is to undertake a thorough assessment of the service user's needs (see Chapter 7). However, you are aware that an assessment would already have taken place prior to admission to the intermediate care programme, so your first source of information will be through gaining access to prior assessment documentation. Through this you discover Delia's date of birth (25 September 1927), the fact that she is single and that her home address indicates that she probably inhabits an owner-occupied house. She has no surviving close relatives: she was the youngest of three children, and her two older brothers died many years previously. Her health prior to the hospital admission was described as generally good; she had seen her GP infrequently, always for 'genuine' reasons. Little is recorded about her past life, her current interests and life-style, and her range of social contacts.

As noted earlier in this chapter, there is a clear danger that functionally dominated approaches to intermediate care could ignore a number of more internal and social aspects. From the existing information, it is possible to hypothesise at an early stage that the following issues would need to be explored. First, not much is known about Delia's personality and the possible effects of this on her recovery of physical and functional abilities. Secondly, there is little information about her social life and the possible range of social support that she may receive. Thirdly, nothing is known about her housing, its suitability and safety. In the absence of this vital detail, any plan that aims to enable her to live independently is likely to be flawed – perhaps fatally so. In the light of this, your first priority is to gain information about all of these issues.

It is perhaps self-evident that your first source of information will be Delia herself, but you are aware that she will be receiving a lot of attention during the course of the intermediate care programme and that you need to dovetail your work with that of other colleagues in the team. Given that it is intended that an individual's stay in the residential settings should be time-limited – six weeks being the notional duration of the programme, in line with government guidance (DoH, 2001c) – you recognise that some of these issues need to be resolved as a matter of urgency. However, you are also aware that you are more likely to obtain better and more usable information if you spend time getting to know Delia and work at her pace. One of the practical advantages of a residential home as a base for this work is the fact that the office accommodation for the intermediate care team has been created in the home, using what had been originally intended as a staff flat. Therefore, you can have more regular and ready access to Delia, to allow the relationship between you to develop gradually. It is decided that an occupational therapist will introduce you to Delia, building on the fact that she has had considerable contact with her, both before and after her admission.

Practice Scenario 9.2

When you first meet Delia, your initial impression is how small and frail she is. However, when you talk to her it is also clear that she is articulate and well able to express herself. She is happy to talk about her past life and her experiences before entering hospital, but is more reticent about discussing her current situation. Despite the fact that there is some pressure on you to gather usable information about Delia's circumstances, you take a conscious decision not to push at this stage, but to ensure that you are able to spend more time with her seeking to gain a measure of trust. You do find out that Delia is very worried about the condition of her house, as she has not been able to see it for many months. You suggest that you would be happy to visit and to check its condition, if that would be acceptable to her. Delia is very grateful for this offer, and immediately seems to relax a little in your company. After conversing on a general level for a while longer, you indicate that you would be able to visit her house in the next day or so and that you will report back on its condition to Delia as soon as you can thereafter.

On the visit to Delia's house you observe that it has not been maintained well over recent months. The garden has become dishevelled, although somebody has recently cut the grass. The outside of the house itself looks in good shape, and there have apparently been no break-ins – you had been concerned about this due to the vulnerability of an empty house to burglary. It is a substantial two-storey detached house, set in large gardens, which looks approximately one hundred years old. When you go inside, the impression of size is confirmed: there are four bedrooms, two reception rooms, a kitchen and conservatory. There is a large bathroom on the first floor, and a small toilet/cloakroom on the ground floor. The house is well furnished: although the furniture appears quite old it is of good quality. The carpets and rugs are showing signs of wear; the house is rather dirty and in need of a general clean-up.

Practice Scenario 9.3

On the following day you make a point of calling in to see Delia to tell her that her house is fine, and to ask if she would be agreeable to you organising cleaning for it because it has been empty for so long. Delia is very pleased with your news and delighted that you are willing to arrange to clean it for her. You comment on what a beautiful house it is, which is the trigger for a lengthy reminiscence about the place of the house in her life. It turns out that her parents were wealthy people, with her father having inherited a thriving textile factory from his own father. In fact, she has lived in the house all her life; it was built for her grandfather, and has passed down the generations. She and her older brothers were all born in the house; the oldest died as an infant, whereas the second son died in the Second World War. After this, Delia herself fell in love with one of her brother's fellow soldiers, and they became engaged to be married. However, he apparently died in the Korean War and she never married thereafter. Her father continued to run his business, but it became gradually less profitable and he sold up in the mid-1960s. Delia continued to live with her parents and looked after both of them during lengthy spells of ill-health before they died during the 1980s. During this time, much of the family's wealth was used up and Delia says that she thinks she doesn't own anything much of value except the house. When you ask if she had ever thought of moving to somewhere more convenient and easier to manage Delia becomes misty-eyed and says that she simply couldn't see herself living anywhere else. She also asks when she can go back home – only having been in the residential establishment for six days of the projected six weeks.

This discussion gives you a clear sense of the psychological and symbolic importance of 'home' to Delia, a potentially critical factor in the therapeutic process. She appears to have a strong motivation to return home, but there is an immediate problem with this idea; the occupational therapist indicates that she has lost many of her functional abilities, probably due to the extended stay in hospital. Although she may be able to regain them, a speedy return home carries with it numerous risks, with which the occupational therapist is presently uncomfortable. Against this, you recognise that her motivation to improve may be directly linked to the prospects of an imminent return home. In discussion with your team colleagues, it is agreed that you should have further discussions with Delia about how she sees the intermediate care process, and what she most desires as its outcome. In addition, you suggest that you will also address the social support to which she might have access, given that there has been very little mention of Delia having any sort of a social life.

Practice Scenario 9.4

When you next meet Delia the first thing she asks about is when she will be 'allowed' to return home. She says that now she is feeling better she longs to return home, and that the thought of not returning makes her very depressed. You discuss with her the team's concerns about her loss of functional abilities and the risks that she would have in trying to manage such a big house, even with assistance. Delia is able to understand these concerns, but she also emphasises that she would be happy to accept these risks because 'it's my life and I should be able to do what I want to do'. She also informs you that she agreed to enter the intermediate care programme because she saw this as the best way to ensure a speedy return home. Having clarified Delia's wishes as far as returning home is concerned, you then discuss the importance of minimising the risks of living independently, explaining that the basic purpose of the programme is to enable her to regain skills and abilities that may have been lost. You also explain that were she to fall and break a bone in her leg or hip she would probably have to experience another lengthy stay in hospital. While Delia accepts the reality of this, she again points out that she would prefer to return to her own home as soon as possible. You then talk about what sort of social contact she would expect to have while living at home. She says that much of her social activity revolves around the local church. She had been a churchwarden for many years, as well as a member of the church choir. She has received numerous visits from the vicar while in hospital and says that there is a wide network of friends to which she has access through church circles. Delia is unsure what if any personal care support she could expect from these sources. You ask how she would respond to the presence of paid carers in her life, possibly for a short time period, to support her in undertaking the practicalities of her life. She indicates that this would not be a problem for her – indeed, if the presence of such helpers enabled her to return home more quickly she would be much in favour. You ask permission to contact her vicar to discuss what if any personal support could be provided from within the church community: this is readily granted.

From this discussion, a number of specific issues and problems can be identified. For example, it confirmed that Delia's desire to return home is indeed very strong; in fact, you are concerned that she may deteriorate psychologically if there is no timetable to effect the return. This may be sooner than might ideally be indicated from a purely functional perspective. Indeed, she clearly stated that she would prefer to return home and live with the level of risk that this would involve. In addition, it would appear that she would return to an active and familiar social life. The degree of informal care support that her social contacts might generate is an issue that remains to be resolved.

At this stage, the key issue is the balance between Delia's urgent desire to return home and the risks that would inevitably attend an early discharge from the intermediate care programme. While the social worker's role at this juncture is to argue for the wishes and desires of the service user, it would be an inadequate and incomplete response to do this without also considering ways in which the risk factors could be minimised. In this respect, it may be more appropriate for Delia to receive intermediate care provision within her own home rather than the residential setting. However, an organisational problem attends such a transfer; community-based intermediate care in this local authority is provided by a separate team, with its own referral and admissions criteria.

Three specific tasks are identified:

- You need to discuss within your own team the impact that Delia's wishes might have on the current intermediate care programme. Given that she remains adamant that an early return home is of paramount importance for her, there is an obvious concern that the success of the programme could become compromised by her reaction if a return home is delayed.
- If it is agreed that a transfer to the community intermediate care team is the best way forward, contact is then urgently needed with this team to discuss the possibility of Delia being discharged home and then receiving support from them.
- At the same time, it is vital to ensure that contact is made with the church community to investigate the extent of social support that might be forthcoming from this quarter.

One of the organisational dynamics that is illustrated by this scenario is the separation that often exists between similar types of service. Due to the piecemeal development of intermediate care, different projects often co-exist within the same geographical locality, providing various types of intermediate care response. This helps to perpetuate boundaries that can work against the interests of service users. As a result, the sensitive management of boundary issues is an important role for all professional groups, including social workers, as Chapters 4 and 5 have discussed.

In terms of the three tasks identified, the first requires considerable discussion within the staff group. While the therapist members of the team indicate that Delia is making progress, they describe this as being relatively slow, and express concerns that she is not ready to return home at this stage in the process. Against this, you note that her overwhelming desire is to return home and that her primary motivation in consenting to the programme was the belief that it would accelerate her homecoming. You argue that any delay could have serious conse-quences for her state of mind, which could compromise her recovery, and that she could at any point simply go home, irrespective of the levels of support avail-able. It is suggested that, in the light of the additional information that you have uncovered, it might have been more appropriate for Delia to have been referred to the community intermediate care team in the first place, even though dis-charges from hospital are customarily managed by the residential team. It is therefore agreed that seeking to negotiate a transfer of responsibility would be in Delia's best interests. Having reached agreement as far as this is concerned, the second action point becomes live. The team manager agrees to contact her coun-terpart in the community team to facilitate this process and all the separate pro-fessionals agree to discuss Delia's progress with the relevant member of the community team if the transfer is agreed. On the third point, it is agreed that you should continue to explore the level of informal care support that might be expected.

With this in mind, you arrange to meet the vicar to identify the nature and extent of this support. At the meeting, the vicar indicates that Delia has been a member of the congregation for many years, since long before his time as min-ister. He describes her as being a very gentle person, but also somebody who knows her own mind. The lengthy illnesses of both her parents occurred not long after he was appointed to the parish; it was during this period that he first came to know Delia well, as he provided considerable 'spiritual guidance' to her and her parents during this period. He says that he thinks that members of the con-gregation will 'rally round', ensuring that Delia is not socially isolated from the community. You specifically raise the team's concerns about the risks to which Delia may be prone at home, and your desire to reduce their impact as much as possible. You suggest that one of the key things that can help in this respect would be ensuring that Delia has continued social contact with a wide range of people. While she will be provided with ongoing support from paid carers when she returns home, in addition to being equipped with an alarm system if she falls, the maintenance of regular social contact will reduce the periods when she is alone, which are the most likely times for falls to occur. In addition, you indicate that such contact is likely to be good for her morale, ensuring that her life con-tinues to have a sense of purpose. The vicar readily agrees to ensure that Delia is provided with as much social contact as she desires.

The process of enabling Delia's transfer to the community intermediate care team takes place without problem or delay. You discuss the progress of the social work issues with your colleague based in this team, with whom you have had considerable prior contact. Given that you have explored many of these issues in some depth and have developed a rapport with Delia, you agree that it is most appropriate for you to see the work through to its conclusion. You are aware that there will be a change in respect of the occupational therapist and physiotherapist involved, due to the pressure of other work. Some degree of continuity of social work is therefore helpful. With this in mind, you agree to discuss the proposed changes with Delia and to manage the transfer of responsibility to the community team, as you will be a consistent presence in the support that Delia receives once at home. It is agreed that you will be able to work towards a planned discharge in a week's time, allowing staff in the community intermediate care team to undertake a gradual assessment of Delia within her home environment on planned preparatory visits. At the same time, this provides an opportunity for you to ensure that the proper levels of both formal and informal care support are in place.

Practice Scenario 9.5

As soon as possible after the key decisions have been made, you visit Delia to inform her of the plans that have been drawn up. She is delighted to have a firm date to return home, and indicates that she is perfectly happy for the preparation for this to take place over the next week. You indicate to her that it will be important to ensure that she has considerable support in place to ensure that she is able to manage living independently. You suggest that she will be given exercise programmes to follow, and that you plan for her to receive assistance from formal services for a time-limited period, if she is prepared to accept them. She indicates that she is happy to have any assistance if that will ensure that she is able to remain at home. You inform Delia that these services will be free of charge for a defined period, but will attract a charge thereafter; although services defined as 'intermediate care' are provided free of charge, 'standard' home care is defined as chargeable. According to agency policy, intermediate care services can only be defined as such for a short period (normally six weeks) for charging purposes. Delia is a little anxious about this, as she says that she doesn't have 'a lot of spare cash' and relies on her pension to support herself from week to week. You reassure her that she would only be liable for the minimum charge in that case, and that this could well be more than offset by additional benefits to which you believe she is entitled. You offer to assist her in the completion of application forms for these benefits, an offer that she is pleased to accept. You also indicate that the care support that is envisaged will be aimed to support her to carry out tasks, rather than do them on her behalf; in this way it will be similar to the work that care staff have been engaged in with Delia in the residential home. Delia says that she understand this, and is able to make a joke of how it feels to be 'bullied' at her age.

While the therapists from the community intermediate care team focus on the functional aspects of Delia's return home, in particular the programmes that will assist her functional rehabilitation, you then focus on ensuring that the formal care services will work to support these efforts. This means having to commission specific care support, avoiding the common problem that home care services are inclined to *do for* as opposed to *do with*. You have to be clear in your instructions about what is required and the way in which it is carried out. Although the local authority has only retained a relatively small home care service, it specialises in the various elements of intermediate care; you are therefore authorised to approach this service without first contacting any of the independent sector service providers, which tend to supply a more generalised response. In discussions with the home care manager you clarify the roles that home care staff should carry out and the times when their assistance will be particularly useful, and are able to conclude an outline contract that you then write up and copy to the manager. You agree that the specific details of this will be concluded following the completed occupational therapy assessment, and that you will arrange a meeting where these tasks can be more fully explained. In addition, you contact the vicar once again to let him know when Delia is to be discharged home. You are careful to describe the sorts of formal support that will be provided, and the purpose of this support. You acknowledge that many people will want to 'help' Delia by doing various household activities on her behalf, but also point out that this could well negate some of the work carried out by formal carers. The vicar understands the desire to ensure that Delia's social contacts do not unwittingly undermine her rehabilitation. He promises to talk to the people who are most likely to have continued social contact with Delia on her return home. In this way you have sought to ensure that you have addressed both the formal and informal dimensions of the care support that Delia will need at home. The final task that you undertake is to ensure that the personal alarm system will be available when Delia is actually discharged; you are assured that this will be completed.

Practice Scenario 9.6

In the week before discharge, Delia has three home visits. On two occasions she is accompanied only by an occupational therapist, who wishes to observe how Delia can manage various functional tasks in the home environment, and thereby establish what aids Delia requires to assist her in these tasks. On the third and final occasion, you accompany Delia and the occupational therapist, and arrange for the home care manager to meet you at Delia's house to ensure that the range of support needs can be clearly established in advance

> *(Continued)*
>
> of Delia's return home, on the basis that it is vital to ensure that all parties are aware of the overall rehabilitation plan. Having made all the preparatory arrangements, you transport Delia home on the day of discharge. After a brief period of acclimatisation, you leave Delia happily back in her own home. You ensure that she has your contact details should there be problems with the care package that will be supporting her, and make an arrangement to visit the following week to see how she is getting on.

Having had no calls from Delia or the home care manager you visit her as planned, to find that nothing untoward has happened in the past week. Delia looks much happier and says that she is managing well with all the help. She also says that she is rarely on her own for long, as friends from church regularly visit her and take her out on local trips. She says that the carers who work with her are 'lovely' and that she is gradually recovering her abilities. She even suggests that she may be able to do without their help 'soon'. After the meeting, you contact the occupational therapist who is providing ongoing support from the community intermediate care team to check whether her assessment is in accordance with Delia's positive comments. She says that there have been improvements in Delia's physical capabilities, and that it would be appropriate to review the formal care package after another month or so. You therefore contact Delia to suggest that her need for formal care support should be reviewed in four weeks' time.

At this review point, you are delighted that the improvements have been maintained, and with the agreement of all parties you agree that the formal support services can now be withdrawn. Delia has obviously improved greatly, both in her physical abilities and in her confidence. She says that she is quite happy to manage on her own; she also says that her friends have organised a cleaning rota for her house, and that one retired man has offered to maintain her garden. Finally, she offers you an invitation to her forthcoming birthday party, to be held in the local church hall.

CONCLUSION

As can be seen from the practice scenario, the social work role with Delia focused predominantly on three areas of activity:

- Understanding her personality and her response to the traumatic events of the last few months, in order to provide appropriate support to her that enables her to recover the self-confidence that these events had shattered.

- Understanding the dimensions of her social circumstances in order to provide the crucial element of social support for Delia.
- Identifying whether her home remained suitable, given the fact that it has been empty and vulnerable for several months, and given its overall internal and external dimensions.

Resolving these elements of Delia's situation will call on all three aspects of social work's history and development – the 'individualist-therapeutic', the 'collectivist' and the 'administrative'. The contribution of the social worker in these areas will complement the more functionally oriented roles of the physiotherapist and occupational therapist. Jointly, a genuinely holistic response to Delia's needs can be provided, which is more likely to make the intervention successful. Although the social work role will encompass a range of administratively oriented elements – arranging for the provision of services, checking benefit entitlements, etc. – the practice scenario demonstrates that these are far from the full extent of the social work contribution. The need for a psychological understanding of Delia's response to her situation is vital, as is the capacity to identify and mobilise sources of informal care and support, part of a more collectivist orientation to practice.

As this book has consistently argued, the essence of social work with older people lies in the combination of these aspects of the social work role. By implication, this requires a reversal of the limited vision of social work that has come to dominate the post-community care world of practice. Through a process of re-engagement with the totality of the social work role, a service can be provided that will assist more older people to live satisfying and productive lives, while also improving the work experiences of practitioners. In the context of intermediate care, and any policies that are subsequently developed that aim to enhance older people's independence, the social work role has the potential to become much more central to policy and practice than is now the case.

CHAPTER SUMMARY

This chapter has examined a neglected area in the literature, the social work contribution to intermediate care. In approaching this subject, the chapter has engaged with a number of different issues.

- It has charted the development of intermediate care as a policy, focusing particularly on the extent to which it has the potential to reduce the use of costly hospital care for older people.

(Continued)

- The fact that the policy has been developed in advance of robust research evidence, despite the fact that it has been considered to be a policy priority for most social services departments. This basic point holds despite the manifold settings within which various types of intermediate care can be developed.
- The place of social work within intermediate care: this is a particular issue given the predominance of other occupational groups in the literature combined with the relative absence of an analysis of what the social work contribution could be.
- The themes of the chapter have been illustrated through the medium of a detailed practice scenario, which identifies the social work role in intermediate care practice.

References

Abbot, A. (1988) *The System of Professions*, Chicago, University of Chicago Press.

Adams, R. (2003) *Social Work and Empowerment* (3rd Edition), Basingstoke, Palgrave.

Adams, R., Dominelli, L. and Payne, M. eds (2002) *Social Work: Themes, Issues and Critical Debates* (2nd Edition), Basingstoke, Palgrave.

Adams, T. and Bartlett, R. (2003) 'Constructing dementia', in T. Adams and J. Manthorpe eds, *Dementia Care*, London, Arnold.

Aldridge, M. (1994) *Making Social Work News*, London, Routledge.

Arber, S. and Ginn, J. (1991) *Gender and Later Life*, London, Sage.

Aronson, J. (1999) 'Conflicting images of older people receiving care: challenges for reflective practice and research', in S.M. Neysmith ed., *Critical Issues for Future Social Work Practice with Ageing Persons*, New York, Columbia University Press.

Audit Commission (1986) *Making a Reality of Community Care*, London, HMSO.

Audit Commission (1997) *The Coming of Age: Improving Care Services for Older People*, London, Audit Commission.

Auslander, G. (2001) 'Social work in health care: what have we achieved?', *Journal of Social Work*, 1, 2, pp. 201–22.

Bailey, R. and Brake, M. eds (1975) *Radical Social Work*, London, Edward Arnold.

Baraclough, J. (1996) '1995 onwards – facing the future', in J. Baraclough, G. Dedman, H. Osborn and P. Willmott, *100 Years of Health Related Social Work 1895–1995*, Birmingham, British Association of Social Workers.

Barclay Report (1982) *Social Workers: Their Role and Tasks*, London, Bedford Square Press/NISW.

Bauld, L., Chesterman, J., Davies, B., Judge, K. and Mangalore, R. (2000) *Caring for Older People: An Assessment of Community Care in the 1990s*, Aldershot, Ashgate.

Beattie, A. (1994) 'Healthy alliances or dangerous liaisons? The challenge of working together in health promotion', in A. Leathard ed., *Going Inter-Professional: Working Together for Health and Welfare*, London, Routledge.

Bell, E.M. (1942) *Octavia Hill: A Biography*, London, Constable.

Bell, E.M. (1961) *The Story of Hospital Almoners*, London, Faber and Faber.

Bennett, G., Kingston, P. and Penhale, B. (1997) *The Dimensions of Elder Abuse*, Basingstoke, Macmillan.

Biggs, S. (1993) *Understanding Ageing*, Buckingham, Open University Press.

Biggs, S. (1999) *The Mature Imagination*, Buckingham, Open University Press.

Blakemore, K. and Boneham, M. (1994) *Age, Race and Ethnicity*, Buckingham, Open University Press.

Bond, J., Coleman P. and Peace, S. eds (1993a) *Ageing in Society* (2nd Edition), London, Sage/Open University.

Bond, J., Briggs, R. and Coleman, P. (1993b) 'The study of ageing', in J. Bond, P. Coleman and S. Peace eds, *Ageing in Society* (2nd Edition), London, Sage/Open University.

Bosanquet, H. (1914) *Social Work in London*, London, John Murray.

Brandon, D., Brandon, A. and Brandon, T. (1995) *Advocacy: Power to People with Disabilities*, Birmingham, Venture Press.

Braye, S. and Preston-Shoot, M. (1995) *Empowering Practice in Social Care*, Buckingham, Open University Press.

Brearley, J. (1995) *Counselling and Social Work*, Buckingham, Open University Press.

Brewer, C. and Lait, J. (1980) *Can Social Work Survive?* London, Temple Smith.

Briggs, R. (1993) 'Biological ageing', in J. Bond, P. Coleman and S. Peace eds, *Ageing in Society* (2nd Edition), London, Sage/Open University.

Brown, L., Tucker, C. and Domokos, T. (2003) 'Evaluating the impact of integrated health and social care teams on older people living in the community', *Health and Social Care in the Community*, 11, 2, pp. 85–94.

Brown, P., Hadley, R. and White, K. (1982) 'A case for neighbourhood-based social work and social services', in the Barclay Report, *Social Workers: Their Role and Tasks*, London, Bedford Square Press/NISW, pp. 219–35.

Bush, R.A.B. and Folger, J.P. (1994) *The Promise of Mediation: Responding to Conflict Through Empowerment and Recognition*, San Francisco CA, Jossey-Bass.

Butrym, Z. (1967) *Social Work in Medical Care*, London, Routledge and Kegan Paul.

Bytheway, B. (1995) *Ageism*, Buckingham, Open University Press.

Bywaters, P. (1986) 'Social work and the medical profession – arguments against unconditional collaboration', *British Journal of Social Work*, 16, 6, pp. 661–77.

Caldock, K. (1996) 'Multi-disciplinary assessment and care management', in J. Phillips, and B. Penhale eds, *Reviewing Care Management for Older People*, London, Jessica Kingsley.

Callaghan, D. (2003) 'When two become one', *Community Care*, 25 September– 1 October, pp. 34–5.

Cambridge, P. and Parkes, T. (2004) 'The case for case management in adult protection', *Journal of Adult Protection*, 6, 2, pp. 4–14.

Cameron, A. and Lart, R. (2003) 'Factors promoting and obstacles hindering joint working: a systematic review of the research evidence', *Journal of Integrated Care*, 11, 2, pp. 9–17.

Carey, M. (2003) 'Anatomy of a care manager', *Work, Employment and Society*, 17, 1, pp. 121–35.

Challis, D., Darton, R., Johnson, L., Stone, M. and Traske, D. (1995) *Care Management and Health Care of Older People*, Aldershot, Arena.

Challis, D. and Davies, B. (1986) *Case Management in Community Care*, Aldershot, Gower.

Charlesworth, J. (2001) 'Negotiating and managing partnership in primary care', *Health and Social Care in the Community*, 9, 5, pp. 279–85.

Clare, A.W. and Corney, R.H. eds (1982) *Social Work in Primary Health Care*, London, Academic Press.

Clark, H., Dyer, S. and Horwood, J. (1998) *'That Bit of Help': The High Value of Low Level Preventative Services for Older People*, Bristol, Policy Press/Community Care.

Clarke, J. and Glendinning, C. (2002) 'Partnership and the remaking of welfare provision', in C. Glendinning, M. Powell and K. Rummery eds, *Partnerships, New Labour and the Governance of Welfare*, Bristol, Policy Press.

Clouder, L. (2003) 'Becoming a professional: exploring the complexities of professional social-ization in health and social care', *Learning in Health and Social Care*, 2, 4, pp. 213–22.

Cohen, S. (1975) 'It's all right for you to talk: political and sociological manifestos for social work action', in R. Bailey and M. Brake eds, *Radical Social Work*, London, Edward Arnold.

Coleman, P. (1993a) 'Psychological ageing', in J. Bond, P. Coleman and S. Peace eds, *Ageing in Society* (2nd Edition), London, Sage/Open University.

Coleman, P. (1993b) 'Adjustment in later life', in J. Bond, P. Coleman and S. Peace eds, *Ageing in Society* (2nd Edition), London, Sage/Open University.

Collins, J. (1965) *Social Casework in a General Medical Practice*, London, Pitman Medical Publishing.

Commission for Social Care Inspection (CSCI) (2004a) *Direct Payments: What are the Barriers?* London, Commission for Social Care Inspection.

Commission for Social Care Inspection (CSCI) (2004b) *Leaving Hospital: The Price of Delays*, London, Commission for Social Care Inspection.

Cooke, P. and Ellis, R. (2004) 'Exploitation, protection and empowerment of people with learning disabilities', in M. Lymbery and S. Butler eds, *Social Work Ideals and Practice Realities*, Basingstoke, Palgrave.

Copeman, J. and Hyland, K. (2000) 'Nutrition issues in older people', in G. Corley ed., *Older People and Their Needs: A Multi-disciplinary Perspective*, London, Whurr.

Cordingley, L., Hughes, J. and Challis, D. (2001) *Unmet Needs and Older People*, York, Joseph Rowntree Foundation.

Cormack, U. and McDougall, K. (1955) 'Case-work in social service', in C. Morris ed., *Social Case-work in Great Britain* (2nd Edition), London, Faber and Faber.

Cornes, M. and Clough, R. (2004) 'Inside multi-disciplinary practice: challenges for single assessment', *Journal of Integrated Care*, 12, 2, pp. 3–13.

Coulshed, V. and Orme, J. (1998) *Social Work Practice: An Introduction* (3rd Edition), Basingstoke, Macmillan.

Crowther, M.A. (1981) *The Workhouse System 1834–1929: The History of an English Social Institution*, London, Batsford.

Cumella, S., le Mesurier, N. and Tomlin, H. (1996) *Social Work in Practice: An Evaluation of the Care Management Received by Elderly People from Social Workers Based in GP Practices in South Worcestershire*, Birmingham, The Martley Press.

Cumming, E. and Henry, W. (1961) *Growing Old: The Process of Disengagement*, New York, Basic Books.

Dalley, G. (1989) 'Professional ideology and organisational tribalism? The Health Service–Social Work divide', in R. Taylor and J. Ford eds, *Social Work and Health Care*, London, Jessica Kingsley.

Davies, M. (1994) *The Essential Social Worker* (3rd Edition), Aldershot, Arena.

Dean, H. (2002) *Welfare Rights and Social Policy*, Harlow, Pearson Education.

Dean, H. (2003) 'The Third Way and Social Welfare: the myth of post-emotionalism', *Social Policy and Administration*, 37, 7, pp. 695–708.

Dedman, G. (1996) '1946–1973: reconstruction and integration: social work in the National Health Service', in J. Baraclough, G. Dedman, H. Osborn and P. Willmott, *100 Years of Health Related Social Work 1895–1995*, Birmingham, British Association of Social Workers.

Department of the Environment, Transport and the Regions (DETR) (1998) *Modern Local Government: In Touch with the People*, Cm 4014, London, The Stationery Office.

Department of Health (DoH) (1989) *Caring for People: Community Care in the Next Decade and Beyond*, Cm 849, London, HMSO.

Department of Health (DoH) (1990) *Community Care in the Next Decade and Beyond: Policy Guidance*, London, HMSO.

Department of Health (DoH) (1995) *NHS Responsibilities for Meeting Continuous Health Care Needs*, London, Department of Health.

Department of Health (DoH) (1997a) *The New NHS: Modern, Dependable*, Cm 3807, London, The Stationery Office.

Department of Health (DoH) (1997b) *Better Services for Vulnerable People*, EL(97)62, London, Department of Health.

Department of Health (DoH) (1998a) *Modernising Social Services*, Cm 4149, London, The Stationery Office.

Department of Health (DoH) (1998b) *Partnership in Action: A Discussion Document*, London, Department of Health.

Department of Health (DoH) (1999) *National Strategy for Carers*, London, Department of Health.

Department of Health (DoH) (2000a) *No Secrets: Guidance on Developing and Implementing Multi-Agency Policies and Procedures to Protect Vulnerable Adults*, London, HMSO.

Department of Health (DoH) (2000b) *The NHS Plan*, London, HMSO.

Department of Health (DoH) (2001a) *The National Service Framework for Older People*, London, HMSO.

Department of Health (DoH) (2001b) *Carers and Disabled Children Act 2000: Carers and People with Parental Responsibility for Disabled Children: Policy Guidance*, London, Department of Health.

Department of Health (DoH) (2001c) *Intermediate Care*, HSC2001/01: LAC (2001)1, London, Department of Health.

Department of Health (DoH) (2001d) *Valuing People*, London, Department of Health.

Department of Health (DoH) (2002a) *Guidance on the Single Assessment Process for Older People*, HSC2002/001: LAC (2002)1, London, Department of Health.

Department of Health (DoH) (2002b) *The Single Assessment Process: Guidance for Local Implementation*, London, Department of Health.

Department of Health (DoH) (2002c) *The Single Assessment Process – Key Implications for Social Workers*, http//www.doh.gov.uk/scg/sap/socialworkers.htm, accessed 28 June 2004.

Department of Health (DoH) (2002d) *Requirements for Social Work Training*, London, Department of Health.

Department of Health (DoH) (2002e) *Fair Access to Care Services: Guidance on Eligibility Criteria for Adult Social Care*, LAC(2002)13, London, Department of Health.

Department of Health (DoH) (2002f) *Fair Access to Care Services: Policy Guidance*, London, Department of Health.

Department of Health (DoH) (2002g) *Intermediate Care: Moving Forward*, London, Department of Health.

Department of Health (DoH) (2003a) *The Community Care (Delayed Discharges etc.) Act 2003: Guidance for Implementation*, HSC2003/009: LAC(2003)21, London, Department of Health.

Department of Health (DoH) (2003b) *Fair Access to Care Services: Practice Guidance – Implementation Questions and Answers*, London, Department of Health.

Department of Health (DoH) (2004a) *The Community Care Assessment Directions 2004*, LAC(2004)24, London, Department of Health.

Department of Health (DoH) (2004b) *Improving Chronic Disease Management*, London, Department of Health.

Department of Health (DoH) (2004c) *The NHS Improvement Programme: Section 2: Chapter 3*, London, Department of Health: accessed at: http://www.publications.doh.gov.uk/nhsplan/nhsimprovementplan-ch3.htm (7 September 2004).

Department of Health (DoH) (2005) *Independence, Well-being and Choice: Our Vision for the Future of Social Care for Adults in England*, Cm 6499, London, Department of Health.

Department of Health/Social Services Inspectorate (DoH/SSI) (1991a) *Care Management and Assessment – Practitioners' Guide*, London, HMSO.

Department of Health/Social Services Inspectorate (DoH/SSI) (1991b) *Care Management and Assessment – Managers' Guide*, London, HMSO.

Department of Health and Social Security (DHSS) (1978) *Social Services Teams: The Practitioners' View*, London, HMSO.

Dinagly, U. and Baillie, E. (2002) 'Psychology and the rehabilitation of the older person', in A. Squires and M. Hastings eds, *Rehabilitation of the Older Person: A Handbook for the Interdisciplinary Team* (3rd Edition), Cheltenham, Nelson Thornes.

Dingwall, R. (1982) 'Problems of teamwork in primary care', in A.W. Clare and R.H. Corney eds, *Social Work and Primary Health Care*, London, Academic Press.

Dröes, R.M., Goffin, J.J.M., Breebaart, E., de Rooij, E., Vissers, H., Bleeker, J.A.C. and van Tilburg, W. (2004) 'Support programmes for caregivers of persons with dementia: A review of methods and effects', in G.M.M. Jones and B. Miesen eds, *Care-Giving in Dementia: Research and Applications* (Volume 3), Hove, Brunner-Routledge.

Eadie, T. and Canton, R. (2002) 'Practising in a context of ambivalence: the challenge for youth justice workers', *Youth Justice*, 2, 1, pp. 14–26.

Ehrenreich, J.H. (1985) *The Altruistic Imagination: A History of Social Work and Social Policy in the United States*, Ithaca NY, Cornell University Press.

Engel, C. (1994) 'A functional model of teamwork', in A. Leathard ed., *Going Inter-Professional: Working Together for Health and Welfare*, London, Routledge.

Estes, C. (1979) *The Aging Enterprise*, San Francisco CA, Jossey Bass.

Estes, C. (2001) 'Political economy of aging: a theoretical perspective', in C. Estes and Associates, *Social Policy and Aging*, Thousand Oaks CA, Sage.

Estes, C. and Associates (2001) *Social Policy and Aging*, Thousand Oaks CA, Sage.

Estes, C., Linkins, K.W. and Binney, E.A. (2001a) 'Critical perspectives on aging', in C. Estes and Associates, *Social Policy and Aging*, Thousand Oaks CA, Sage.

Estes, C., Wallace, S.P., Linkins, K.W. and Binney, E.A. (2001b) 'The medicalisation and commodification of aging and the privatisation and rationalisation of old age policy', in C. Estes and Associates, *Social Policy and Aging*, Thousand Oaks CA, Sage.

Etzioni, A. (1969) *The Semi-Professions and their Organization*, New York, Free Press.

Evandrou, M. (1997) 'Social care: today and beyond 2000', in M. Evandrou ed., *Baby Boomers: Ageing in the 21st Century*, London, Age Concern.

Evans, D. and Kearney, J. (1996) *Working in Social Care: A Systemic Approach*, Aldershot, Arena.

Fleming, S., Blake, H., Gladman, J., Hart, E., Lymbery, M., Dewey, M., McCloughry, H., Walker, M.F. and Miller, P. (2004) 'A randomised controlled trial of a home care rehabilitation service to reduce long term institutionalisation for elderly people', *Age and Ageing*, 33, 4, pp. 384–90.

Forman, J. and Fairbairn, E. (1968) *Social Casework in General Practice*, Oxford, Oxford University Press.

Freidson, E. (1970) *Professional Dominance: The Social Structure of Medical Care*, New York, Atherton Press.

Freidson, E. (1986) *Professional Powers*, Chicago, University of Chicago Press.

Giddens, A. (1998) *The Third Way*, Oxford, Polity.

Gilchrist, R. and Jeffs, T. (2001) 'Introduction', in R. Gilchrist and T. Jeffs eds, *Settlements, Social Change and Community Action*, London, Jessica Kingsley.

Glasby, J. (2003) *Hospital Discharge: Integrating Health and Social Care*, Oxford, Radcliffe Medical Press.

Glasby, J. (2004) 'Social services and the Single Assessment Process: early warning signs?', *Journal of Interprofessional Care*, 18, 2, pp. 129–39.

Glasby, J. and Littlechild, R. (2004) *The Health and Social Care Divide: The Experiences of Older People* (2nd Edition), Bristol, Policy Press.

Glendinning, C. and Rummery, K. (2003) 'Collaboration in primary health and social care: From policy to practice in developing services for older people', in A. Leathard ed., *Interprofessional Collaboration: From Policy to Practice in Health and Social Care*, Hove, Brunner-Routledge.

Glendinning, C., Powell, M. and Rummery, K. eds (2002) *Partnerships, New Labour and the Governance of Welfare*, Bristol, Policy Press.

Godfrey, M. and Callaghan, G. (2000) *Exploring Unmet Needs*, York, Joseph Rowntree Foundation.

Golan, N. (1978) *Treatment in Crisis Situations*, New York, Free Press.

Goldberg, E.M. and Neill, J.E. (1972) *Social Work and General Practice*, London, George Allen and Unwin.

Goldsmith, M. (1996) *Hearing the Voice of People with Dementia*, London, Jessica Kingsley.

Gorman, H. (2003) 'Which skills do care managers need? A research project on skills, competency and continuing professional development', *Social Work Education*, 22, 3, pp. 245–59.

Gorman, H. and Postle, K. (2003) *Transforming Community Care: A Distorted Vision?*, Birmingham, Venture Press.

Gregson, B., Cartlidge, A. and Bond, J. (1991) *Interprofessional Collaboration in Primary Health Care Organizations*, London, Royal College of General Practitioners.

Griffiths, R. (1983) *NHS Management Inquiry: Report*, London, DHSS.

Griffiths, R. (1988) *Community Care: Agenda for Action*, London, HMSO.

Grimley Evans, J. and Tallis, R.C. (2001) 'Editorial: A new beginning for care for elderly people?', *British Medical Journal*, 322, 7290, pp. 807–8.

Hadley, R. and McGrath, M. (1981) *Going Local: Neighbourhood Social Services*, London, Bedford Square Press.

Ham, C. (1999) *Health Policy in Britain* (4th Edition), Basingstoke, Macmillan.

Hardiker, P. and Barker, M. (1999) 'Early steps in implementing the new community care; the role of social work practice', *Health and Social Care in the Community*, 7, 6, pp. 417–26.

Hardy, B., Leedham, I. and Wistow, G. (1996) 'Care manager co-location in GP practices: effects on assessment and care management arrangements for Older People', in R. Bland ed., *Developing Services for Older People and their Families*, London, Jessica Kingsley.

Harris, J. (1998) 'Scientific management, bureau-professionalism, new managerialism: the labour process of state social work', *British Journal of Social Work*, 28, 6, pp. 839–62.

Hart, E., Lymbery, M. and Gladman, J.R.F. (2005) 'Away from home: an ethnographic study of a Transitional Rehabilitation scheme for older people', *Social Science and Medicine*, 60, 6, pp. 139–48.

Hart, E., Lymbery, M. and Gladman, J.R.F. (in press) 'Methodological understandings and misunderstandings in inter-professional research: experiences of researching transitional rehabilitation for older people', *Journal of Interprofessional Care*.

Herod, J. and Lymbery, M. (2002) 'The social work role in multi-disciplinary teams', *Practice*, 14, 4, pp. 17–27.

Hockey, J. and James, A. (2003) *Social Identities across the Life Course*, Basingstoke, Palgrave.

House of Commons Health Committee (2002) *Delayed Discharges*, London, HMSO.

Howe, D. (1996) 'Surface and depth in social work practice', in N. Parton ed., *Social Theory, Social Change and Social Work*, London, Routledge.

Hudson, B. (1990) 'Social policy and the new right – the strange case of the community care White Paper', *Local Government Studies*, 16, 6, pp. 15–34.

Hudson, B. (2002) 'Interprofessionality in health and social care: the Achilles' heel of partnership,' *Journal of Interprofessional Care*, 16, 1, pp. 7–17.

Hudson, B. and Henwood, M. (2002) 'The NHS and social care: the final countdown?' *Policy and Politics*, 30, 2, pp. 153–66.

Hughes, B. (1995) *Older People and Community Care*, Buckingham, Open University Press.

Hughes, B. and Mtezuka, M. (1992) 'Social work and older women: where have older women gone?', in M. Langan and L. Day eds, *Women, Oppression and Social Work*, London, Routledge.

Hugman, R. (1995) 'Contested territory and community services: interprofessional boundaries in health and social care', in K. Soothill, L. Mackay and C. Webb eds, *Interprofessional Relations in Health Care*, London, Edward Arnold.

Hugman, R. (1998a) 'Social work and de-professionalization', in P. Abbott and L. Meerabeau eds, *The Sociology of the Caring Professions* (2nd Edition), London, UCL Press.

Hugman, R. (1998b) *Social Welfare and Social Value*, Basingstoke, Macmillan.

Humphrey, J.C. (2003) 'New Labour and the regulatory reform of social care', *Critical Social Policy*, 23, 1, pp. 5–24.

Huntington, J. (1981) *Social Work and General Medical Practice*, London, George Allen and Unwin.

Huntington, J. (1986) 'The proper contributions of social workers in health practice', *Social Science and Medicine*, 22, 11, pp. 1151–60.

Huxham, C. (2000) 'The challenge of collaborative governance', *Public Management*, 2, 3, pp. 337–57.

International Federation of Social Workers (IFSW) (2000) *Definition of Social Work*, http://www.ifsw.org/Publications/4.6e.pub.html, accessed 1 July 2005.

Jefferys, M. and Sacks, H. (1983) *Rethinking General Practice: Dilemmas in Primary Medical Care*, London, Tavistock.

Johnson, J. ed. (2004) *Writing Old Age*, London, Centre for Policy on Ageing.

Johnson, P., Wistow, G., Schulz, R. and Hardy, B. (2003) 'Interagency and interprofessional collaboration in community care: the interdependence of structure and values', *Journal of Interprofessional Care*, 17, 1, pp. 69–83.

Johnson, T. (1972) *Professions and Power*, Basingstoke, Macmillan Education.

Jones, C. (1983) *State Social Work and the Working Class*, London, Macmillan.

Jones, C. (1996) 'Regulating social work: a review of the review', in M. Preston-Shoot and S. Jackson eds, *Educating Social Workers in a Changing Policy Context*, London, Whiting and Birch.

Jones, C. (2001) 'Voices from the frontline: state social workers and New Labour', *British Journal of Social Work*, 31, 4, pp. 547–62.

Jones, G.M.M. (2004) 'Metaphors for teaching about changing memory and cognition in Alzheimer's disease', in G.M.M. Jones and B. Miesen eds, *Care-Giving in Dementia: Research and Applications* (Volume 3), Hove, Brunner-Routledge.

Jordan, B. (1984) *Invitation to Social Work*, Oxford, Martin Robertson.

Jordan, B. (2004) 'Emancipatory social work? Opportunity or oxymoron', *British Journal of Social Work*, 34, 1, pp. 5–19.

Jordan, B. with Jordan, C. (2000) *Social Work and the Third Way*, London, Sage.

Kemshall, H. (2002) *Risk, Social Policy and Welfare*, Buckingham, Open University Press.

Kitwood, T. (1997) *Dementia Reconsidered*, Buckingham, Open University Press.

Klein, R. (2001) *The New Politics of the NHS* (4th Edition), Harlow, Pearson.

Langan, M. (2003) 'Social work inside out', in V.E. Cree ed., *Becoming a Social Worker*, London, Routledge.

Larson, M.S. (1977) *The Rise of Professionalism: A Sociological Analysis*, Berkeley, University of California Press.

Leathard, A. ed. (2003) *Interprofessional Collaboration: From Policy to Practice in Health and Social Care*, Hove, Brunner-Routledge.

Levin, E., Davey, B., Iliffe, S. and Kharicha, K. (2002) 'Research across the social and primary health care interface: methodological issues and problems', *Research, Policy and Planning*, 20, 3, pp. 17–30.

Lewis, J. (1995) *The Voluntary Sector, the State and Social Work in Britain*, Aldershot, Edward Elgar.

Lewis J. (2001) 'Older people and the health–social care boundary in the UK: half a century of hidden policy conflict', *Social Policy and Administration*, 35, 4, pp. 343–59.

Lewis, J. and Glennerster, H. (1996) *Implementing the New Community Care*, Buckingham, Open University Press.

Lister, R. (2001) 'New Labour: a study in ambiguity from a position of ambivalence', *Critical Social Policy*, 21, 4, pp. 425–47.

Littlejohn, P. and Victor, C. eds (1996) *Making Sense of a Primary Care-Led Health Service*, Oxford, Radcliffe Medical Press.

Lloyd, M. (2002) 'Care management', in R. Adams, L. Dominelli and M. Payne, eds, *Critical Practice in Social Work*, Basingstoke, Palgrave.

Loxley, A. (1997) *Collaboration in Health and Welfare*, London, Jessica Kingsley.

Lymbery, M. (1998a) 'Care management and professional autonomy: the impact of community care legislation on social work with older people', *British Journal of Social Work*, 28, 6, pp. 863–78.

Lymbery, M. (1998b) 'Social work in general practice: dilemmas and solutions', *Journal of Interprofessional Care*, 12, 2, pp. 199–209.

Lymbery, M. (1999) 'Lessons from the past – learning for the future: social work in primary health care', *Practice*, 11, 4, pp. 5–14.

Lymbery, M. (2000) 'The retreat from professionalism: from social worker to care manager', in N. Malin ed., *Professionalism, Boundaries and the Workplace*, London, Routledge.

Lymbery, M. (2001) 'Social work at the crossroads', *British Journal of Social Work*, 31, 3, pp. 369–84.

Lymbery, M. (2003) 'Collaborating for the social and health care of older people', in C. Whittington, J. Weinstein and T. Leiba eds, *Collaboration in Social Work Practice*, London, Jessica Kingsley.

Lymbery, M. (2004a) 'Managerialism and care management practice', in M. Lymbery and S. Butler eds, *Social Work Ideals and Practice Realities*, Basingstoke, Palgrave.

Lymbery, M. (2004b) 'The changing nature of welfare organisations', in M. Lymbery and S. Butler eds, *Social Work Ideals and Practice Realities*, Basingstoke, Palgrave.

Lymbery, M. and Butler, S. eds (2004) *Social Work Ideals and Practice Realities*, Basingstoke, Palgrave.

Lymbery, M. and Millward, A. (2000) 'The primary health care interface', in G. Bradley and J. Manthorpe eds, *Working on the Fault Line: Social Work and Health Services*, Birmingham, Venture Press/Social Work Research Association.

Lymbery, M. and Millward, A. (2001) 'Community care in practice: social work in primary health care', *Social Work in Health Care*, 34, 3/4, pp. 241–59.

Lymbery, M. and Millward, A. (2004) 'Delayed discharge: preparing for reimbursement', *Journal of Integrated Care*, 12, 4, pp. 28–34.

McDonald, A. (1999) *Understanding Community Care: A Guide for Social Workers*, Basingstoke, Macmillan.

MacDonald, G. and Sheldon, B. with Gillespie, J. (1992) 'Contemporary studies of the effectiveness of social work', *British Journal of Social Work*, 22, 6, pp. 615–43.

MacFarlane, A. (2004) 'Disability and ageing', in J. Swain, S. French, C. Barnes and C. Thomas eds, *Disabling Barriers – Enabling Environments* (2nd Edition), London, Sage.

McNally, D., Cornes, M. and Clough, R. (2003) 'Implementing the single assessment process: driving change or expecting the impossible?', *Journal of Integrated Care*, 11, 2, pp. 18–29.

Manchée, D. (1944) *Social Service in a General Hospital*, London, Bailière Tindall and Cox.

Mandelstam, M. (1999) *Community Care Practice and the Law* (2nd Edition), London, Jessica Kingsley.

Manthorpe, J. (2002) 'The potential of social services', in A. Squires and M. Hastings eds, *Rehabilitation of the Older Person: A Handbook for the Interdisciplinary Team* (3rd Edition), Cheltenham, Nelson Thornes.

Manthorpe, J. and Bradley, G. (2000) 'Care Management across the Threshold', in G. Bradley and J. Manthorpe eds, *Working on the Fault Line: Social Work and Health Services*, Birmingham, Venture Press/Social Work Research Association.

Marshall, M. ed. (1990) *Working with Dementia: Guidelines for Professionals*, Birmingham, Venture Press.

Marshall, M. and Dixon, M. (1996) *Social Work with Older People* (3rd Edition), Basingstoke, Palgrave.

Mathew, D., Brown, H., Kingston, P., McCreadie, C. and Askham, J. (2002) 'The response to No Secrets', *Journal of Adult Protection*, 4, 1, pp. 4–14.

Matthews, J. and Kimmis, J. (2001) 'Development of the English settlement movement', in R. Gilchrist and T. Jeffs eds, *Settlements, Social Change and Community Action*, London, Jessica Kingsley.

Meads, G. (2003) 'New primary care policies: from professions to professionalism', in A. Leathard ed., *Interprofessional Collaboration: From Policy to Practice in Health and Social Care*, Hove, Brunner-Routledge.

Means R. and Smith R. (1998) *From Poor Law to Community Care* (2nd Edition), Bristol, Policy Press.

Means R., Morbey H. and Smith R. (2002) *From Community Care to Market Care?*, Bristol, Policy Press.

Means, R., Richards, S. and Smith, R. (2003) *Community Care: Policy and Practice* (3rd Edition), Basingstoke, Palgrave.

Mercer, G. (2004) 'User led organisations; facilitating independent living', in J. Swain, S. French, C. Barnes and C. Thomas eds, *Disabling Barriers – Enabling Environments* (2nd Edition), London, Sage.

Middleton, L. (1997) *The Art of Assessment*, Birmingham, Venture Press.

Miesen, B. and Jones, G.M.M. (2004) 'The Alzheimer Café concept: a response to the trauma, drama and tragedy of dementia', in G.M.M. Jones and B. Miesen eds, *Care-Giving in Dementia: Research and Applications* (Volume 3), Hove, Brunner-Routledge.

Miller, C. and Freeman, M. (2003) 'Clinical teamwork: the impact of policy on collaborative teamwork', in A. Leathard ed., *Interprofessional Collaboration: From Policy to Practice in Health and Social Care*, Hove, Brunner-Routledge.

Milner, J. and O'Byrne, P. (2002) *Assessment in Social Work* (2nd Edition), Basingstoke, Palgrave.

Morris, C. ed. (1955) *Social Case-work in Great Britain* (2nd Edition), London, Faber and Faber.

Mountain, G. (2001) 'Social rehabilitation: concepts, evidence and practice,' *Managing Community Care*, 9, 2, pp. 8–15.

Mowat, C.L. (1961) *The Charity Organisation Society*, London, Methuen.

Mullaly, R. (1997) *Structural Social Work* (2nd Edition), Oxford, Oxford University Press.

Nancarrow, S. (2004) 'Dynamic role boundaries in intermediate care services', *Journal of Interprofessional Care*, 18, 2, pp. 141–51.

Neysmith, S. and MacAdam, M. (1999) 'Controversial concepts', in S.M. Neysmith ed., *Critical Issues for Future Social Work Practice with Ageing Persons*, New York, Columbia University Press.

Nocon, A. and Baldwin, C. (1998) *Trends in Rehabilitation Policy – A Literature Review*, London, King's Fund.

Nolan, M., Davies, S. and Grant, G. (2001a) 'Quality of life, quality of care', in M. Nolan, S. Davies and G. Grant eds, *Working with Older People and their Carers*, Buckingham, Open University Press.

Nolan, M., Davies, S. and Grant, G. (2001b) 'Integrating perspectives', in M. Nolan, S. Davies and G. Grant eds, *Working with Older People and their Carers*, Buckingham, Open University Press.

Norman, A. (1985) *Triple Jeopardy: Growing Old in a Second Homeland*, London, Centre for Policy on Ageing.

Office for National Statistics (ONS) (2001) *Living in Britain*, www.statistics.gov.uk, accessed 28 June 2004.

Oliver, M. (2004) 'If I had a hammer: the social model in action', in J. Swain, S. French, C. Barnes and C. Thomas eds, *Disabling Barriers – Enabling Environments* (2nd Edition), London, Sage.

Osborn, H. (1996) 'One Door – Many Mansions: 1974–1995', in J. Baraclough, G. Dedman, H. Osborn and P. Willmott, *100 Years of Health Related Social Work 1895–1995*, Birmingham, British Association of Social Workers.

Otton Report (1974) *Report of the Working Party on Social Work Support for the Health Service*, London, HMSO.

Parker, G., Bhakta, P., Katbamna, S., Lovett, C., Paisley, S., Parker, S., Phelps, K., Baker, R., Jagger, C., Lindesay, J., Shepperdson, B. and Wilson, A. (2000) 'Best place of care for older people after acute and during subacute illness: a systematic review', *Journal of Health Services Research and Policy*, 5, 3, pp. 176–89.

Parry-Jones, B. and Soulsby, J. (2001) 'Needs-led assessment: the challenges and the reality', *Health and Social Care in the Community*, 9, 6, pp. 414–28.

Parsloe, P. ed. (1999) *Risk Assessment in Social Care and Social Work*, London, Jessica Kingsley.

Payne, M. (1995) *Social Work and Community Care*, Basingstoke, Macmillan.

Payne, M. (1996) *What is Professional Social Work?* Birmingham, Venture Press.

Payne, M. (1997) *Modern Social Work Theory* (2nd Edition), Basingstoke, Macmillan.

Payne, M. (2000) 'The politics of case management and social work', *International Journal of Social Welfare*, 9, 2, pp. 82–91.

Peckham, S. and Exworthy, M. (2003) *Primary Care in the UK: Policy, Organisation and Management*, Basingstoke, Palgrave.

Petch, A. (2003) 'Intermediate care or integrated care: the Scottish perspective on support provision for older people', *Journal of Integrated Care*, 11, 6, pp. 7–14.

Phillips, J. and Waterson, J. (2002) 'Care management and *social* work: a case study of the role of *social* work in hospital discharge to residential or nursing home care', *European Journal of Social Work*, 5, 2, pp. 171–86.

Phillipson, C. (1982) *Capitalism and the Construction of Old Age*, London, Macmillan.

Phillipson, C. (1989) 'Challenging dependency: towards a new social work with older people', in M. Langan and P. Lee eds, *Radical Social Work Today*, London, Unwin Hyman.

Phillipson, C. (1993) 'The sociology of retirement', in J. Bond, P. Coleman and S. Peace eds, *Ageing in Society* (2nd Edition), London, Sage/Open University.

Pilcher, J. (1995) *Age and Generation in Modern Britain*, Oxford, Oxford University Press.

Pinker, R. (1982) 'An alternative view', in the Barclay Report, *Social Workers: Their Role and Tasks*, London, Bedford Square Press/NISW, pp. 236–62.

Pithouse, A. (1998) *Social Work: The Social Organisation of an Invisible Trade* (2nd Edition), Aldershot, Ashgate.

Plant, R.D. (2002) 'Rehabilitation Concepts', in A. Squires and M. Hastings eds, *Rehabilitation of the Older Person: A Handbook for the Interdisciplinary team* (3rd Edition), Cheltenham, Nelson Thornes.

Postle, K. (2002) 'Working "between the idea and the reality": ambiguities and tensions in care managers' work', *British Journal of Social Work*, 32, 3, pp. 335–51.

Powell, M. (2000) 'New Labour and the third way in the British welfare state: a new and distinctive approach', *Critical Social Policy*, 20, 1, pp. 39–60.

Pugh, R. (2002) *Rural Social Work*, Birmingham, Venture Press.

Quality Assurance Agency (QAA) (2000) *Subject Benchmark Statements – Social Policy and Social Work*, Gloucester, Quality Assurance Agency for Higher Education.

Rachman, R. (1997) 'Hospital social work and community care: the practitioners' view', in G.K. Auslander ed., *International Perspectives in Health Care: Past, Present and Future*, New York, Haworth Press.

Randall, L. and Glasgow, L. (2000) 'Independence and rehabilitation', in G. Corley ed., *Older People and Their Needs: A Multi-disciplinary Perspective*, London, Whurr.

Ratoff, L. (1973) 'More social work for general practice?', *Journal of the Royal College of General Practitioners*, 23, pp. 736–42.

Rawson, D. (1994) 'Models of inter-professional work: likely theories and possibilities', in A. Leathard ed., *Going Inter-Professional: Working Together for Health and Welfare*, London, Routledge.

Richmond, M. (1917) *Social Diagnosis*, New York, Russell Sage Foundation.

Riley, M.W. (1986) 'On the significance of Age in Sociology', *American Sociological Review*, 52, 1, pp. 1–14.

Roberts, M. (1997) *Mediation in Family Disputes: Principles of Practice* (2nd Edition), Aldershot, Arena.

Robinson, J. and Stevenson, J. (1999) 'Rehabilitation', *Managing Community Care*, 7, 4, pp. 39–44.

Robinson, J. and Turnock, S. (1998) *Investing in Rehabilitation*, London, King's Fund/Audit Commission.

Rodgers, B.N. and Stevenson, J. (1973) *A New Portrait of Social Work*, London, Heinemann Educational Books.

Rose, M. (2001) 'The secular faith of the social settlements: "If Christ came to Chicago"', in R. Gilchrist and T. Jeffs eds, *Settlements, Social Change and Community Action*, London, Jessica Kingsley.

Rowlings, C. (1981) *Social Work with Elderly People*, London, Allen and Unwin.

Rummery, K. and Glendinning, C. (2000) *Primary Care and Social Services: Developing New Partnerships for Older People*, Oxford, Radcliffe Medical Press.

Salter, B. (1998) *The Politics of Change in the Health Service*, Basingstoke, Macmillan.

Sanderson, I. (2001) 'Performance management, evaluation and learning in "modern" local government', *Public Administration*, 79, 2, pp. 297–313.

Schön, D.A. (1991) *The Reflective Practitioner*, Aldershot, Arena (first published 1983).

Seebohm Report (1968) *Report of the Committee on Local Authority and Allied Personal Social Services*, London, HMSO.

Seed, P. (1973) *The Expansion of Social Work in Britain*, London, Routledge and Kegan Paul.

Shaw, C. (2004) '2002-based national population projections for the United Kingdom and constituent countries', *Population Trends*, 115, pp. 6–15.

Sheppard, M. (1995) *Care Management and the New Social Work: A Critical Analysis*, London, Whiting and Birch.

Shield, F. (1998) 'Developing a therapy-led community rehabilitation team', *Managing Community Care*, 6, 4, pp. 160–8.

Simpkin, M. (1983) *Trapped within Welfare* (2nd Edition), London, Macmillan.

Simpkin, M. (1989) 'Health issues, social services and democracy: steps towards a radical reintegration', in M. Langan and P. Lee eds, *Radical Social Work Today*, London, Unwin Hyman.

Slater, R. (1995) *The Psychology of Growing Old: Looking Forward*, Buckingham, Open University Press.

Smale, G. and Tuson, G. with Biehal, N. and Marsh, P. (1993) *Empowerment, Assessment, Care Management and the Skilled Worker*, London, HMSO.

Squires, A. (2002a) 'The rehabilitation of the older person – past, present and future', in A. Squires and M. Hastings eds, *Rehabilitation of the Older Person: A Handbook for the Interdisciplinary Team* (3rd Edition), Cheltenham, Nelson Thornes.

Squires, A. (2002b) 'The National Service Framework for Older People: timely and challenging', in A. Squires and M. Hastings eds, *Rehabilitation of the Older Person: A Handbook for the Interdisciplinary Team* (3rd Edition), Cheltenham, Nelson Thornes.

Stevenson, O. (1999) 'Old people at risk', in P. Parsloe ed., *Risk Assessment in Social Care and Social Work*, London, Jessica Kingsley.

Sturges, P. (1996) 'Care management practice: lessons from the USA', in C. Clark and I. Lapsley eds, *Planning and Costing Care in the Community*, London, Jessica Kingsley.

Sutherland Report (1999) *With Respect to Old Age: Long Term Care – Rights and Responsibilities: A Report by the Royal Commission on Long Term Care*, London, The Stationery Office.

Tanner, D. (2003) 'Older people and access to care', *British Journal of Social Work*, 33, 4, pp. 499–515.

Taylor, G. (1993) 'Challenges from the margins', in J. Clarke ed., *A Crisis in Care: Challenges to Social Work*, London, Sage/Open University.

Taylor, I. (2000) 'New Labour and the enabling state', *Health and Social Care in the Community*, 8, 6, pp. 372–9.

Thompson, N. (1995) *Ageing and Dignity*, Aldershot, Arena.

Thompson, N. (1998) 'The ontology of ageing', *British Journal of Social Work*, 28, 5, pp. 695–707.

Thompson, N. (2001) *Anti-Discriminatory Practice* (3rd Edition), Basingstoke, Palgrave.

Thompson, N. (2003) *Communication and Language*, Basingstoke, Palgrave.

Tinker, A. (1997) *Older People in Modern Society* (4th Edition), Harlow, Addison Wesley Longman.

Torkington, C., Lymbery, M, Millward, A., Murfin, M. and Richell, B. (2003) 'Shared practice learning: social work and district nurse students learning together', *Social Work Education*, 22, 2, pp. 165–75.

Torkington, C., Lymbery, M., Millward, A., Murfin, M. and Richell, B. (2004) 'The impact of shared practice learning on the quality of assessment carried out by social work and district nurse students', *Learning in Health and Social Care*, 3, 1, pp. 26–36.

Townsend, P. (1962) *The Last Refuge*, London, Routledge and Kegan Paul.

Townsend, P., Davidson, N. and Whitehead, M. eds (1992) *Inequalities in Health*, Harmondsworth, Penguin.

Training Organisation for the Personal Social Services (TOPSS) (2002) *National Occupational Standards for Social Work*, London, TOPSS.

Valios, N. (2004) 'What's the deal?', *Community Care*, 22–28 January, pp. 28–30.

Vaughan, B. and Lathlean, J. (1999) *Intermediate Care: Models in Practice*, London, King's Fund.

Victor, C.R. (1997) *Community Care and Older People*, Cheltenham, Stanley Thornes.

Webb, A. and Wistow, G. (1987) *Social Work, Social Care and Social Planning*, London, Longman.

Webb, B. (1926) *My Apprenticeship*, London, Longman, Green & Co.

Whittington, C. (2003) 'Collaboration and partnership in context', in C. Whittington, J. Weinstein and T. Leiba eds, *Collaboration in Social Work Practice*, London, Jessica Kingsley.

Wilding, P. (1982) *Professional Power and Social Welfare*, London, Routledge and Kegan Paul.

Willmott, P. (1996) '1895–1945: the first 50 years', in J. Baraclough, G. Dedman, H. Osborn and P. Willmott, *100 Years of Health Related Social Work 1895–1995*, Birmingham, British Association of Social Workers.

Wilson, G. (2001) *Understanding Old Age*, London, Sage.

Wilson, K.V. (2003) 'Intermediate care: from innovation to . . . post-mortem?', *Journal of Integrated Care*, 11, 6, pp. 4–6.

Woodroofe, K. (1962) *From Charity to Social Work*, London, Routledge and Kegan Paul.

Wootton, B. (1959) *Social Science and Social Pathology*, London, George Allen and Unwin.

Wyatt, M. (2002) 'Partnership in health and social care: the implications of government guidance in the 1990s in England, with particular reference to voluntary organisations', *Policy and Politics*, 30, 2, pp. 167–82.

Younghusband, E. (1955) 'Conclusion', in C. Morris ed., *Social Case-work in Great Britain* (2nd Edition), London, Faber and Faber.

Younghusband, E. (1978) *Social Work in Britain 1950–1975 (Volume 1)*, London, George Allen and Unwin.

Index